Social and Political Pl

'John Christman has a wonderful grasp of the large layout of the field and of the detailed positions within it. He writes with tremendous clarity. It was a joy to read . . . I can't recommend the book more highly.'
Michael Morgan, *Indiana University, USA*

'I marvel at how well Christman has been able to capture particularly the internal critique among many liberals concerning the substance of their view. Christman is himself an important contributor to this discussion and, therefore, he writes not as someone who simply observes the discussion from afar. This is a clear advantage to the work.'
James Sterba, *University of Notre Dame, USA*

Social and Political Philosophy: A Contemporary Introduction offers a broad survey of many of the fundamental philosophical questions about social and political life in the modern world. It contains clear and accessible discussions of the philosophical issues central to political thought. Issues that are given in-depth treatment include: the foundations of political authority, economic justice, the limits of tolerance and the challenges to mainstream political thought raised by considerations of community, race, gender and culture, as well as the perspective of post-modern thought.

This accessible and user-friendly text will be of value to any student coming to social and political philosophy for the first time. It contains the following textbook features:

- chapter summaries
- examples and case studies
- annotated further reading.

John Christman is Associate Professor of Philosophy at Pennsylvania State University, USA. He is the author of *The Myth of Property: Toward an Egalitarian Theory of Ownership* and the editor of *The Inner Citadel: Essays on Individual Autonomy*.

Routledge Contemporary Introductions to Philosophy

Series editor:
Paul K. Moser,
Loyola University of Chicago

This innovative, well-structured series is for students who have already done an introductory course in philosophy. Each book introduces a core general subject in contemporary philosophy and offers students an accessible but substantial transition from introductory to higher-level college work in that subject. The series is accessible to non-specialists and each book clearly motivates and expounds the problems and positions introduced. An orientating chapter briefly introduces its topic and reminds readers of any crucial material they need to have retained from a typical introductory course. Considerable attention is given to explaining the central philosophical problems of a subject and the main competing solutions and arguments for those solutions. The primary aim is to educate students in the main problems, positions and arguments of contemporary philosophy rather than to convince students of a single position.

Epistemology
Robert Audi

Ethics
Harry Gensler

Metaphysics
Second Edition
Michael J. Loux

Philosophy of Art
Noël Carroll

Philosophy of Language
William G. Lycan

Philosophy of Mind
John Heil

Philosophy of Religion
Keith E. Yandell

Philosophy of Science
Alex Rosenberg

Social and Political Philosophy
John Christman

Social and Political Philosophy

A contemporary introduction

John Christman

London and New York

First published 2002
by Routledge
11 New Fetter Lane, London EC4P 4EE

Simultaneously published in the USA and Canada
by Routledge
29 West 35th Street, New York, NY 10001

Routledge is an imprint of the Taylor & Francis Group

© 2002 John Christman

Typeset in Garamond by M Rules
Printed and bound in Great Britain by
MPG Books Ltd, Bodmin

All rights reserved. No part of this book may be reprinted or
reproduced or utilised in any form or by any electronic,
mechanical, or other means, now known or hereafter
invented, including photocopying and recording, or in any
information storage or retrieval system, without permission in
writing from the publishers.

British Library Cataloguing in Publication Data
A catalogue record for this book is available from the British Library

Library of Congress Cataloging in Publication Data
A catalog record has been requested

ISBN 0–415–21797–0 (hbk)
ISBN 0–415–21798–9 (pbk)

*To the memory of my aunts Lorraine Fleming and
Virginia 'Minette' Jilek,
and to all the members of my family.*

Contents

Preface	xi
Acknowledgements	xiii

1	INTRODUCTION	1
	The liberal democratic paradigm	6
	Preliminaries I: Method	9
	Preliminaries II: Moral theory and political philosophy	14
	Structure of the book	17
	Chapter summary	21
	Notes on further reading	22

PART I: BASIC ISSUES WITHIN THE LIBERAL PARADIGM   23

2	THE PROBLEM OF POLITICAL AUTHORITY	25
	The social contract tradition	26
	Hobbes's social contract: Mechanism, egoism, and rationality	28
	Locke: Reason, morality, and freedom	41
	Lessons from Rousseau and Kant	48
	From consent to legitimacy	52
	Chapter summary	56
	Case to consider	58
	Notes on further reading	58

3	DISTRIBUTIVE JUSTICE	60
	Distributive justice and equality	61
	Libertarianism	65
	Rawlsian distributive justice	74
	Varieties of egalitarianism	80
	From equality to the welfare state	87

	Chapter summary	90
	Case to consider	92
	Notes on further reading	93
4	**TOLERATION, PLURALISM, AND THE FOUNDATIONS OF LIBERALISM**	**94**
	The canons of liberalism	94
	The perfectionist challenge	103
	Utilitarian liberalism: Perfectionism in disguise?	108
	The response of political liberalism	111
	Liberalism, public discourse, and democracy	117
	Chapter summary	119
	Case to consider	121
	Notes on further reading	121

PART II: CRITIQUE OF THE LIBERAL PARADIGM: CHALLENGES AND DEPARTURES   123

5	**CONSERVATISM, COMMUNITARIANISM, AND THE SOCIAL CONCEPTION OF THE SELF**	**125**
	Conservatism	126
	Communitarianism	130
	Liberalism, freedom, and culture	145
	Chapter summary	148
	Case to consider	149
	Notes on further reading	150
6	**RACE, GENDER, AND THE POLITICS OF IDENTITY**	**152**
	Ideal theory and ongoing injustice	153
	Critical race theory	157
	Gender, sex, and the challenge of feminism	163
	Identity, injustice, and democracy	179
	Chapter summary	180
	Case to consider	183
	Notes on further reading	184
7	**RADICAL CRITIQUE: MARXISM AND POST-MODERNISM**	**185**
	The legacy of Marx and Marxism	186
	Post-modern departures	199

CONTENTS

Epilogue: The hope of liberalism	207
Chapter summary	212
Case to consider	213
Notes on further reading	214
Notes	216
Bibliography	230
Index	245

Preface

This book is intended to serve two related purposes. The first is to provide a text that would be useful in general survey courses on contemporary political philosophy or as a companion text for more focused classes on related topics. The series in which this book appears is designed to provide mid-level undergraduate textbooks for students with some background in philosophy but new to this particular subject matter. With this in mind, this book contains an admittedly selective account of current trends in (for the most part) Anglo-American social and political philosophy over the last thirty years or so. The book is designed to serve as a main text but also could be paired with primary material from the authors discussed.

The second aim of the book is to provide a general rendering of that material for an audience outside of academia, though one with some familiarity with philosophical methods and topics. The general reader should not need any specialized background in the history of philosophy or political theory to benefit from this work, though a taste for abstract theorizing may well be a prerequisite.

The organizing principle of the book is to lay out in some detail the guiding paradigm of political philosophy which currently dominates the field – the 'liberalism' inherited from the European Enlightenment which undergirds the constitutional democracies of the modern West – and to discuss particular controversies within that paradigm. It then places that paradigm under scrutiny and raises deep questions about the methodology, fundamental value commitments, and philosophical presuppositions of that view. In this way, the book marks what I take to be a profound shift in political philosophy (and perhaps Anglo-American philosophy generally) toward asking fundamental questions about its own methods and bases. Questions about 'mainstream' philosophy from various quarters – from feminists, critical race theorists, post-modern theorists, and others – have caused many philosophers to rethink the standard techniques of philosophical analysis that have dominated philosophy (in the analytic tradition) since the seventeenth century. This book reflects the rumblings of that challenge by considering some of the

PREFACE

basic questions raised, for political philosophy at least, from those perspectives.

But this book is still very much an account of what counts as the 'mainstream' of political philosophy. And while chapters are given over to critiques concerning feminism, race theory, and the like, the bulk of the book is a discussion of theories that do not mention gender, race, class, ongoing political struggles, or any of the considerations that these critics want to place at center stage. The reason for this is that, despite the author's sympathy with many of these calls for a new orientation in social philosophy, it would be inaccurate to write an introduction to the current state of the art in this field without reflecting the actual material which makes up this current practice. Perhaps another, even more valuable, book would be entitled 'A Revisionist Introduction to Current Political Philosophy' where such a reorientation is carried out. But the present work has different aims.

Similarly, the book reflects whatever biases, narrowness, and exclusionary tendencies are found in current academic philosophy in the English-speaking world where 'analytic' philosophy is the reigning method. For example, two broad areas of political thought that are not covered here – again because they have not been (yet?) fully brought into the parameters of most current work in the field – are American pragmatism (from which some recent analytic philosophers have claimed inspiration) and the legacy of 'Critical Theory' that emerged from the Frankfurt school in Germany and continued in the United States (except for brief discussions in Chapter 7 and references to the work of Jürgen Habermas). Both these traditions offer profound insights into questions of political philosophy, and theorists currently working in this area would do well to include them to a greater degree in their discussions.

But again, for the general reader who is interested in current trends in political thought and for the student learning about mainstream social philosophy, the constellation of topics included here offers, I hope, the best overview of that landscape. I also hope, however, that the methodological and theoretical challenges to this mainstream raised here will make the boundaries of that landscape less secure.

Acknowledgements

The writing of this book benefitted greatly from a number of persons to whom I would like to express my thanks. My friends and colleagues in both the Philosophy and Political Science Departments at Penn State University have been particularly helpful through the process of writing this book, as have been numerous other dear friends who always expressed interest and support and made valuable suggestions on various aspects of the book. An anonymous reader for Routledge gave me excellent suggestions (and induced me to rewrite a section of Chapter 3 in a way that greatly improves the discussion), and the editorial staff for the press was immensely helpful throughout the (alas extended) process. Lori Watson read the entire manuscript and offered countless valuable suggestions, both stylistic and substantive; I want to express my gratitude for her time and thoughtfulness. Thanks also to Ella Campi and Daniel Campos for their help with gathering bibliographical materials. Finally, as with all of my endeavors, Mary Beth Oliver has been a tireless supporter and a constant inspiration. I thank her here deeply (and again).

CHAPTER 1

Introduction

- The liberal democratic paradigm
- Preliminaries I: Method
- Preliminaries II: Moral theory and political philosophy
- Structure of the book
- Chapter summary
- Notes on further reading

This is an exciting time to be studying political philosophy. Critical discussions in political theory have raised deep and perplexing questions about the nature of philosophical inquiry generally: what role should 'reason' play in our abstract reflections; is 'objective' theorizing from a detached and neutral perspective really possible, or is this always a front for surreptitiously biased and ultimately self-serving thought; is *thinking* ultimately political?

Also, events in the world have profoundly reshaped the ideological terrain within which political theorizing is taking place. Debate about political principles outside of philosophy for a long time played out a clash between socialism and capitalism, framed (oversimply) as a conflict between valuing (economic) equality and valuing (political) liberty. However, in the current landscape, especially since the fall of the Soviet Union, the model of a constitutional democracy with regulated but competitive economic markets has come to predominate political understanding in most parts of the world, including most former Communist regimes. But this does not mean that such a framework is therefore acceptable uncritically – quite the opposite – for what political philosophy has now focused on are the fundamental evaluative presuppositions of that framework, and the perhaps controversial principles about individual citizens, social life, and sources of value that such a model presupposes. When examined at that level, liberal democracy faces questions about its very foundations, raised in a way which forces us to inquire into the ultimate legitimation of political power itself. Questions of distributive justice, though still alive in current discussions, have been upstaged by questions of basic political legitimacy.

Moreover, increased social mobility, broader cultural awareness, and economic globalization have made traditional assumptions of insulated, homogeneous societies in political thought more suspect. Societies have become manifestly multicultural, containing (or at least finally recognizing) a more fully diverse population. Increased international communication has made interaction *between* cultures and traditions more robust as well. This interaction has thrown into doubt centuries-old assumptions about the uniform identity, interests, and needs of human beings; so theorizing about 'the rights of man' without inquiring into the different kinds of 'men' (people) being conceptualized is now highly controversial.

And of course there are times when such cross-cultural encounters threaten the very limits of political communication. Acts of terrorism and mass violence place before us fundamental questions about the *possibility* of politics, the possibility that a normative framework could be found within which peaceful, and mutually respectful solutions to deep conflicts can be achieved. Are there some disagreements that are so profound that no argument, no acts of reasoning, negotiation, deliberation or collective understanding could produce such a framework? How does one draw the boundary around the possibility of peaceful co-existence?

More generally, in many areas of the academic world the presuppositions of 'modernity' – the cultural and philosophical orientation of the Western world since the seventeenth century – have come under basic challenge. *Post*-modernism in its various forms has raised fundamental questions about meaning, power, the self, and the possibility of human knowledge that strike at the heart of the world views that inform political and social theory. Moreover, post-modern critiques are often expressed in explicitly *political* terms, where models of rational thought, language, and self-hood that are presumed in the justifications of human rights and justice are replaced by complex pictures of the dynamics of power, decentered agency, unstable meanings, and the like. And such power dynamics are alleged to *structure* self-consciousness, conceptual schemes, and philosophical traditions, undercutting the pretensions of objectivity and detached rationality assumed in them (and in the theories of justice they support). Even when thinkers conclude that such critical challenges ultimately fail, the force of that critique nevertheless changes the terms in which political thought is couched. In this way,

INTRODUCTION

political philosophy is engaged with debates about the fundamental elements of thought, language, and identity.

Political philosophy is the study of people living in societies, governed by institutions and practices that mold, constrain, and in many ways constitute the lives they lead. It is not merely an explanatory or descriptive enterprise, such as sociology or (most parts of) political science, though it freely utilizes such material; nor is it an historical recounting of how such institutions and practices arose, though again, historical material is directly relevant to it. Rather, political philosophy interprets and evaluates these phenomena. It constructs theoretical accounts of the meaning and justification of social practices and institutions. Its main task is normative, asking whether a particular social organization is good or right or justified. Though it also includes the interpretive, asking how such organization should be best understood so that such normative questions can be asked most clearly.

Political philosophy focuses on individuals in social settings and, more particularly, on those norms and laws that shape citizens' lives. Its subject matter is 'people,' whether viewed as individuals or as groups, but people as they live within rule-governed social institutions. The most important of such institutions is the state, with its various legal, political, and economic functions, but many other institutions govern the way people live in societies and hence are the proper focus of political philosophy. One could say, then, that at the most general level, political philosophy is simply the study of *power*, of the institutional centers of social power that shape and constrain the lives of people living together.

Central to political philosophy are such questions as these: what is the ultimate justification of political authority in an area to begin with; what is the most fair and just distribution of material goods and social benefits for a society (and to what degree should inequalities in wealth that capitalist economic markets produce be left uncorrected); how tolerant must the state be toward dissidents and subversive groups; and to what extent should the state attempt to promote the good of its citizens, as opposed to simply protecting their liberty to pursue their own good (even if they predictably fail in doing so)? These last issues lead to more abstract but also more fundamental questions of political philosophy: when we theorize about what is just in a society, do we automatically (and problematically) assume only one kind of citizen to whom such justice will apply, surreptitiously leaving out of account those who do not fit the mold; what priority should be given to the rights and liberties of *individuals* in a society as opposed to the protection of communities and cultures, especially when those aims conflict; can we formulate a set of principles of justice for a society in a way that abstracts from historical and continuing injustice found in that society, injustice such as racism and sexism; and do the methods that we use to philosophize about all these issues themselves mask patterns of exclusion, a privileged position of thought, or an unsustainable reliance on objectivity and reason? These are the sorts of questions we will examine here.

This book will focus on contemporary political philosophy as developed in Europe and the North Atlantic states, and primarily in the Anglo-American philosophical tradition. It will tend to utilize the language and style of the so-called 'analytic' approach to philosophy, one usually contrasted with the 'Continental' tradition. But it must be emphasized that political philosophy lately has increasingly blurred this distinction, where the ideas of Hegel, Marx, Nietzsche, Heidegger, and Foucault (considered in the 'Continental' tradition) are placed alongside arguments by Locke, Mill, and Rawls (names associated with the analytic mode). Nevertheless, while the broad title of this book may indicate otherwise, it should be clear that this will be a survey of recent philosophical work in political philosophy in the European and North American tradition, for the most part framed by the analytic philosophical method.

But this geographical and cultural localism should not prevent us from asking pointed questions about its own privilege: why *does* a book purportedly surveying contemporary political philosophy say nothing at all about theoretical reflections on politics from places like Japan, India, Africa, or South America? I won't try to answer that question, except to say that it is a question that is itself one of political philosophy: why are social institutions like universities arranged in a way that topics labeled in general ways ('history of philosophy') actually exclude many traditions of philosophy that occur on non-European or North Atlantic traditions?

This book is structured in line with a certain shift in emphasis in (Anglo-American) political philosophy that has occurred in the last thirty years or so. Attention has moved from asking questions about political principles from *within* the framework of what I will call the 'liberal paradigm' to raising questions about the legitimacy of that paradigm itself. For example, through much of the 1970s and 1980s (in the analytic tradition), philosophers focused a great deal on such questions as what economic justice amounts to and what the legitimate basis of political obligations is.[1] But the various positions on these issues were articulated within a framework where the rights and interests of autonomous individuals, conceived as undifferentiated by race, gender, culture, or communal connection, and generally motivated by the

INTRODUCTION

rational pursuit of self-interest, were the assumed subject of the principles under debate. And while questions of economic justice and the like continue to be important, political philosophers have also begun asking more basic questions about the assumptions lying behind this framework, questions relating to the identity and motivations of the people assumed within them, the metaphysical orientation presupposed by them, and various facts about social dynamics, psychology, and institutional structure taken as true. In this way, controversies over such things as the separation of church and state or affirmative action are no longer necessarily seen as merely disputes within an accepted tradition of political thought – one where the rights and liberties of the autonomous individual are always paramount for example – but as disputes about the neutrality and inclusiveness of that tradition itself.

Interestingly enough, the work of John Rawls – one of the most important political philosophers in the Anglo-American tradition in the twentieth century – manifests the shift I am describing. Rawls's *A Theory of Justice* (Rawls 1971) is often credited with not only bringing up to date the tradition of enlightenment liberalism which inspired, for example, the US Constitution, but also with providing a framework for the discussion of political principles that had direct relevance to actual controversies in the real world (such as the distribution of wealth in society).[2] Many philosophical controversies were played out within the framework Rawls's work presented, a view that saw all questions of obligation and right as fundamentally focused on the free and equal *individual* person. But things began to change in the 1980s when thinkers began questioning the basic assumptions underlying that model. Spurred greatly by the 'communitarian' challenge to liberalism as well as the work of feminists, race-theorists, and other philosophers aligned with ongoing political struggles in the real world, questions were raised about whether arguments over political principles presupposed an overly narrow conception of the persons on whose behalf those principles were meant to be justified, one that reflected the 'individualism' of traditional Enlightenment liberalism at the expense of more socially embedded conceptions of the self.

Things had changed, however, by the time of the publication of Rawls's second book, *Political Liberalism*, where he attempted to respond to these challenges to the liberal tradition (Rawls 1993). In this work, Rawls attempted to recast the basic justification of the framework for deciding questions of political principle he had earlier utilized in a way that did not presuppose any controversial conceptions of citizens' personalities, value commitments, or sense of identity. He argued that the traditional liberal principles he earlier defended – the priority of liberty, the protection of equality of opportunity and the limitations of material inequalities – could be justified without reference to universal, all encompassing moral theories but as a view that fundamentally *different* kinds of people could commit themselves to in a spirit of mutual respect. (We will discuss Rawls's views in greater detail below.) This, however, indicates where we are in the current landscape, where central questions of political philosophy concern how *any* set of political ideals can be justified for a population that is marked by deep and irreducible differences in culture, social identity, and moral and religious commitment.

This relocation of philosophical attention provides the motivation for the structure of this book. The 'liberal democratic paradigm' will first be spelled out and utilized in order to discuss various controversies in political life, such as the nature of obligations to the state and the justice of the distribution of material resources. Then, however, the entire framework of liberalism will be challenged from a variety of viewpoints, ones which all question its basic presuppositions as well as its policy implications. Parts I and II of the book manifest these two orientations, respectively. To make this clearer, let me explain further what I mean by the 'liberal' paradigm of political philosophy.

The liberal democratic paradigm

In one's initial encounter with political philosophy, the term 'liberalism' conjures up rather specific political programs, ones associated with the Democratic party in the USA, for example, or (to some degree) the Labour and Liberal Democratic parties in Britain. It is thought to be contrasted, as well, with the 'conservatism' of American Republicans, British Tories, and European Christian Democrats. But the concept of liberalism in political philosophy is meant to apply much more broadly than this, to the philosophical principles underlying the model of the constitutional democracies that emerged in Europe and the north Atlantic in the seventeenth and eighteenth centuries, regimes which are generally committed to the rule of law, popular sovereignty, and the protection of human rights. Under that rubric, philosophical liberalism, as we might call it, encompasses much if not all of what is called 'conservative' in contemporary Western politics. (Though, in Chapter 5, we will consider a philosophical view meant as a challenge to philosophical liberalism which we will label 'conservativism.') I will expand on the basic components of the liberal model in the next chapter (and in Chapter 4), but first, some preliminaries.

I will refer to the paradigm of political philosophy being discussed

INTRODUCTION

here as (interchangeably) 'the liberal democratic model,' 'philosophical liberalism,' 'political liberalism' (though this last term will be narrowed in scope in Chapter 4), and simply 'liberalism.' It is a general approach to the justification of political authority that sees such authority as resting fundamentally on the rights and choices of individual citizens, whose rational autonomy and freedom to choose for themselves is respected by such authority. In particular, liberalism is the view that the most fundamental role of the state is to secure *justice* for citizens and not, for example, to promote their good or their virtue. Protecting their rights and regulating social relations among them is the first priority of political institutions, not trying to make sure such citizens live fulfilling or flourishing lives.

So the protection of individual liberty, in particular the liberty to form and revise one's own conception of the good life, is fundamental. This means that religious freedom, freedom of association, speech, and privacy will have basic importance. This priority is based on the equality of status that all citizens enjoy in regimes organized by liberal principles. This equality of moral status is attributed to all persons because they are rational, autonomous agents. Therefore, the concept of the 'person' or 'citizen' assumed in liberal theory is that of an independent rational agent, one who has the capacity to reflect upon and alter her choices and to form commitments with others (and with traditions, religions, families, and nations) by way of this rational reflection.

In short, the liberal state is committed to a kind of *neutrality* regarding its citizens' pursuit of their own good. This is because such neutrality is required by the more basic principle that every citizen is autonomous and of equal moral standing and so deserving of respect. And given that citizens pursue (autonomously) diverse conceptions of value, the state violates that respect if it is not neutral concerning those conceptions. This is why the liberal state is also committed to a principle of tolerance, tolerance for any value system or set of beliefs that citizens may hold, as long as their pursuit of that value system does not inhibit similar pursuit on the part of others. The question that we will have to consider, however, is how to draw the line defining the limits of this tolerance: for example should liberal states tolerate those who advocate sexist or racist (or any non-liberal) policies?

But a question that will snap constantly at the heels of liberal theorists will be whether a liberal state can maintain the kind of neutrality to which it is committed in light of the extreme *diversity* of its population. The increasing globalization mentioned above makes the assumption of a culturally homogenous population no longer tenable. Along with increasing multiculturalism comes greater plurality of values, ways of thinking, social structures, religious faiths, and political outlooks, many of which include views that are diametrically opposed to certain aspects of a liberal culture. A trenchant issue for liberalism will be whether it can retain its supposed neutral stance in light of such heterogeneity, or whether liberal philosophy itself is just one more contender in the arena of political disagreement and not the impartial, objective, framework within which all such disagreements can be worked out that it pretends to be.

Indeed, what we are calling liberal political philosophy here emerged in Europe out of the intellectual milieu of the Enlightenment, where faith in the power of rational thought and the search for universal objective principles of knowledge, science, and morality predominated. In the shadow of the Protestant Reformation and the development of the Newtonian mechanistic world view came the idea that individuals themselves must be the source of judgments of what is good or right for them (within severe limits of course). So political authority, formerly considered to rest on the divine right of monarchs working within a larger natural (and divine) order, came to be thought of as resting ultimately on the consent of the governed, expressed most notably by the idea of a social contract.

The social contract approach to political authority initially was meant to manifest a conception of justice that conformed to the strictures of natural law, where such law includes fundamental reference to the natural *rights* of individuals (such as the rights to life, liberty, and property). Further, this whole picture – that political authority is grounded in a social contract – was considered to be determined by objective reason and applied universally. It is not just English or French people that ought to be governed by a social contract, but *humanity as such*. Reason told us so.

So liberalism arose out of a framework in which it is presumed that moral conclusions can rest on ineluctable reason and apply to all human beings. Of course, in their original versions, these political theories never in fact applied to all persons as such, nor were they really meant by their defenders to do so. Women, enslaved peoples, indigenous victims of colonial expansion, non-property owners, and others were explicitly left out of the social contract. So the claim to universalism, and perhaps also the 'objectivity' with which these conclusions were reached, might be brought into serious question. The issue that remains for more recent versions of the liberal view is this: given the history of exclusion in defining the groups to which these supposedly 'universal' liberal principles applied, can such principles *ever* claim to be universal and objective?

INTRODUCTION

However, before proceeding to consider such controversies, let us be clear about some preliminary matters that will be of relevance throughout these discussions.

Preliminaries I: Method

The humanities in general, and philosophy in particular, has no 'method' securely its own, comparable to the experimental and statistical methods of the sciences. However, one might be able to detect an amalgam of 'standard' modes of approaching philosophical issues (moral and political issues in particular). The reigning 'method' for moral and political philosophy, at least in the Anglo-American analytic school of philosophy, directs that such thought proceeds basically by analyzing the meanings of key concepts (such as 'freedom,' 'rights,' or 'neutrality') and combining that analysis with logically structured arguments showing the implications of particular positions using those concepts. Reference to our 'intuitions' is also thought to be important in assessing specific moral principles based on the practical implications that can be drawn from them. So, for example, when a principle implies that killing innocent people is sometimes permissible, we quickly reject this position for having 'counterintuitive' implications. In both moral and political philosophy, then, much attention is given to interpreting and analyzing key concepts, constructing arguments built up from them, and scrutinizing the implications of views for their intuitiveness. (Though, as we will see, intuitions alone are not the sole measure of plausibility for a position.)

This method of argumentation yields a structure with the following components: a set of basic, axiomatic ideas, along with analysis of the key terms in those ideas; and a set of deductive inferences that lead to normative conclusions whose implications in the real world are acceptable intuitively. Such a model of philosophical method, simplified as it is, is most at home in analytic philosophical traditions, where emphasis is placed on clarity of meaning of key concepts and the testability of the hypotheses put forward (the resemblance to scientific method here is not accidental). But it is important to keep in mind various limitations of this method, not only as seen from alternative philosophical traditions (such as continental philosophy) but also from within analytic philosophy itself. The most obvious point to make about relying on (deductive) arguments like this is that they will, at best, show that some conclusion or criticism is true only if the axiomatic first principles from which it is derived, as well as any other premises imported into the argument, are also true. But this just pushes the inquiry back to those premises and first principles themselves. It might have once been thought (and is still thought by some) that substantive normative conclusions can be drawn from 'first principles' – claims that no reasonable person could reject – so that conclusions then are irresistible. But the belief that 'first philosophy' of this sort is likely to succeed is very dubious, since there are many reasons to think that basic claims (upon which such philosophical systems are built) are not indubitable or even meaningful *by themselves*, independent of their place in a system of thought and belief which includes the conclusions they imply (Larmore 1996: 4–16). This is especially so in political philosophy, where the assumption of shared starting points, universal values, and undeniable basic propositions is often precisely what is at issue.

And of course argumentation of this sort never really tells the whole story: there are always unmentioned assumptions lurking in the background whose truth is required for the argument's cogency. Such background assumptions may concern contingent facts about the world to which the conclusions are meant to apply, or the psychological characteristics of the people governed by them, or the sociological facts assumed for the societies they cover. This is not to say that argumentation can somehow be avoided – indeed, arguments are ubiquitous in this book – but only that such deductive moves are always functioning on the backs of countless unstated assumptions whose truth may be contestable, but which are crucial for the cogency of the arguments.

The point holds similarly for the analysis of concepts. Terms that wield such normative power as 'freedom' or 'justice' cannot simply be analyzed impartially, where their inner structure is laid open for all to see and understand. Such terms are as contestable as the normative conclusions they are used to support. If I argued, for example, that freedom means . . . (fill in the blank) and that therefore private property should be abolished because it interferes with freedom, those who disagree with my conclusion will immediately question the particular understanding of the concept of freedom I proposed to support it. Such a conception is only as acceptable as the normative (and other) implications it carries with it. Moreover, terms such as this are made meaningful by their *use* (sometimes officially codified use) in institutional and social settings. We cannot merely find the inner conceptual structure of such terms in a dictionary somewhere in order to settle political controversies. We must see how they are used in real life, in legal settings for example or in the charters and policies of institutions, to see what work they generally do in the social practices of the real world. This makes conceptual understanding a complicated matter indeed (perhaps a never ending process) but nevertheless one that is not settled by purely detached reflection alone.

INTRODUCTION

Relevant to this point is an issue that has received a great deal of philosophical attention at least since the eighteenth century: the supposed distinction between 'facts' and 'values.' David Hume observed that whenever he saw an argument that went from descriptive, non-normative premises (facts) to evaluative, normative or moral conclusions (values), there inevitably occurred a surreptitious moral statement somewhere in the premises, or else the supposed deduction did not really succeed (Hume 1739). That led to the general assumption that there was a fundamental distinction between propositions stating matters of fact ('candidate Jones garnered 57 percent of the vote in the election') and propositions expressing values, norms or moral principles ('candidate Jones did wrong in accepting the bribe'). Methodologically, this underlies the separation between the sciences (the social sciences among them) and moral and political theories, at least those philosophical theories which include evaluations of morality and politics.

The 'fact-value' distinction runs parallel to the assumption that propositions reporting facts about the world, so-called synthetic or contingent propositions, are fundamentally distinct from propositions that merely express the meanings of words and are thereby true by definition (the supposed analytic-synthetic distinction). But both of these distinctions have been thoroughly questioned, and for related reasons. In both cases, it is very difficult to express exactly where the line should be drawn between the two kinds of propositions and what grounds there are (independent of the distinction itself) for drawing it. A seemingly neutral factual claim, such as 'his father left him at the entrance of the airport' contains concepts such as 'father' which embody a number of normative ideas about power and responsibility which can be grasped only by knowing about various social categories and norms. (Such assumptions would help explain the alarm we would feel upon learning that the son in question was only one year old.)

However, one connection between so-called facts and values that continues to be seen as valid is that expressed by the principle 'ought implies can.' This claim, whose force really lies in its converse, is that no obligation – no 'ought' – can validly apply unless the action in question is at least possible. So if one *cannot* carry out the action, then it is not the case that one *ought* to do so (the obligation is not really valid). In this way, all normative claims carry with them some presumption about what is possible, and that presumption rests on any number of descriptive or factual claims about the world and the people in it. In this way, once again, we see the difficulty of keeping completely separate the world of factual investigation from that of normative or philosophical analysis. (For this reason, it should be noted, political philosophy has become increasingly interdisciplinary, utilizing work from the social and behavioral sciences as well as the other humanities as part of its overall enterprise.)

Another important function of philosophical reflection that is not often stressed in standard approaches is that of *interpretation*, where phenomena or concepts are explicated not to reveal their necessary and sufficient conditions (their definitions), but rather to creatively produce new ways of understanding them. Instead of analyzing concepts as free-standing entities, the project of interpretation produces rich explications of ideas and phenomena understood as part of a larger context, similar to the project of interpreting a literary text. While admittedly not objective in the manner of a scientific investigation (whose 'objectivity' is itself a matter of debate), interpretive activity brings forth new, but not groundless or unfounded, revelations about activities, ideas, and practices. At home in the 'hermeneutic' tradition of philosophy (a school most closely associated with the philosopher Hans Georg Gadamer but which arises out of the hermeneutic techniques of literary scholarship), interpretive analysis is unavoidable in any rich theoretical understanding of political phenomena (Rorty 1991). Certain gestures, for example – a raised fist, a song of protest, a street demonstration – have an expressive power that cannot be reduced to the true-or-false propositions that one might deduce from them. And in so far as understanding such gestures is part of understanding the mechanics of democratic action, then a fully worked out political theory will have to make use of interpretive reflections of this sort that go beyond conceptual analysis and deductive argumentation.

Indeed, the analysis of concepts cannot take place outside of the real world of politics – where meanings of key terms are fixed in part by the historical backdrop against which they are used, the practices in which they function, the institutional sense given to them, and the like. For this reason, political theories which formulate principles that are meant to be stable, clear, and unchanging in their meaning and applications may appear suspect. Because of this suspicion, some theorists will insist that, in the end, the meaning and scope of principles must be the result of real-world, ultimately political, discussion and debate rather than detached philosophical theorizing (Young 1990a, Habermas 1996a, 1998, Benhabib 1996b, Fraser 1997). All that political *theory* can do is specify the necessary conditions for such discussion to take place.

In addition to putting forward an influential political theory, Rawls also developed an approach to the methodology of political theorizing that we should mention here, one which departs from merely analyzing concepts or constructing foundationalist arguments from axiomatic first principles. This method is called 'reflective equilibrium.' This approach demands that we evaluate a given moral or political view by testing it against our 'considered judgments at all levels of generality' (Rawls 1999a: 286–302; cf. also Rawls 1971: 19–21, 48–51). That is, we consider the general coherence of the abstract principles comprising the theory in terms of their internal relations and general surface plausibility (given the arguments supporting them); we then examine the particular judgments that such principles imply about specific cases in the world; and we consider the entire package for its overall acceptability, considering its abstract plausibility, internal coherence, and 'intuitive' adequacy in particular cases.

So the test of reflective equilibrium is a coherentist account of the validity of normative claims. In calling it 'coherentist,' I mean to contrast it, on the one hand, with various forms of 'foundationalism,' in that it does not demand that we proceed from indubitable first principles and derive conclusions via deductive argument from them alone. It can, on the other hand, also be contrasted with 'intuitionism,' which demands that we merely look at the street-level judgments in isolation. But notice that this means that normative claims are always subject to review in light of new understandings either of the moral principles themselves or aspects of the world to which the principles are meant to apply, aspects that may change or be seen in a new light by some powerful new interpretation of them. In this way, we see again both the role that interpretation will play in political theorizing and also how interdisciplinary the whole enterprise will be. It also indicates that political judgments are seldom a hard and fast affair, but rather always open to reconsideration in light of new insights or information.

This rather detailed table-setting about method was necessary not just to be clear about what will be going on in the coming pages, but also to introduce ideas that will become relevant when we consider challenges to the liberal model of political philosophy. For many of these challenges will question not only the substantive principles of liberalism (the priority of individual rights for instance), but also the methods by which political principles are justified and evaluated in that tradition. Relying on detached reflection on concepts and arguments, where the historical location or personal characteristics of the person reflecting is not mentioned, will be the focus of critique for those who think that such philosophical reflections inevitably conceal the more basic power dynamics driving the defense of theories and policies in question. (See Chapters 6 and 7 below for discussion.)

Preliminaries II: Moral theory and political philosophy

It will be useful to outline the general features of moral philosophy in the Western, Anglo-American tradition that are often brought to bear in political philosophy. However, it is generally the case that political theories include their own methods of justification, as was just described. But the three dominant approaches to morality which will be relevant in discussions of political theories in the tradition assumed here are these: utilitarianism and other forms of consequentialist morality; deontology (or Kantian ethics); and virtue ethics.

Utilitarianism is a straightforward view about morality that is (roughly) summed up by the slogan that what is morally right is that which produces 'the greatest happiness for the greatest number.' In general, it is the view that actions, rules, character traits, policies, and institutions should be evaluated according to the level of 'good' (utility) they produce. So what is *right* – what is acceptable or right to do – is defined in terms of what is *good* – utility itself. Only the consequences of the act (rule, character trait, and so on) matter, not its intrinsic nature. Judgments are never based on the act or norm in question, always on its consequences, in particular on whether it produces the maximum good (utility) compared with all feasible alternatives.

But 'utility' – the good that is to be maximized according to the theory – is subject to a variety of interpretations, each suggesting a variant of utilitarian theory. (Variants can also be defined according to whether 'acts,' 'rules,' 'institutions,' and so on are the primary focus of evaluation.) Utility is traditionally thought of as a measure of human happiness or pleasure. In the original formulation by Jeremy Bentham and his followers, utility was defined as pleasure, measured only by its intensity, duration, and such, as experienced by the agent. Later utilitarians such as John Stuart Mill put forth more complex theories of utility meant to encompass aspects of life not reducible simply to pleasure or felt experience. But in general, either 'utility' is taken to refer to subjective, psychological states, such as pleasure or felt contentment, or it is understood more abstractly as a state of a person apart from her experiences, such as the degree to which her preferences have been satisfied (where preferences are just things a person *has* rather than something she necessarily *feels*). Also, utility can be considered either as something that can be compared across individuals or not. Understanding utility as pleasure (measured by its intensity and duration, say) might imply that it is meaningful to measure the different degrees of utility that two (or more) people experience (as the intensity and duration of their states of pleasure). But if one thinks of utility as just an index of the satisfaction

INTRODUCTION

of a person's preferences, then it will not be possible to meaningfully compare the different levels of utility different people experience. All one can then ask is whether people are better or worse off than, or the same as they each used to be (individually).

However, all variants of utilitarianism share a certain canonical structure comprised of three main components: (a) only consequences matter; (b) consequences are evaluated only in terms of the utility contained in them; and (c) maximum levels of utility in such consequences ought to be aimed at by the acts, rules (and so on) being evaluated (Sen 1997: 111).

Deontological theory is the approach to morality that grew out of the work of Immanuel Kant, who developed a highly complex and interconnected philosophy of knowledge, morality, judgment, and politics in the eighteenth century (though versions of this approach to morality has much older roots). In general, deontological theory defines what is morally right in terms of certain objectively valid duties, derived purely from reasoned reflection on the structure of rational agency (and without reference to the consequences of acting on the duty in question). More particularly, Kantian deontology defines morality as that set of necessarily obligatory principles derived from the structure of practical reason itself. Morality is based on the self-imposition of objectively valid moral imperatives grasped through reflective reason alone (without reference to contingencies of time, place, or consequence). Reason and autonomy, then, are the basic foundations of morality, for Kant.

In this way, Kantian deontology is a morality based squarely on the ultimate moral value of the *person*, and in two related ways. Moral principles are derived from the point of view of the reasonable person and are binding only in so far as she can impose such principles on herself, and hence manifest autonomy in doing so (she is 'self-governing'). Kant argued that every rational person, by virtue of the structure of her reason and freedom (autonomy), is bound by certain universal principles that she is able to apprehend and impose upon herself, principles manifested in the Categorical Imperative that says that one should act only if one can consistently will one's intended act (one's 'maxim') to be a universal law for everyone (Kant [1785] 1983: 14). Second, Kantian morality views persons themselves as fundamentally valuable, as the seat of dignity and moral worth, so that no act or policy can be justified if it ignores or exploits some person in order to achieve some valuable goal (the end *never* justifies the means). The second version of the Categorical Imperative states that one must never treat humanity in oneself or others as a mere means, only as an end in itself (ibid.: 36). In this way, Kantianism is fundamentally anti-paternalist – one can never interfere with a reasonable person for her own good – and anti-utilitarian, since it is never right to sacrifice the rights of one person for the greater good of others.

The duties not to use people, not to interfere with them against their will, and the like that Kantian ethics sees as fundamental can best be expressed in terms of the basic rights that all human beings enjoy, rights they hold simply in virtue of their humanity and not based on any contract or convention. In this way, doctrines of 'human rights' are at home in Kantian theory (though a moral theorist can justify the importance of protecting individual rights on other grounds as well). This aspect of Kantian theory makes apparent how the dominant strand of liberal political philosophy – where the protection of individual rights is fundamental and the state is enjoined not to promote the good of citizens against their will – rests on Kantian assumptions, as we will see. The fundamental obligation to respect persons as rational agents able to choose their moral values for themselves is at once a Kantian demand as well as a paradigmatically liberal one.

The third approach to morality that has dominated philosophical thinking in the analytic tradition of late is what has come to be called 'virtue ethics' or 'virtue theory.' Arising from the work of Aristotle, virtue theory begins with the conception of the ideal human life, one where the person enjoys a high degree of moral happiness – where she *flourishes* in the fullest sense of that term – as the fundamental moral good. The view then defines a variety of character traits – virtues – that are thought to be necessary for the person to lead such a flourishing life, hence to achieve that good. Institutions and social practices can be evaluated, then, according to how they allow that development and accord with the demands of such virtues. The highest achievement of a state will be to ensure that its citizens flourish in this sense.

Moreover, human beings from this view are understood as fundamentally *social* beings, whose happiness can only be understood in terms of the social context in which they live and grow. This may add a degree of relativism to the view (such that what counts as courage in ancient Greece is different from what courage demands in inner-city America). For this reason, as we will see, virtue ethics will provide the spring board for specifically *anti*-liberal viewpoints, in particular for communitarianism (see Chapter 5).

In addition to these standard views, moral theorists have been pressing alternative perspectives, motivated often by basic criticisms of these traditions. For example, spurred by feminist critiques of both utilitarianism and Kantianism, 'care ethics' has been put forward as better expressing the experiences of, and the elements of life associated with, women. Care ethics stresses the importance of protecting relations with others, and places in a secondary position universal obligations to do one's objective duty or to maximize utility overall. (Some have seen care ethics as somewhat congenial to a certain understanding of virtue theory – see, for example, Stocker 1987.) What is especially distinctive about this approach to morality is its insistence that one's obligations are thoroughly contextual and local, and that no amount of detached, impartial, and impersonal theorizing can capture the specific nature of our moral needs and directives (see Noddings 1984 for discussion). A mother has a set of obligations to a *particular* child or children, for example, and those obligations are subtly shaped by the contingencies of both (all) their lives. So one can notice straight away the sharp contrast with, say, Kantian moral philosophy, in that the focus is on our relational, affective, and contextually embedded moral commitments rather than our capacity for detached reflection and individual choice (our rational autonomy). (We will discuss this view in greater detail in Chapter 6.)

Other approaches to morality will be mentioned as we proceed. Such alternatives will often be part of the critical motivation that guides challenges to liberal political philosophy, so that not only the substantive politics, but also the whole approach to moral philosophy that liberalism presupposes will be questioned. For this reason, as I mentioned, doing political philosophy these days involves one in some rather basic (and hence very complex) philosophical conundrums.

Structure of the book

The core of the book will be the presentation of the general framework that dominates political thought in current philosophy – liberalism – and then consideration of fundamental criticisms of that framework. Part I is concerned with laying out the contours of the liberal approach to political philosophy, both methodologically and in terms of substantive principles. We will proceed by considering various controversies that arise from *within* the liberal paradigm, controversies that reveal its fundamental commitments and (perhaps) weaknesses. The first such controversy involves the basic question of political authority: how can centralized political power be justified at all in a way that does not violate the basic moral claims of individual people whose lives are shaped by that power (Chapter 2)? Included in this examination will be a look at the 'social contract' tradition of liberal thought which claims that only when individuals have somehow *agreed* to the existence and pattern of operation of political authorities are they acceptable.

Next, the issue of how to distribute society's resources will be addressed (Chapter 3). If people are considered as having fundamentally equal moral status (as they are in the liberal tradition), what mechanism of property rights and economic justice should be adopted in a just society? It is here that we will take up the questions of distributive justice that, as I mentioned, have dominated the philosophical landscape in the 1970s and 1980s, pitting free-market libertarian views against radically egalitarian stands. More recently, however, there has been much discussion of how to cash out the 'equality' that must be recognized in all citizens: even if we grant that all people are owed respect for their basic equality, this still leaves open the question 'equality of what?'

In each of these cases, however, the overall liberal approach to political philosophy will be used as a paradigm within which these more particular questions can be raised. But we will then consider in more depth the nature of that paradigm – the basic contours of liberal theory that, in the fundamental challenges to that model, receive so much critical scrutiny. Central to our inquiry will be the liberal claim that the fundamental obligation of the state is to secure justice for its citizens while remaining neutral concerning their individual conceptions of moral value and the good life. This will be challenged by 'perfectionists' who claim that advancing the good for people should be the primary aim of governments, with protecting their rights (specified in principles of justice) merely part of that project. This discussion will bring the fundamental commitments of liberalism into sharper focus (Chapter 4).

It is here that liberalism will begin to be put on the defensive, particularly concerning its allegedly neutral and universal applicability. Now, in some recent variations of the liberal approach, philosophers have specifically given up on the universalist pretensions of classical liberalism. That is, instead of insisting that the moral values supporting liberal democratic regimes are universal principles grounded in reason and so applicable in principle to all peoples at all times in history, these thinkers claim that liberalism is justified only as a 'political' device for establishing stable and peaceful relations among diverse people and groups who exist at a certain point in history. The principles of liberalism, then, such as the priority put on protecting individual liberty, equal opportunity, and the reduction of unjustified inequalities, are said to be justified as a useful set of principles around which some consensus can be gained among increasingly pluralistic and multicultural citizens in order to achieve stability and peace in their societies. (We mentioned earlier Rawls's articulation of this position.) Other defenders of liberalism, however, continue to stick more closely to the classical model, saying that the liberal framework can be justified by comprehensive moral considerations, backed up by philosophical arguments, to which we are all morally committed. So we will have to discuss whether liberalism is best seen as a political compromise around which people with very different moral outlooks can commit themselves (for their own reasons) or as a fundamental moral outlook itself, of which clear-thinking reasonable people can all be convinced but which remains neutral toward the wide variety of differences found in the modern world.

But in either case, we will consider fundamental challenges to this approach to political philosophy in Part II. On the one hand, it will be charged that liberalism is too *individualistic* in its outlook – insisting as it does that individual freedoms be protected prior to any promotion of a person's or group's good. On the other hand, some claim that people gain their identity, outlook, moral motivation and self-understanding through their membership in *communities* and *groups* of various kinds. Therefore, unless the state protects the existence and promotes the flourishing of those communities and groups, people's real interests will not be properly protected by it. Amid discussion of this challenge will be the consideration that liberalism is not only not a universal, neutral approach to political philosophy generally, but that it is specifically aligned with the 'liberalism' in social policy that we put to the side above, and that an alternative 'conservative' approach is equally viable. The connection between this conservative alternative and the communitarian critique of liberalism will be explored (Chapter 5).

Next, it will similarly be claimed that liberalism fails as a neutral and unbiased philosophy in that it reflects a point of view and set of interests that many people do not share. In particular, the fact that liberal philosophy narrowly reflects a white, male, mostly middle-class perspective about value and justice will be made the centerpiece of critiques which thematize race and gender (Chapter 6). This will connect with the previous chapter's emphasis on the model of the 'person' presupposed by liberalism, a model that will be given increased scrutiny. In addition, we will consider in this chapter a challenge not just to liberalism, but to the entire mode of political theorizing dominant in analytic philosophical contexts, a challenge that points to the way such theorizing abstracts from the actual histories of struggle and oppression found in modern societies. Such struggles, it will be argued, manifest profound *injustice* that tends to get ignored by the traditional philosophical emphasis on detached, timeless reflections. These criticisms will claim that political philosophy must be as much about (actual) injustice as it is about (idealized) justice.

Finally, we will subject the liberal paradigm to even more radical critique (Chapter 7). This will include a challenge from contemporary versions of Marxism that argue that liberal theory utilizes a philosophical method which serves merely to reflect the interests of the dominant powers in society (capitalism), and it does this by ignoring the more basic material and economic forces that structure thought and value, including the thoughts and values reflected in that very philosophical method. In addition, the liberal view will be charged with complicity in a more general pattern of thinking typical of the post-Enlightenment, European world view (that is, of *modernity*). The reliance on rationality, both in assumptions about citizens and in its own philosophical methods, will be challenged by those who claim that rationality is itself an illusion – one resting on an outdated faith in the settled nature of language, in the clear-cut meanings of signs and symbols, and in the ability of people to understand their own motives and thought processes. Once it is understood just how open-ended, variable, and fuzzy meanings are (as are the thought processes, language, and motivations that inform people's choices), the philosophical method that liberalism rests upon will be shaken. And liberalism will be forced to confront the profoundly variable nature of identity and thought: it will once again have to confront the phenomenon of *difference*.

Along the way, through all of this abstract theorizing, I hope to explain how disagreements at this level directly effect decisions of policy and public controversy in everyday politics (the 'Case to consider' at the close of each chapter). These are presented as both examples to discuss as well as test cases for the particular policies that abstract theories may be committed to supporting. For example, the liberal model posits a strict priority for the protection of individual freedom (such as the freedom of speech) over the promotion of other interests (such as promoting greater racial harmony). Does this mean that codes on college campuses forbidding 'hate speech' are always unjust? Or does this mean that in so far as liberal theory implies that such codes are unjust, liberal theory is itself biased and parochial? As we will see, debates such as this one will make salient disagreements about the fundamental principles of social and political institutions, where principles such as freedom of expression come into direct conflict with the goal of promoting a healthy community atmosphere of mutual respect. In all these cases, discussion can center around both the question of whether some dominant view supports the policy in question as well as whether, given that it *does* support such a policy, that view is therefore problematic. In this way, the technique of testing theories by the method of 'reflective equilibrium' can be put to use.

INTRODUCTION

As with any finite survey of such a complex array of material such as this, the focus will admittedly be highly selective. As already mentioned, the philosophical world being covered in these pages is that of the European (particularly English-speaking) and North American philosophical traditions (and even within that locale, only certain strands are examined). Given that, many powerful philosophical movements and issues will be left out. This is inevitable, though no less unfortunate. Charges of narrowness of the scope of this study, then, will be inevitable and understandable. My only response, in addition to mentioning obvious limitations of both space and of my own abilities, is that I want to make questions of exclusion, artificial claims of universality, and presumptions of objectivity *themselves* central to the discussion, so that readers of this survey will be afforded the theoretical space to raise questions about the structure of the work itself, its own exclusionary structure and silent (and perhaps silencing) background assumptions.

Chapter summary

This chapter aimed to set the stage for the subsequent discussions in the book. We considered why political philosophy has special poignancy these days in light of recent geopolitical, cultural, and intellectual changes. We noted, in particular, a shift in the focus of this philosophy from considering various controversies from *within* a given paradigm of political thought – liberal theory – to asking fundamental questions about the viability of that paradigm itself. We then considered the basic contours of the liberal model of political philosophy, emphasizing its commitment to grounding all political authority in the rights of citizens themselves and the priority of justice over promoting good lives or virtue. This last tenet connects with the neutrality to which liberalism is committed concerning citizens' diverse moral, religious, cultural, and political orientations, a neutrality that must be maintained while recognizing the deep diversity among those orientations found in the modern world.

It was also necessary to spell out some preliminaries to our later discussions. First, the methods of moral and political theorizing were examined, where the role of intuitions as basic tests of given principles, the analysis of concepts, and the use of deductive argument to support positions were considered. We also introduced (while at the same time questioning) the alleged distinction between statements of 'fact' and statements of 'value,' and added that interpretation must also be included in political philosophy as an activity which neither derives values from basic principles, nor merely describes phenomena from a value-free standpoint, but rather mixes both to produce richer and more enlightening pictures of the social world. This discussion was rounded off by a consideration of 'reflective equilibrium' as an independent, coherentist, standard for measuring the plausibility of normative principles.

Next, we considered the major approaches to moral theorizing that play a role in political philosophy today; these include utilitarianism, Kantian theory (or deontology), and virtue theory, while noting additional views which do not fit neatly into any of those categories. Finally, the overall structure of the book was laid out, mentioning the strategy of setting out the details of the liberal paradigm, considering problems that arise within it (Part I), and then turning to fundamental challenges to that paradigm moved by considerations of community, race, and gender, and Marxism and post-modernism (Part II).

Notes on further reading

For a general overview of contemporary political philosophy, see Kymlicka 1990 and Hampton 1997. A very comprehensive collection of articles on political philosophy can be found in Kymlicka 1992. Introductions to moral theory of the sort relevant to the topics discussed here abound, but some examples are LaFollette 2000, Pojman 1999, Rachels 1993 and Singer 1993 (though an excellent supplement to these standard treatments is Sterba 2001.) For a discussion of utilitarianism specifically, see Sen and Williams 1982. Since Kantian moral thought figures prominently in the versions of liberal theory we will focus upon here, further reading into his moral philosophy might be recommended, for example O'Neill 1989, Hill 1992, and Korsgaard 1996. For a discussion of virtue ethics, see Slote 1992. For alternative approaches to morality, for example developing the 'care' perspective, see Gilligan 1982, Kittay and Meyers 1987, and Noddings 1984.

Rawls's work will be discussed in detail in upcoming chapters. His two major works are Rawls 1971 and 1993, though his collected papers are available in 1999a. For overviews of liberalism and its problems, see Kymlicka 1989, Larmore 1996, and Gray 1989 and 1993.

PART I

Basic issues within the liberal paradigm

CHAPTER 2

The problem of political authority

- The social contract tradition
- Hobbes's social contract: Mechanism, egoism, and rationality
- Locke: Reason, morality, and freedom
- Lessons from Rousseau and Kant
- From consent to legitimacy
- Chapter summary
- Case to consider
- Notes on further reading

As I described in the Introduction, the liberal approach to political philosophy involves a variety of theoretical and methodological commitments, ones that will be the subject of controversy as we proceed. First, however, I want to discuss various issues *within* the liberal paradigm, questions that arise against the backdrop of liberal philosophy without putting the components of that paradigm themselves in question. This will serve its own independent purpose, but it will hopefully also set the stage for our critical discussion of liberalism in Part II. The issue to be dealt with in this chapter is, for many thinkers, the fundamental question of political philosophy: what justifies the authority that political institutions wield over citizens? In short, what justifies the state?

First, we must be clear about what we mean by 'authority.' Clearly, to have authority over someone is to have power over them, to be in a position to shape their actions and reasons for acting. To be under authority, then, is to be in a position where one's actions and reasons for acting are shaped by that force. But this suggests an important distinction, between authority simpliciter (or *de facto* authority) and rightful or legitimate authority (*de jure* authority). Generally speaking, then, authority can be defined as a relation between a person or institution and another person (the subject of authority), which relation provides reasons for the subject to act that override her own reasons. That is, the presence of the authority gives the subject reasons that she otherwise would not have to act in a way that pre-empts her authority-independent reasons. One could go further and claim that legitimate authority is conceptually connected to obligation, such that when a person or institution has rightful authority over others, those others have a moral obligation to obey the dictates of that person or institution (within the bounds of its authority) (Raz 1986: 23–37).

The question of this chapter then can be put this way: what conditions would justify the exercise of legitimate political authority? Before asking this question, it is useful to reflect why it arises as a particular problem at all in political philosophy. Why does the presence of the *de facto* authority of the state – its power – demand a justification? The answer – almost too obvious to notice but which has ramifications in other areas of inquiry – is that it is assumed as a background condition that people are, and should remain, *free* unless sufficient justification is given for the limitation of that freedom.[1] This presumption, that we are all 'born free' as Rousseau put it, is part of the traditional setting within which questions of legitimate political authority have been asked (see Hart 1979). As we will see below, this presumption has often taken the form of imagining a 'state of nature' where people live without such political authority and to which life in such societies is compared.

The social contract tradition

The general proposition we will be considering in this section is the claim that state power is justified only if such power has been agreed to, by way of a contract of some sort, by those living under that power. Before considering historical examples of contract theory, let us be clear about the elements that go into any claim that an obligation rests on a previous contractual act. Such acts are undertaken by individuals who must negotiate over the terms of the contract with the resources they have access to, including mental and physical resources (to persuade others for example) and the capacities to understand their own desires and the opportunities before them. Differences in people's access to any such resources figure in the kind of terms they will agree to, hence the outcome of contractual negotiations are in large part a function of such access. Relevant also will be the criteria by which *participation* in the negotiations is allowed – just who are the parties whose interaction results in the contract? Such interaction takes place against a background of a non-contractual world – the world before or without the contract. The details of this pre-contractual condition are important because the contractees' relative position in such a condition will greatly affect what it will be rational for them to contract into. In the tradition we will now examine, the pre-contractual condition is understood as *the state of nature*.

Although this book is a look at contemporary political philosophy, the historical development of the liberal conception of justice is of crucial importance in understanding its main features. The liberal answer to the problem of political authority has the unique character it does in part because of the particular circumstances out of which it arose, circumstances that in many ways remain in place in the contemporary world. The tradition of thought that answers questions about political authority by reference to a social contract is thought to have begun in Europe in the seventeenth century, though its roots go further back than this. Prior to the sixteenth century, European thinkers understood the universe in an Aristotelean, teleological manner, where nature was thought to be organized according to an interlocking functional matrix whose operation contributed to an overall end, a *telos*. Royalty took their place, not sanctioned from below by the consent of the governed, but by their superior place in the overall structure of humanity (in the 'great chain of being'); and states and kingdoms were evaluated according to how they flourished rather than whether they were 'just' in some modern sense (Skinner 1978).

Replacing this teleological picture of things was what was called the 'New Science,' a mechanistic world view where natural phenomena (including human thought and action) were explained not with reference to final functions and purposes, but rather in terms of the chains of causes and effects that produced them. Parallel to this intellectual transformation was the Protestant Reformation, which rejected the idea of a hierarchically structured, metaphysically grounded view of the world where individuals' identity and value were defined solely by their place in this order. The idea of a contract among citizens and rulers, then, emerged as the prime source of the justification of state authority consistent with Protestant individualism and non-teleological metaphysics.

Also important is that this transition occurred following almost two centuries of bloody conflict by religious groups fighting for geopolitical dominance and motivated by differing conceptions of divine mandate, the so-called 'Wars of Religion.' The seemingly interminable nature of this warfare provided the historical backdrop to the idea that toleration and mutual respect for difference could co-exist with overall popular consent to a single (and increasingly secular) locus of power. This can be seen as the germinal form of the idea of mutual respect for individual autonomy and the inescapable plurality of moral outlooks that characterize modern liberal political theory (cf. Schneewind 1998).

Returning to the social contract theorists themselves, the concept of 'natural rights' plays an important role in these approaches to political justification. Indeed, the idea that individuals are endowed with certain innate rights to justifiably act according to their individual wills – so familiar a concept to contemporary ears – was indeed radical at the point when the social contract view was beginning to flourish. The overarching principles that specified the order of nature and dictated its proper functioning – natural law – came to be seen in increasingly secular terms, as scientific laws rather than theological principles. Natural right also evolved from the specification of what it is objectively *right* for a person to do (in the way it is 'naturally' right for a plant to grow and reproduce) to what, subjectively, a person *chooses* to do. Conditions that resulted from free choice within people's natural rights, then, were just, simply because such people rationally chose to produce those conditions (Tuck 1979).

Also, it is presumed that natural rights are exercised according to *Reason*, in that the rights specified were ones that allowed rational and moral action only. One did not have a natural right to act whimsically or in an evil manner. Putting these ideas together, then, political justification came to be seen to rest on the choices people made within the dictates of reason and natural right. As we will see below, this combines two ideas that can in principle be separated – the idea that a person's *choice* justifies a state of affairs and the idea that such a state is justified because it is in the person's or persons' rational *interest*. In the sixteenth and seventeenth centuries, however, a person's right to act and choose was seen as coterminous with what that person would reasonably choose, and hence what would be in her rational interest to do.

These considerations, then, generally characterize the approach to political authority that will later evolve into the liberal paradigm for justice. First, however, let us look more closely at the historical precedents for that development.

Hobbes's social contract: Mechanism, egoism and rationality

Thomas Hobbes (1588–1679) lived at a time when widespread warfare raged throughout Europe: the wars of religion in the sixteenth century and the Thirty Years' War in the seventeenth are particularly bloody examples. He was also a witness to a great upheaval in English political life, where parliamentary armies rose up against, and overthrew, Charles I. The idea that life without a strong central authority would result in a 'war of all against all' was not difficult for him to imagine.

Hobbes was both a mechanist and a materialist, believing that natural phenomena were made up (only) of physical elements that functioned according to deterministic laws of cause and effect. Human beings were no different, nor were their voluntary actions. For Hobbes, voluntary movement (what he called 'animal' motion) was caused by the external impact of some force on the senses proceeding to internal motions that are either helped (pleasure) or hindered (pain), issuing eventually (or not) in external movement. Such a system would operate according to a fundamental principle of continual motion, so that the most aversive eventuality would be death (the ceasing of all motion). So, for Hobbes, the most fundamental drive for all human beings was self-preservation, a drive that necessarily outranked any other competing desire, such as the possible desire to advance another's welfare (Hobbes [1651] 1986: 118–21, 183–87).

Similarly, Hobbes is widely understood as the prototypical representative of 'psychological egoism.'[2] Psychological egoism is the descriptive claim that, as a matter of psychological fact, the fundamental motive for all human beings is self-interest. Although people may at times act to serve the interests of others or take others' concerns into account, their *ultimate* aim is to advance their own interests, treating the satisfaction of others' needs as purely instrumental in the final accomplishment of their own goals. But we should be careful here to understand precisely what this claim of psychological egoism amounts to. For it is not (merely) the view that people act on *their own* desires, for this is consistent with saying that the most charitable person we could imagine would not disconfirm the theory since their desires to help others are still *their own desires* (making the view true of all self-motivated action by definition, and hence empty). Rather, an egoist such as Hobbes must claim that all people have as an actual *aim* the advancement of their own good, no matter how other-directed such action at first appears. Egoists of this sort must say that such apparently charitable people really have their *own* welfare in mind, even subconsciously, when they act on others' behalf (they want to avoid punishment or guilt, they are pursuing some reward or positive feeling, or the like).

With this psychological picture before us, we can now see how Hobbes's vision of life outside of society would be structured. Since people are completely selfish in the way described, they will act in others' interests only as a result of social conventions – laws, social practices, rules of behavior – backed up by formal and informal sanctions. Without these sanctions, people would have no immediate motive not to willfully pursue their own aims. Also, without established institutions (such as armies, police forces, and the like), all individuals would enjoy roughly the same level of power to accomplish their aims. No person or group of people (groups which would be internally unstable in any case) could dominate others to accomplish their goals (Hobbes

[1651] 1986: 183). And, finally, given the inevitable conflicts of desires among individuals, there would be constant violence and danger, for all would do what they could to accomplish their own goals and naturally encounter others of equal power doing the same, resulting in what Hobbes famously called a 'warre . . . of every man, against every man' where life would be 'solitary, poor, nasty, brutish, and short.' (ibid.: 185, 186) For Hobbes, then, any escape from this horrific state would be justified for those involved, in that it would be in keeping with reason in light of people's fundamental motives (and the laws of nature). What is justified about political power is equated with what is rational for those living under it to accept.

In order to understand this approach to political authority, it is necessary to grasp the full nature of the problem of social coordination among self-interested individuals acting rationally, but separately, and without any pre-existing mechanism of enforcement or rules. If two people encounter each other in such a situation, they may face an interactive situation that game theorists have labeled a Prisoner's Dilemma. This well-studied problem involves a choice situation where two independent actors must make a decision which will affect their respective well-being. In very general terms, a Prisoner's Dilemma (PD) obtains when the two actors face a choice situation where they would both be better off if they chose one option *together* (cooperated) but individually advantaged if they did not do so (defected). If they both could be assured that their counterparts would cooperate, they would be made best off by cooperating, but short of having that assurance, it is better for each of them to not cooperate. Since *each* of them is made individually better off by choosing the non-cooperative option – and without enforcement mechanisms in place to assure them that the other person will act cooperatively, they cannot be assured that they will – they both choose the non-cooperative option, despite its being less advantageous than if they both acted cooperatively together.

The simplest way to understand the dilemma is to picture the prospect of a two-person exchange without any way to enforce the agreement underlying the exchange. Picture, for example, a nefarious exchange of money for contraband, where the only factors relevant to the choice of action is the outcome of the exchange (and that no enforcement of choices is available, such as from the police). Imagine that the agreement is for you to leave a briefcase of money on a pre-assigned park bench while another person simultaneously leaves the contraband at a park bench four blocks away. By the time you get to the other briefcase to find out if the contraband is in it, your counterpart will be looking at the case you left to see if you left the money in it. You (supposedly) will never see this person again and will suffer (you hope) no repercussions if you leave an empty case (the other person can hardly go running to the police!).

What is it rational for you to do? You certainly would prefer making the deal to not doing so (after all, you're buying the contraband because you want it). But, surely, you also would love to have it for free, leaving an empty briefcase while getting the goods. So your best option is to leave an empty case. But your counterpart's choice situation is exactly the same – preferring a deal to none at all but most preferring both packages (and most dreading getting left with nothing). So if you are rational (and various other minor details hold true), you will leave an empty case and so will your counterpart. No deal!

Also, a parallel choice problem arises when a *group* decides to gather together to perform some joint task (this is called the 'collective action problem'). If there is no enforcement mechanism to induce compliance – like suffering from a bad reputation or losing friends and the like, or experiencing the joy of commingling with friends for its own sake – it will be in everyone's individual interest to stay home and let the others perform the task. For either enough people will show up and you will not be needed, in which case you waste your time and energy going out there, or they won't, in which case you *really* blow your day since you show up for nothing. (There are, of course, situations where you might be the crucial person tipping the balance between not having enough folks and having just enough; but we are imagining cases where the nature of the task makes that extremely unlikely, ones involving very large groups of people for example.) Now you, like everyone else, would prefer the task to be accomplished. But since everyone acting individually and with self-interested motives reasons the same way you do, then everyone fails to show up (though interestingly enough, selfishness is not strictly necessary for this problem to arise). So again, although everyone *acting together* would prefer outcome A (the exchange made or the task getting done) to outcome B (no deal or no task), B results because everyone acts as an individual to maximize her own interests. So, as a group, everyone loses.

One important additional detail should be mentioned here. If the interaction with another person were to happen more than once, if the exchange took the form of an 'iterated' Prisoner's Dilemma, then the considerations bearing on your choice change considerably. For one must then take into account the effect your choice has on the possibility of future cooperation with the person. (If you tried to run off with the money and the goods in the first deal, you can hardly be trusted in the future!) In iterated PDs, depending on how easy it is to identify those who have cooperated in the past and whether you can predict how many times you will interact again, it will likely be in your interest to cooperate – make the exchange for example – as long as the other person does also. (As soon as you encounter a lack of cooperation you should defect in the future though.) Although it might be a bit mysterious how things could ever get *started*, since the first encounter mirrors a PD, once people do start cooperating, such continued cooperation, even among self-interested individuals, could occur spontaneously and without external enforcement mechanisms.[3]

Returning now to Hobbes, in a state of nature where all individuals are rationally self-interested in the way specified, the interactions among people take on the structure of a PD (and a collective action problem). For Hobbes, there are no enforceable covenants or promises in the state of nature. Morality, including rights and obligations, only holds power over people when there is some enforcement mechanism in place to give them reasons to conform to it; without such things, morality does not exist. Indeed, Hobbes discusses the 'Foole' who has 'said in his heart' that there is no real justice, that one has no reason not to break promises whenever 'it conduces to one's benefit' (Hobbes [1651] 1986: 203). But his answer to the Foole is not that moral obligation is self-evidently binding. Rather, it is that as long as one will be in need of some 'confederates' with whom one wants some social interaction, then it is within reason to obey the conventions of morality; only if they never found out about the Foole's betrayals will others trust him enough to interact with him in the future. That is, with an iterated interaction, the problem of the Prisoner's Dilemma is altered so that mutual cooperation is actually rational among self-interested actors.

Like other thinkers in this tradition, Hobbes also specifies the Natural Laws that apply to human behavior. The general definition of a law of nature for human beings, says Hobbes, is that of a general rule 'found out by Reason, by which a man is forbidden to do, that, which is destructive of his life' (ibid.: 189). The first, fundamental law of nature, then, is to seek peace, and when that is not possible, to do whatever is necessary to defend oneself. In a state of nature (a war of all against all), it follows that everyone has a 'right' to everything, 'even to one another's body,' when that is necessary for survival. But the second fundamental law of nature, for Hobbes, is that a person should be willing, *when others are also*, to lay down his right to invade his neighbor's possessions in so far as peace and security can be established as a result. Hobbes then lists seventeen further laws of nature, such as that one should keep one's covenants, return good will to those who benefit you, cooperate with others, pardon offenses, and the like (ibid.: 201–14).

But one might be surprised to see such other-regarding obligations as *laws of nature* for Hobbes, the psychological egoist! The explanation is that such laws apply only when there is assurance that others in one's vicinity are acting in the same way; as Hobbes says: 'For he that should [obey the laws of nature] where no man els should do so, should but make himselfe a prey to others, and procure his own certain ruine, contrary to the ground of all Lawes of Nature' (ibid.: 215). The assurance in question can only be secured, however, when mechanisms of enforcement are erected in order to supply the correct incentives for general compliance, incentives appealing to the self-interest of all involved. Moreover, one can reasonably predict that many in the area (and even oneself on occasion) will be so moved by 'ambition, avarice, anger, and other Passions' (ibid.: 196) that even if it were perfectly rational to cooperate, many will not; and it will always be better to pre-emptively renege on a bargain than to be left holding the (empty) bag while another breaks her promise and acts non-cooperatively. So natural cooperation among people will not occur, even though the establishment of such cooperation would make it reasonable to continue to cooperate (see our discussion of the iterated PD above). Only when an external power is constructed, one to which all the rest of us hand over our individual abilities to exact our will (our weapons, say), will there exist a mechanism to enforce promises, contracts, laws, and, indeed, all the rest of morality and public law.[4]

This is the beginning of civil society, for Hobbes, and the ground for its justification as well. For citizens' granting complete sovereign power to one entity while forsaking all of their individual abilities to act on selfish interests establishes political authority and delivers them all from the state of nature, a state of endless war and conflict. Moreover, and this is crucial, since the state of nature was so full of conflict and opposition, meaning that no plans could be made, peaceful lifestyles pursued, property protected, or even survival assured, any civil society that ensures some measure of peace and survival will be in one's rational interest to enter. And since justification for Hobbes just means being in the rational interest of those affected, then such a state is justified, no matter how absolute the power of the sovereign.

This implies, then, that a state which denied citizens all basic freedoms (of speech, religion, association, privacy, and so on), but which nevertheless protected their bare existence, would be justified. For while such a state would surely enmiserate its citizens, it would still be preferable to the all-out war of a state of nature. The only justification for disobeying or attempting to destroy an existing sovereign would be protection of one's own life, a right which one never forgoes for Hobbes. So rebellion against tyrannical rulers, except when necessary to protect one's life, is *never* justified.

This sovereign could be embodied in 'one Man, or upone one Assembly of men' (Hobbes [1651] 1986: 227). Hobbes even claimed that a sovereign could be a democracy (though he strongly doubted that such a system could ever be stable – ibid.: 243–45.) But the social compact that secures and justifies the sovereign authority here is not a contract between the citizens and the sovereign (as will be the case with Locke, discussed below). For the sovereign cannot be bound by any contract or promise; to say otherwise would be to assume the presence of a third power, more powerful than both the sovereign and citizens, who could enforce such a contract, and there exists no such third power in this scenario.

Sovereignty is established, on Hobbes's view, out of the voluntary, rational action of those governed, at least some of the time. At others, it is imposed by force, either as an invading force or an internal consolidation of power. But although we can make a conceptual distinction between rule by conquest and rule by collective agreement (what Hobbes calls 'Sovereignty by Acquisition' and 'Sovereignty by Institution' – ibid.: 228–51), the grounds for the authority of a ruler, once in place, are the same in both cases. For even if a foreign power invaded one's territory and forcefully imposed a government, even a tyrannical one, one is still better off with such a government than in the state of nature.

Further, if in the initial decision to create a commonwealth (Sovereignty by Institution) one is in the minority in voting for this or that government, one is still bound by the result. Indeed, Hobbes provides a striking justification for the normative force of majority rule: the majority should hold sway merely because, based on superior numbers and hence superior might, they could 'destroy' the minority (ibid.: 221). The greater physical power of the larger numbers grounds their authority, on this view. So while Hobbes envisions a 'Congregation' coming together to decide whether or not to create a sovereign authority, whether one goes along with the others in this deliberation or not, one will either be a subject of the newly formed commonwealth or remain in a state of nature relative to it, which is worse of course. Therefore, one's obligation to an existing sovereign is completely independent of any act of choice on your part; you are obligated simply because the existence of such authority is in your *interest*, based on the assumptions about life outside of society we are making here.

The sovereign, for Hobbes, then stands in an 'agency' relation to the citizens (see Hampton 1997: 41). That is, however he, she or they (let us assume 'he') acts, unless he directly attacks the citizens and threatens their lives, he always acts in their interests. His power to protect the citizens from each other and from foreign enemies justifies his actions. For this reason, Hobbes claimed that the sovereign cannot ever injure the citizens, by definition, for to injure someone is to act in a way contrary to their interests. But his existence and all his (non-murderous) acts are effectively an extension of the citizens' individual wills, and since we cannot injure ourselves when we (rationally) decide to do something, he as our agent cannot injure us.

But there is a problem with this explanation/justification of absolute sovereignty: Hobbes is claiming that it will be rational for self-interested individuals in a state of war with each other to agree to lay down their weapons and allow an external authority to assume complete power over them all. This is because mutual cooperation cannot be expected to arise spontaneously – without the imposition of sanctions of some sort from outside. People's natural proclivities toward avarice, ambition, vainglory, and the like will prevent them from ever beginning the kinds of mutually cooperative enterprises that, along the lines of the iterated PD, would make it rational to continue to cooperate (that is, engage the Laws of Nature). David Hume would later argue, in fact, that a social contract cannot be the fundamental basis for political obligations, for conventions of promise keeping would not be in place unless one already had stable social relations with one's compatriots, that is, lived in a society with them. (Hume thought, in fact, that property rights must be established before one had anything to make promises *about*.) (Hume [1739] 1978: 516–25).

The problem in the Hobbesean context is complex, however, for it is unclear from the text whether Hobbes thought that spontaneous cooperation *could* arise out of the purely rational self-interested action of strangers in a state of nature (even absent disruptive passions) (for discussion, see Hampton 1986: ch. 2). In his answer to the Foole, he claims that 'without the help of Confederates' no one in the state of nature could 'hope by his own strength, or wit, to defend himself from destruction' (Hobbes: 204). Yet Hobbes repeatedly declares that such a society of cooperative individuals is impossible without an external power; indeed, this is what makes the state of nature so horrible in the first place. He claims that no one could rationally 'be received into any Society, that unite themselves for Peace and Defence, but by the errour of them that receive him' (ibid.: 205), implying that a rational person (a non-fool) would never join in confederation and 'society' with others without an already existing enforcement mechanism, something this line of argument is attempting to justify.

But this, then, gets to the heart of the difficulty for the Hobbesean view: for people in a state of nature as Hobbes describes it must find a way to cooperate among themselves *at least to the extent of setting up a sovereign*. That is, if the creation of a sovereign involves the mutual laying down of all defenses among the proto-citizens, presumably simultaneously since the person who did so first could be attacked by the others, then some minimally cooperative behavior is necessary to create a sovereign in the first place (to choose a form of government, actually appoint a particular person as leader, and so on). But if *this* amount of cooperation is indeed possible – whether through the gradual emergence of cooperative behavior along the lines of an iterated PD or by some miracle of sudden fellow feeling – then after this proclivity is established, people would presumably be able to cooperate without the need of an *all-powerful* external authority. They could see that such cooperation is beneficial to all (as long as non-cooperators could be identified). So if some common mode of internal defense could be set up – a police force that helped locate and prosecute non-cooperators (criminals) – then there is no need for the absolute sovereign that Hobbes is so famous for defending.

But this problem of spontaneous cooperation arises on the Hobbesean model only if we interpret it as a justification based on *will*, the actual rational choices of those affected by the authority structure in question. But as I noted above, on Hobbes's view there is no distinction where obligation is concerned between sovereignty by 'Institution' (based on will or choice) and sovereignty by 'Acquisition' (based on conquest). In either case, the existence of the sovereign prevents the reversion to the unpalatable state of nature. So we shouldn't worry about how the creation of the commonwealth actually arose – that is, always by force, if only the force of a majority whose superior numbers could destroy the rest of us; the claim is that its existence is in our *interest*.

The initial attractiveness of granting political authority through a social contract stems from the assumption that individuals are legitimately bound only by an authority that they have, in some sense, chosen for themselves. Like all other voluntary actions, the decision to live under the authority of a political regime is an extension of our own free will; so the authority we live under is simply a case of obeying ourselves. But on the Hobbesean view, we are bound not because we chose to be so but because, given the background assumptions, it is *best* for us. (This is despite Hobbes's own explicit claim that there exists 'no obligation on any man which ariseth not from some act of his own' (ibid.: 268).) The Hobbesean social contract is one which grounds the authority of the state in the *interests* rather than the explicit *will* of the citizens.

Another basic difficulty with Hobbes's attempt to ground political authority in the rational interests of citizens (relative to a state of nature) concerns the precarious picture of human psychology and motivation he posits. It is easy to observe scenarios other than those Hobbes sketches where patterns of cooperative behavior arise spontaneously because of dispositions instilled widely in the population, perhaps due to common experiences (virtually everyone was nurtured in a *family* after all, and a huge number of human beings find no problem 'cooperating' with the young that they give birth to and nurture). Hobbes's view that, left to their own devices and outside of society, people would all act as individual, self-interested maximizers of their own good looks all the more doubtful when it is seen to imply that no societies could ever reasonably arise by voluntary agreement under these assumptions; yet people *do* often agree on such arrangements. Let us probe deeper into this issue by looking at more recent attempts to use Hobbesean models to justify political power.

Contemporary Hobbeseanism

Several philosophers have followed in the Hobbesean path by constructing arguments for the authority of the state based generally on the rationality of obeying such authority, utilizing the psychological profile of people as self-interested rational choosers of their own good. This picks up on Hobbes's 'egoism,'[5] though in contemporary writing this term refers to a complex set of doctrines, some of them descriptive and some normative (see Pojman 2000: 539–67). As we will see, however, it is not the kind of egoism that Hobbeseans defend that is the source of difficulty for this way of justifying the state as much as the failure to recognize the separation between the *rationality of obedience* and the *legitimacy of authority*.

The problem of going from a state of nature to civil society (considered either as an actual transformation or a hypothetical scenario) points to a difficulty that, for some commentators, damns the entire social contract approach to political justification (Skinner 1978: 164; cf. Simmons 1979). For how can individuals who are described as lacking the capacities for cooperation, peaceful living, consistent judgement – in short, whatever factors that make life in the state of nature relatively unpalatable – suddenly become able to enter into a relationship which itself demands cooperation, peaceful attitudes toward others, and consistent judgement? If people had the wherewithal to construct a civil society, then they would have the wherewithal to live peacefully in a state of nature.

However, some contemporary Hobbeseans have argued that social organization should not be seen as a solution to a problem of direct conflict and lack of cooperation among agents. Rather social institutions are seen as the solution to what is called a 'coordination problem,' a scenario where people all want to find some means of coordinating their desires and simply need a procedure for doing so.[6] Unlike the Prisoner's Dilemma (a conflict game), agents here don't have an individual interest in 'defecting' (not cooperating) if the other person cooperates. Both want cooperation, it's just a trick to find the point around which to organize that cooperation. Desires don't conflict directly necessarily (where I want what you have and you want what I have), but they cannot be all satisfied together unless some arrangement is made involving our mutual collaboration. (The little dance that people do when they encounter each other on the sidewalk, each trying to get out of the other person's way but going to the wrong side each time, is an example of a coordination game; both would prefer walking on opposite sides from each other and don't care which side is chosen as long as they are mutually complementary.)

Establishing the rationality of supporting state authority in this light means abandoning the strict Hobbesean assumption that people are so naturally selfish that without a powerful state to keep them apart, their directly conflicting desires would bring them to blows at every turn. Moreover, the problem of explaining how it is rational to enter society from an initial state of nature is avoided since people can be assumed to all benefit from both organizing a society initially as well as remaining cooperative within it when it operates in minimally beneficial ways. In the Hobbesean scenario discussed above, it is always in one's individual interest to defect from group cooperation – one gets the benefits of what the group activity provides with none of the costs of contributing to it. Here, however, we assume more realistically that people are more naturally social and benefit from cooperation itself.

The claim that states are solutions to coordination games rather than conflict games rests on the assumption that people would all prefer being in some cooperative social relation or other rather than being the lone defector while others are cooperating. This view trades on the various benefits of social life itself, assuming that people would prefer living in society with others, all things being equal. Moreover, if one were the lone rebel in an otherwise stable state, one would be vulnerable to oppression from the collective power of the existing social system. Seeing social life in this way implies that the state is a *convention,* a set of institutions that help citizens coordinate their desires and not simply a power center keeping them apart. The rationality of supporting such a state – obeying its laws generally, not fomenting rebellion, not looking for opportunities to emigrate – is based on the general advantage of living under a cooperative scheme relative to being an outsider (and hence comparatively powerless). Moreover, it will be rational for people to participate in the creation and maintenance of the state in either actively supporting the operation of its institutions or forgoing opportunities to undermine them. The latter kind of activity would be irrational because it involves, in effect, defecting from the cooperative organization whose existence is personally beneficial.

In this way, a legitimate state authority can be justified without an explicit contract either among the citizens or between the citizens and the newly established sovereign, and this legitimacy is based on the collective rationality of citizens' supporting such a state. Individual subjects 'consent,' but only in the sense that their behavior is generally supportive of, or at least not resistant to, the operation of governmental authority (what Hampton calls 'convention consent' – Hampton 1997: 94). Although this paradoxically explicates the Hobbesean social contract model without the use of a contract, it avoids what we noted above as one of the most serious shortcomings of the orthodox Hobbesean view, namely that it problematically assumed that people who were not capable of making or keeping binding contracts suddenly form a commonwealth based on a contractual promise. This also avoids the problem we will note below when discussing Locke that virtually no one in the generations that come *after* the founding members of the commonwealth ever make an explicit agreement to obey the authority of the state.[7]

However, it is the very connection between the rationality of the state's power and its legitimacy that motivates criticisms of this approach. For this revised Hobbesean justification of state power still eliminates the gap between the rationality of obedience to state authority and the legitimacy of that authority. For example, it may well be my best option to obey the commands of my captor who holds me under violent threat, even for a long period of time, but we would never say that her commands are thereby legitimate. In the story we have just told, citizens support the convention of state authority simply because, as things stand, it is their best option (see Hampton 1997: 89). Whether a particular state will deserve the support of its citizens depends entirely on the level of well-being a person would enjoy in the alternative cooperative regimes (or states of nature) accessible to her. If we assume a background of equal bargaining power and full participation in all government-creating conventions, this structure sounds quite acceptable. But nothing in what justifies political authority in this story *requires* that background conditions be equal in this way; that is altogether a contingent matter. What grounds the justification of the authority is simply the rationality of living under it. As soon as an alternative coalition can be established and secession from the dominant authority be carried out with impunity, the authority vanishes. But how can one say that a political institution has *legitimate* authority when some of its citizens (perhaps) are merely biding their time until the moment is right for a revolt? How, indeed, can this be distinguished from sheer mastery? What we see here are the ramifications of the Hobbesean reliance on *interests* rather than *will* in justifying political institutions.

Collapsing the moral legitimacy of the state into the rationality of obeying its dictates also founders on the variability of speculations concerning not only the various motivations that citizens may find themselves with, but also concerning the alternatives open to them. We are aware of the weakness of Hobbes's original view that people are so selfishly motivated and anti-social that life with even tyrannical rulers is justified. But contemporary Hobbeseans face similar difficulties, in that the plausibility of claims justifying state authority will vary with differences in the motives and personality structures of the people living under them, as well as the alternatives to continued obedience open to them. We know, for example, that 'states of nature' are no longer to be found in the modern world. There are few (if any) realistic options of reverting to life without a government at all or moving to some unincorporated area (where would that be?). What we are talking about, then, is not starting a government from an a-political state of nature, but rather the decision to *remain loyal* to an already established power structure. (This question can be further broken down into the questions of whether to support, resist, revolt against, etc. an existing power.) The rationality of doing so will depend, of course, on one's options, including the opportunities for successful emigration to alternative societies. But the level of welfare one would enjoy in each of these alternative states of affairs, whichever ones are open, varies widely, and hence the kind of sovereign to which it is rational for one to be obedient is itself indeterminate.

This variability in conditions in which choices about state authority are made shows how these Hobbesean arguments are all, in a crucial respect, *hypothetical*. That is, they do not claim specifically that obedience to any particular state is in fact rational and so that authority legitimate. Rather, they claim that such obedience *would be* rational if various (usually contrary-to-fact) conditions hold. Claims about what would be rational for people living in counterfactual circumstances cannot be applied to us, actual people, facing choices about obedience to existing political institutions. Saying it does is akin to using the argument that it is rational for you to do X because, under alternative conditions, it would be rational for you to do X. But this form of argument is clearly invalid and is, in any event, unavailable to Hobbeseans, for their conclusions must all rest on the rationality of *actually* taking some action (obeying a sovereign for example). Hypothetical circumstances where other actions might be advisable are irrelevant.[8]

Before leaving the subject of Hobbes, however, let us note some of the features of this approach to justifying political authority which are relevant to liberal political philosophy generally as well as serve to mark out a distinct line of thought within it. As should be clear from what we've said here, Hobbes is a 'radical individualist' in his analysis and evaluation of social phenomenon (Hampton, 1986, Macpherson 1962). That is to say, the claims he makes about societies take as the fundamental unit of analysis the individual person, a person described with characteristics that never necessarily include her or his relation to others. While such individuals may well be members of families, be part of a religious tradition that defines their values, understand themselves as fundamentally molded by tradition, or the like, none of that is directly relevant to understanding what it is rational for them to do, for Hobbes, and hence not directly relevant to the question of whether the sovereign under which they live is justified or not.

Second, Hobbesean evaluations of political institutions are grounded in the rationality of the choices of the individuals living under them. That is, the question of whether a political or social structure, such as the state, is to be created or maintained is always a question of whether it is rational for this to occur. And this question of the 'rationality' of an institution is explicated in terms of the rationality of those living under it (to create it, maintain it, or obey its dictates). The legitimacy of authority, in this approach, is translated simply as the rationality of obedience. This 'rational choice' approach to social analysis marks out a distinct and controversial strain of liberalism, one where the justification of the state rests solidly in claims about persons' *interests*, not their expressed *will*. This latter idea – that a state's legitimacy is only secured via the actual willing acceptance of that state's authority – leads us to another dominant version of the social contract approach to justifying political power.

Locke: Reason, morality, and freedom

When Hobbes claimed that people, both in the state of nature and in civil society, were moved by 'reason' or 'rationality,' all he meant by that is that they were able to choose the best means of satisfying whatever it is they desired. Nothing about *what* they desired figured in the appraisal of their reasonableness. This implies that rationality did not include reference to morality; to be rational said absolutely nothing, by itself, about whether or not one was moral or had the capacity for moral action (however that is defined). As we will presently see, that is precisely where the political philosophy of John Locke, and those following in his train, departs from the Hobbesean framework.

John Locke (1632–1704) was also active in the development of the 'new science' in the seventeenth century which opposed the Scholastic, teleological, world view inherited from the Middle Ages in Europe, and he is broadly known for his defense of empiricism, the view that particular ideas, even moral ideas and principles, could not be 'written on the soul' or understood by reason alone without generalizations from ideas arising from sensation (Locke [1689] 1996). But he is also known for his development of the theory of the social contract. Before considering those views, we should not neglect certain other arguments Locke makes that are relevant to our inquiry here. In his *Letter Concerning Toleration*, Locke defends religious 'toleration' toward various sects of Protestantism (he explicitly argues that Catholics and atheists lack the requisite moral framework to merit toleration). The general outline of the argument he uses there, while not unique to Locke (cf. Milton [1660] 1950), is relevant to the development of one of the basic lines of liberal thought. That argument is that external coercion for the purpose of inducing religious faith is not so much morally abhorrent as it is *ineffective*, and so, in a sense, absurd. For to have faith is to grasp internally, for one's own reasons, the truth of the theological doctrine which is being apprehended (as well as the moral obligations that arise from it). No external force can *induce* a person to understand the truth of such doctrines, for Locke; for if that were attempted, the person would be assenting to the doctrine for reasons of expediency (avoiding the punishment threatened for example) rather than its truth (Locke [1689] 1955). So we see here a nascent form of the psychological model of moral commitment that will play a central role in liberal political thought: to validly bind individuals, moral obligations must be apprehended by the person bound by them 'from the inside', as it were, rather than imposed on her by an external force.

Like Hobbes, Locke attempts to justify political authority on the basis of a social contract among the governed. These arguments are contained in the second of his *Two Treatises of Government* (Locke [1690] 1963). Locke begins his argument with a picture of the state that man is 'naturally in,' the state of 'perfect freedom' and equality, 'wherein all power and jurisdiction is reciprocal' (ibid.: 309). This refers, of course, to the state of nature, the backdrop against which state authority will be justified. But the contrast with Hobbes regarding the key concepts in this picture is crucial, for Locke intends something quite different by 'freedom' and 'equality' in his description of the natural state of pre-political human beings.

As I mentioned, Locke's empiricism committed him to the view that no complex ideas can arise outside of experience and remain valid – we can have no true beliefs based on reason alone. Yet, in the *Second Treatise* he states boldly that, because we are God's handiwork (and He would not have created us unless we had the capacity to follow norms that are necessary for our survival), we all have a natural capacity for Reason, which gives us direct access to the moral law (for Locke, the laws of nature. He writes, '[t]he *State of Nature* has a Law of Nature to govern it, which obliges everyone: And Reason, which is that Law, teaches all Mankind, who will consult it, that being all equal and independent, no one ought to harm another in his Life, Health, Liberty, or Possession' (ibid.: 311). Putting aside the question of where we get these ideas, the basis of Locke's political theory is that, independent of social conventions and civil obligations, all human beings have certain natural moral rights that all other human beings are obliged, and know by reason they are obliged, to respect. This means that the state of nature, for Locke, is a very different place from the chamber of horrors described by Hobbes. Despite our natural freedom, we have no right to destroy ourselves and we have no right to harm others. Indeed, we have an obligation 'to preserve the rest of Mankind' when doing so does not threaten our own lives, a view quite at odds with the Hobbesean right of all to all things. Further, we have no right to violate others' natural rights to life, liberty, and possessions.[9]

But this conception of people's natural understanding of morality indicates why, eventually, all people would want to move into civil society, on Locke's view. For just as every person has rights to health, liberty, and possessions, everyone also has a right to *enforce* the protection of those rights by way of punishing violators. Indeed, someone whose natural capacities do not prevent him from either understanding or following the moral law is like a 'wild Savage Beast' and may be 'destroyed as a *Lyon* or a *Tyger*' (ibid.: 314–15). However, individuals are not always precise in their estimations of the amount of punishment deserved for particular transgressions. And those accused of crimes will often react violently against such punishments, and so such a spiral of conflict will make continued life in the state of nature 'inconvenient.' There will lack any superior common judge with the authority to settled disputes such as this, and people will naturally come together to create political institutions that will function as such a judge. This means that although by nature we all have certain rights and duties, we cannot effectively enjoy such rights securely unless we live under a common political authority. This, then, is the motive for civil society for Locke.

The authority created in such a society, then, is based solely on the consent of those governed, the act creating the authority in question and authorizing its coercive powers. We should note, though, that the assumption that even without a centralized political authority people nevertheless are obliged by various rights and duties, on Locke's view, obviates the problem which plagued Hobbes's picture, namely how those not subject to promissory obligations can make a promise to create a centralized authority to enforce promises. For Locke, individuals *are* bound by their promises and agreements in the state of nature by virtue of the natural rights we all enjoy and which we all recognize through reason, even where there is no enforcement mechanism to support anyone's claim of a breach.

When people in Locke's state of nature are imagined to congregate to create a civil society, two separate acts of agreement take place. The first is the initial decision to gather as a society at all, and this agreement must be unanimous to be binding on all participants; anyone dissenting from such an agreement simply remains in the state of nature relative to the others. However, subsequent to this initial social formation, another agreement is made, an agreement to form a *particular* governmental structure; and this agreement need not be unanimous for Locke, but can proceed simply by majority rule (ibid.: 375).

These original contracts, then, create civil society and put in place the centralized political authority of the state, with whatever legislative and executive apparatus are chosen by the contractees. However, past agreements by one's ancestors of this sort would have no force for contemporary citizens (and Locke seemed to think such initial contracts actually took place for all stable societies – Locke [1690] 1963: 378ff.), so these would not be sufficient to justify the coercive authority of a present government. In response to this observation, Locke argues that one can be bound by current governments by virtue of 'tacit consent,' consent which can be inferred from one's ongoing voluntary actions. When someone asks you if you are OK with what they are doing, and you sit passively, for example, when you clearly could object or leave, it can be inferred that you have tacitly consented to the proceedings even if you fail to utter the specific words 'I agree.'

Locke writes, 'every Man, that hath any Possession, or Enjoyment, of any part of the Dominions of any Government, doth thereby give his *tacit Consent*, and is as far forth obliged to Obedience, to the Laws of that

Government, during such Enjoyment' (ibid.: 392), see also Simmons 1993: ch. 4). If the person did not accede to the operations of the government, he could merely emigrate: 'there are no Examples so frequent in History . . . as those of Men withdrawing themselves, and their Obedience, from the Jurisdiction they were born under . . . and *setting up new Governments* in other places' (ibid.: 389). So the act that tacitly expresses one's consent to be governed, even when one was not a party to the original agreement setting up a society, is that of remaining in the jurisdiction in question.

The natural rights one exercises in consenting to adhere to a political authority fixes the grounds for the legitimacy of that authority. For this reason, Locke argues that rebellion is justified whenever a sovereign acts in ways that are in violation of citizens' natural rights. In specific opposition to Hobbes, then, arbitrary or absolute power on the part of the sovereign is never justified and is automatically grounds for resistance and rebellion, for Locke. As he claims: 'It cannot be supposed that [citizens] should intend, had they the power so to do, to give any one, or more, an *absolute Arbitrary Power* over their persons and estates' (ibid.: 405). Any sovereign act which runs counter to the protection of the natural rights of the governed automatically nullifies the legitimate authority of that sovereign.

But Locke's reliance on actual (albeit tacit) consent raises the most serious difficulty for his view.[10] On the one hand, it is unrealistic to think that anyone in a sufficiently large society has ever directly expressed consent to the general structure of governmental authority. And on the other hand, relying on tacit consent spurs the same difficulty, though for different reasons. First, any criterion of obligation which relies on tacit consent must admit that any actual expression of *non-consent* completely erases that prior obligation. If instead of sitting passively and smiling while those around you begin to act as if you had agreed, you stop them by saying: 'Listen, don't take what I'm doing here as a sign that I agree to what you are doing,' you are then not bound by a promise to comply. Therefore, whatever actions are taken by the consent theorist to indicate 'tacit' agreement, a citizen can always simply announce that she does not agree to the governmental authority or its actions. Clearly, tacit consent cannot bind someone against her expressed will. (This is not to say that a person can simply go back on an agreement once it is made, but rather she can make it clear that her ongoing actions, say enjoying the benefits of civil society, should not be taken as grounds for agreement to obey its rules.) But since legitimate governments bind all those living under them, even dissenters to some degree, this line of argument seems weak if used to ground such legitimacy.

Moreover, any view that reads one's continuing to live and work in an area as tacit acceptance of the authority of that area must come to grips with the extreme costliness (and in some ways impossibility) of emigration from that area. As historical commentators on Locke's theory have famously made clear, consent cannot be inferred from the actions of someone for whom alternatives to so acting (moving one's household and livelihood) are extremely costly (see Hume [1739] 1978: 547–49, Simmons 1979: 95–100). (Even contemporary writers who continue to use consent as a basis for political obligations admit that actual states could be legitimated on such a basis only if both national and international law were radically altered, allowing, for example, opportunities to express approval or disapproval of the constitutional structure as well as for inexpensive emigration and relocation (see Beran 1987).

Locke relied, then, on a 'will' theory of political authority: such authority is justified because of a direct relationship between acts of will on the part of the governed and the power of the government. Moreover, the limits of political obligation are specified with reference to the alternative non-political world that Locke imagines as the natural state definitive of our basic liberties. But as was the case with Hobbes, this 'natural' state is described by him based on an explicit view of human psychology. On Locke's picture of human nature, people have the fundamental capacity to understand and be bound by the strictures of the moral law, including the natural rights of others. These natural rights, moreover, are expressed in particular terms – the rights to life, liberty, health, and possessions. However, an alternative list of basic human rights, say one which included a right to a fulfilling cultural life or the right to revel in one's ethnic heritage, would yield a radically different picture of the state of nature and hence a very different baseline against which political authority is measured. In this way, the Lockean strategy for justifying the state rests not only on a specific picture of human nature, but also a specific list of our basic rights. What this shows is that it is not consent alone which provides the justification of state authority, but also a specific view of the basic moral rights and duties applicable to all human beings by nature. So in so far as those prior moral strictures are contentious or questionable, so are the moral obligations to respect state authority which they support. (We will discuss this in detail in later chapters.)

Contemporary Lockeanism

Recent followers of Locke include, most notably, libertarian thinkers who argue that the existence of state power is at best a necessary evil and, in order to be consistent with our natural rights, must be confined only to the functions of protecting people against overt harm. Political obligation, on this view, rests on the degree to which such states succeed in protecting these pre-political prerogatives that all human beings enjoy independent of the existence of any government. For Lockean libertarians, most notably, such rights include the right to private property, so states are legitimate only if they protect the rights of property owners from incursions of such rights, including unapproved governmental regulation, taxation, or the like.

A famous example of such a view can be found in Nozick (1974), where he argues that all human beings enjoy a certain array of moral rights, such as the right to liberty and the right to secure property, that legitimate governments must protect. One can imagine that a state could arise in the form of a 'dominant protection agency' in a way that did not violate those natural rights (therefore Nozick holds off challenges from anarchists who claim that such rights are always violated by a government's very existence and so all governments are unjust – see, for example, Wolff 1970). However, such a state is consistent with the demands of justice (individual rights) only when it confines itself to that minimal protective role. Any such further functioning, such as instituting welfare-state policies to help the poor, redistributing income via coercive taxation, or in promoting other cultural or moral values, directly violates the requirements of justice.

Other libertarian thinkers in the Lockean tradition utilize the notion of a hypothetical contract to justify state authority (see Lomasky 1987, Narveson 1988). That is, a political authority is justified if, under certain idealized conditions, one *would* agree to its dictates. But here also the claim is made that the only government that meets such a standard is a minimal government, since the natural rights which define the idealized conditions (under which agreement is meant to take place) are 'negative' rights to liberty and property (among other things), rights against interference by others. So state action that intrudes on individuals' property rights or rights to liberty is always unjust, on this view. What makes these strategies Lockean is that they rely on a conception of pre-political rights to provide the framework for justification of political authority.

However, these views of the justification of states and limitations on their authority rest on the background moral considerations that are postulated as the pre-political ground of social obligation – the view of natural rights assumed. We will discuss in the next chapter the libertarian claim that such rights include rights to property (of the sort that would preclude government limitations on free market capitalism). But the chief worry raised here is whether such a voluntarist conception of state authority, set against the background of individualist morality, can ever succeed in establishing the legitimacy of any particular state regime (see Simmons 1999). What is distinctive of contemporary Lockeans in general, however, is the view that legitimate state authority rests on the consent of the governed when such consent expresses the natural rights they all enjoy independent of the existence of the state. But as we saw, the 'consent' portion of this argument is either implausible or otiose: if one argues that actual consent is required to legitimate political authority, most modern societies are illegitimate since citizens in such societies rarely ever give such consent; and if one claims that mere tacit consent is all that is required, one must accept that any declaration of disagreement with the government undercuts its authority. But, moreover, the consent element in this theory is not the most basic component of justification of state power, rather it is the view of universal natural rights of a specific sort, and the conception of morality this view expresses, that underlies it. And as we will discuss in later chapters, this is hardly an uncontroversial moral view.

Lessons from Rousseau and Kant

If this were a study focused solely on the social contract tradition, it would be appropriate to add detailed analyses of the views of the other two major contractualist thinkers of this era, Jean-Jacques Rousseau and Immanuel Kant. But we will also briefly describe some of the insights that these philosophers add to the social contract model of political authority, insights that will shape the discussions to follow.

Rousseau is famous for his work *On the Social Contract*, where he argued that only when society is arranged so that individuals can participate directly in the development of legislation can a type of sovereignty be established where a person 'obeys only himself' and remains free (Rousseau [1760] 1987; see also Levine 1976). The type of freedom Rousseau had in mind in these arguments was a type of 'positive' freedom, where to be free means to be self-governing. But since others in one's society also have interests and needs that they will insist upon satisfying, one retains one's freedom in this sense only when one interacts with those individuals in finding a solution to such conflicts of interest, a solution expressed in a collective decision called the 'general will.' The individual citizen, then, must submit completely to the general will, since that expression of collective interest just *is* the best balance of competing interests that collective interaction in a society can produce. In any other case, one is either dominating others from a position of superior power or being dominated by them. So to be individually self-governing, for Rousseau, is to participate (and have one's interests reflected) in collective self-government. (While Hobbes based political legitimacy in its consistency with rationality, and Locke on its consistency with natural rights, Rousseau bases such legitimacy on the demands of *freedom*.)

However, Rousseau was quite critical of Locke and Hobbes (especially the latter) for speculations about the primordial state of nature based either on observations of contemporary, socialized, human beings or on armchair reflections. Rousseau argued that one must consider human beings not in some fanciful hypothetical state but as they really were, and as they have developed through various stages of social organization (Rousseau [1755] 1987). When one gets an accurate general understanding of such development, one striking lesson that must be learned is the extreme contingency of the dispositions and interests that human beings find themselves with, and with which they enter civil society. There is no 'natural' proclivity toward either selfishness or morality, for Rousseau, in that such inclinations arise in human beings only as a result of the happenstance of population growth and proximity, technological developments, and family organization, among other things. Although human beings might be said to possess a 'natural' tendency toward self-preservation and pity, there is no fixed human condition that can be laid out as a backdrop against which to construct normative theories of justice (ibid.).

So for Rousseau, a society is just (free) only when governed by a social contract which embodies the general will of the people. Contemporary followers of Rousseau (J. Cohen 1986, Gould 1988) stress the need for citizen participation in democratic institutions and emphasize the connection between such institutions and individual (positive) freedom. The standard criticism of Rousseauian approaches, however, is that modern complex states cannot function without various methods of representation, ones which Rousseau himself would have claimed to be oppressive. At best, critics claim, Rousseauian democracy could only be established in small, homogeneous societies where citizens are willing to spend their time at town meetings, government planning discussions, and the like. Such a model is hardly applicable, they argue, to large complex societies (see Christiano 1996: 106–09). From another direction, critics of Rousseau's politics have pointed out the frightening manner in which the 'general will' is meant to subsume all individual citizens' particular claims (for example, Berlin 1969); for Rousseau, one must completely alienate one's own interests to the general will: (see Rousseau [1760] 1987: 148). The claim is that without assuming certain pre-political rights to resist the will of the collective, such arrangements will manifest the worst aspects of tyranny of the majority.

Nevertheless, Rousseau is important in stressing that normative political principles must be evaluated in light of the contingent circumstances which shape interests and guide values rather than as idealized norms abstracted from real social histories. Classical social contract theories, and some of their contemporary heirs, often forget this lesson and proceed as if the profile of the rational chooser, whose needs and interests can be determined theoretically and independently of contingent social and historical features of her existence, can be postulated as the basis of theories of justice and the good. Rousseau's arguments alert us to the need to temper such armchair theorizing with attention to the contingencies of history and social life within which those needs and interests have emerged. (We will revisit this issue in Chapters 6 and 7.)

In the arena of normative philosophy, Immanuel Kant is best known as the source of 'deontological' or duty-based moral theory, an approach to moral reasoning that demands that rational agents consider the generalization of their proposed action when judging its moral acceptability (as we discussed in the Introduction above). This procedure is one expression of Kant's Categorical Imperative, with its dictates to universalize our maxims for action, never use another as merely a means to our ends, and to act as if we were legislators in a kingdom of ends (Kant [1785] 1983). Kant also developed important views concerning political philosophy. The social contract, for Kant, expresses the equal freedom to which all have a right in a just civil society. It is not an historical contract, just as the state of nature is not an actual past state, but rather an 'idea of reason,' a 'regulative' ideal that guides our action and shapes the rule of law. Kant argued that there is a moral imperative to 'establish' a social contract and 'remove' oneself from the state of nature, which would be a non-juridical state where human interaction was governed solely by force and power (though it is unclear that such verbs as 'establish' or 'remove' should be taken literally as implying movement from one state to another, rather than implying that one make sure one is *in* such a state). Under the rule of law – the social contract – interactions are governed (ideally) by the juridical relations of right and wrong which would conform to the principle of equal freedom. This is the principle that one's actions in a society are right only if such actions can coexist with everyone else's freedom organized under a general law (Kant [1797] 1999: 113–50).

On Kant's view, one has a moral obligation to bring about a just juridical state of affairs, a republican government where the general will of the people is expressed in legislation, and where sovereignty rests on a social contract. However, this must come about only by non-violent means, as one is never allowed to commit violence as a means to bringing about even justified ends; this would violate the moral law itself. For these reasons, Kant claimed that revolution, even waged against the most oppressive of states, was never justified; such rebellion always involved, or foreseeably would produce, violence. (For discussion, see Korsgaard 1997.)

The Kantian social contract, like Rousseau's version, is not a specifiable act of origination for a society (a constitutional convention for example), but rather an abstraction that can be used to define legitimate political authority. Only when society is governed by the general will of the people rather than coerced by a superior power will the equal freedom required by justice be protected. And Kant argued that only a republican form of government, with representative assemblies and an elected legislature, would embody the kind of popular sovereignty required by the social contract.

Notice that Rousseau and Kant represent a fundamental shift from the approach taken by Hobbes and Locke, namely that the legitimation of state authority no longer relies on factors bearing on its *origin*. Nothing about an initial organizing convention or original consent is relevant to the justice (and hence legitimate authority) of political structures. With Hobbes, we saw that no act of will was necessary for the legitimation of the state, but the movement from the state of nature to a civil society must have been one that was consistent with the rational interests of those making such a move. With Locke, actual expressions of consent, even if tacitly expressed through indirect means, were necessary for political justification. A shift occurs with Rousseau, who still maintains a focus on the will as the source of legitimacy, but no longer requires that outward acts of consent to the beginnings of a civil society be in evidence. In Kant, the shift in strategy is complete, for the legitimating force of the idea of a social contract is now no longer grounded in the actual consent or participation of the citizens. Rather, political power is justified if (and only if) it conforms to the universal standards of morality – that is, if it is *just*. However, unlike Hobbes, states cannot be justified simply because they happen to answer to the perceived needs and interests of the citizenry; Kant is still a 'will' theorist, as we are using that term. But the expression of the rational will is now construed strictly hypothetically, as what a rational being *would* accept, consistent with maintaining equal freedom with her co-citizens. This last step is picked up in contemporary discussions of political authority and transformed to a general definition of legitimacy: justified political authority is that which could be approved of by rational agents living under such rule. Let us, then, move on to consider such discussions.

From consent to legitimacy

Our survey of the prominent historical figures in the social contract tradition mobilizes various themes in the theoretical structure of liberalism, a principle one of which is that the justification of political authority must be a function of the individual approval of those subject to that authority. What was noted, however, was that in so far as such actual, even tacit, consent is a necessary condition for legitimacy, there arise serious objections to the view that state authorities for complex societies are ever legitimate. Another option pursued by contemporary followers of the social contract tradition is the use of the model of *hypothetical* consent in order to justify political institutions. Instead of (problematically) demanding that citizens actually express their acceptance of the political authority under which they live (however tacitly), one could claim that state authority is justified if such citizens *would* accept that authority under conditions of fair choice, and consequently they are thereby bound by its principles. Indeed, these theorists argue, in so far as such hypothetical consent can be secured, such a state is *just*.

The most famous purveyor of this approach to justice is John Rawls. Rawls's view picks up on the Kantian claim that justice is a matter of what rational individuals would choose for themselves when not swayed by factors that would bias their choices, such as their own narrow self-interest; justice amounts to those principles chosen in this manner for a well-ordered society in which these choosers would be citizens. Such 'biasing' factors filtered out of the choice mechanism are any factors that would be perceived as 'arbitrary from a moral point of view,' characteristics whose contingency and personal particularity would make principles chosen in light of them clearly the product of self-interest rather than of impartial reasoning applicable to all affected. The factors that bias the choice of principles are personal factors such as one's gender, race, place in society, class, natural talents, and one's particular conception of the good life. Justice, then, is that set of principles chosen by those who will live according to them from a perspective insensitive to these personal factors. Rawls calls this view 'justice as fairness' (Rawls 1971).

The conditions under which such hypothetical choice occurs is labeled the 'original position' and the mechanism for establishing blindness to one's own particularities Rawls calls the 'veil of ignorance' (Rawls 1971: 10–19). Such choosing representatives are free, in the sense that they choose without constraint from previously accepted principles of justice, and they are equal, in that they occupy reciprocal positions of power concerning the decision process. But since those choosing would not know what they themselves, in real life, think is good or bad, they must utilize some *general* index of a good life which would apply to them independent of their own particular life plans. Rawls calls such goods 'primary social goods' and they include such things as basic rights and liberties, freedom of movement and occupation, powers and prerogatives of positions of responsibility, income and wealth, and the social bases of self-respect (Rawls 1971: 78–81, 1982). Justice is then defined by the principles chosen in the original position applied to the basic institutions of society.[11]

Rawls goes on to argue that specific principles would be chosen under these conditions and hence define justice. These principles are:[12] (1) each person has an equal right to the most extensive scheme of equal basic liberties compatible with like liberties for all (the Basic Liberties Principle); and (2) social and economic inequalities (measured by primary goods) are allowed but only in so far as: (a) they are attached to positions and offices open to all under conditions of fair equality of opportunity; and (b) they work to the benefit of the least advantaged members of society (the Difference Principle). These principles should be applied to the institutions of the basic structure of society in lexical priority, where violations of the first principle are not allowed simply for greater enforcement of the second, and similarly for the second and third (2a and 2b).

The first principle simply reflects the higher order interest that we all have in pursuing a life plan of our own choosing. The second principle is more complex, especially the second part, which is called the Difference Principle. For Rawls argues that if one had no knowledge of one's place in society, the first obvious guiding principle to choose would be strict equality of primary goods – you know that no matter where you ended up, you are not worse off than anyone else. And such would be the first consideration in the original position. But it would make sense also to choose to *allow* inequalities if they made even the least advantaged person better off than she would have been without them. Then, even if one ended up among the worst off, the inequalities in society are better for you than the alternative condition of absolute equality. In the end, only the primary goods of income and wealth are subject to this kind of inequality, for only these could ever benefit those with less of them (inequalities of basic rights and liberties never benefit those with fewer of such rights and so are always equally guaranteed).

What Rawls argues, then, is that society's main institutions should, first, protect basic liberties, next, guarantee equality of opportunity, and finally, ensure that only those inequalities of income and wealth that benefit the least fortunate are allowed. These are the principles that we all would choose for ourselves if we were choosing under condition of fair and impartial selection; and justice, he claims, is defined as the outcome of such hypothetical agreement.

But that last point – that the hypothetically chosen rule should apply to actual society – makes salient one of the major difficulties raised against Rawls's system, at least in its initial formulation (later revisions of his theory will be considered in Chapter 4). For what ground is provided for an obligation in the *real* world by a contract agreed to in a *hypothetical* one (see Simmons 1979)? That is, even if justice can be defined as the outcome of fair bargaining of this sort, what foundation is really provided for citizens of an actual society by a hypothetical bargain that would have been struck in alternative circumstances?

Rawls anticipated this objection and claimed that the reason we (real people in society) should be bound by principles chosen in artificial circumstances is that the 'conditions embodied in the . . . original position are ones that we do in fact accept. Or if we do not, then perhaps we can be persuaded to do so by philosophical reflection' (Rawls 1971: 19). The philosophical reflection Rawls has in mind is characterized by the 'reflective equilibrium' described in the Introduction above – settling on principles because they cohere among themselves, as well as with other abstract judgments that seem reasonable, and because they yield acceptable concrete directives in the real world.

But Rawls's critics have claimed that such reflection will, at best, be indeterminate, unless one has already assumed a previous commitment to the method of selection of principles and the values which motivate it that Rawls sets out. Rawls claims that the values of freedom and equality are fundamental to the operation of the original position and the veil of ignorance. But what is the argument that we should all accept *this* interpretation of freedom and equality (or even the values of freedom and equality at all), short of some basic moral argument such as the Lockean claim for universal natural rights? (And Rawls does not want to claim that justice is based on a foundational moral system of this sort for such systems are inherently controversial.) For example, in Rawls's system, principles of justice should not allow people to profit from their natural talents in ways that do not benefit the worst off person. This is reflected in the fact that knowledge of our natural talents is forbidden in the original position. But if one thought, for example, that it is perfectly acceptable that the random distribution of natural talents determine one's (probably unequal) place in society independent of how this affected others, then one will reject the way that Rawls sets up the original position in the first place (Nozick 1974: 189–204). Therefore, the justification of the two principles of justice rests on values that are implicit in the mechanism for choosing those principles, and those values are as controversial as the resulting principles themselves (at least Rawls's interpretation of them (Barry 1989)).

Other uses of hypothetical consent have also gained prominence since Rawls developed his view (see, for example, Buchanan and Tullock 1965, Lomasky 1987, Narveson 1988, Scanlon 1982, Gauthier 1986). Some of these follow the Hobbesean tradition of seeing political institutions as the result of a compromise that would be struck among rational, self-interested individuals. But as we saw above, the normative force of that compromise turns on the contingencies of that imagined choice situation (as well as the distance between such a situation and the actual world we live in). But also, seeing justice as a result of bargaining among competing agents amounts to viewing rules of society as a compromise in a power struggle and not a set of ideals with moral weight. And for those non-Hobbeseans who build normative values *into* the choice situation, so that the result of the bargain rests not only on the operation of self-interest but on the background moral obligations within which people bargain, the criticism just waged against Rawls applies as well: those background moral values are as up for grabs as the principles themselves that result from them. The use of a hypothetical choice procedure that rests on them merely begs the question at issue, namely: what values are we all committed to as a matter of justice?

But perhaps we should take stronger inspiration from Rousseau here, specifically the lesson we learned above that one cannot raise the question of political obligation apart from the actual already given facts of our place in a society and the contingencies of its history. For we *are* members of states, so that the question of whether we want to *join* a society is moot, rather it is a question of whether we are in fact obligated, morally, to obey the dictates of the government to which we have cultural, personal, and psychological ties. The answer to that question depends on whether the principles guiding that state are just (in Rousseau's view, whether we can maintain our freedom within it), more particularly, whether they function in a way that expresses respect for us as free and equal persons. Those who move about so much that they can choose their citizenship are in a different boat, but their obligation then turns on the actual overt acts of securing citizenship, which they voluntarily undertake, in a particular place. For the rest of us, the question of political obligation becomes the question of justice.

But what is it for a government to function in a way that expresses respect for our freedom and equality? And should legitimacy rest on respect for these values, rather than say, a commitment to advancing our good? We will attend to those questions in Chapter 4 below. For now, let us merely note that such a view rests on a 'will' theory of political obligation rather than an 'interest' view, as discussed above. Moreover, freedom and equality is respected only if there is some mechanism by which that will can be expressed and show some general approval of the existence and operation of that government. The tradition of popular sovereignty in which this view develops demands as much.

One final word about legitimacy and participation. If the legitimacy of a state is secured only when those living under it can in some way express approval of it, how does this not imply the implausible conclusion that only small states run by a direct democracy (where all citizens are legislators) are legitimate, as was the case with Rousseau's view? We will return to this question in a later chapter, but for now, let us say that what may be required for legitimation of a political authority is not the direct expression of our will in its operation, but rather merely the *opportunity* to participate in activities that support or resist its operations? Either through voting (the weakest form of such an opportunity) or through more active participation in political parties, associations with political programs, community groups, and the like, we might say that opportunities to approve or resist the power structures that operate in one's area are provided. What can be claimed is that with such opportunities in place, as long as they are meaningful and not merely formal, citizens can be said to express their will concerning the general structure and policies of the state. This, then, would connect legitimacy to actual willing, but would not demand the impractical necessity of general and explicit expressions of consent.

But such a view, if fully worked out, would require a more robust theory of *democracy*, for that is the process being referred to here, the opportunity to participate in the democratic activities of a commonwealth. Such theories abound in the literature and bear close examination (see, for example, Christiano 1996 and Held 1987); for now, let us say merely that an acceptable theory of democracy may well succeed in preserving the connection between political legitimacy and the actual wills of citizens, a view central to the liberal conception of justice arising from the work of Locke, Rousseau, and Kant.

Chapter summary

The central issue in this chapter was the question of what justified the authority of the state. After defining 'authority,' we turned to the social contract approach to the question of political authority. Such theories always assume a set of agents who are party to the contract, and a set of conditions (both concerning the agents and surrounding circumstances) in which the contracts are made.

The social contract view of Thomas Hobbes was examined, bringing out its basic commitment to an egoistic conception of human beings and a justification of the authority of the state based on the rational self-interest of those governed by it (against the backdrop of a state of nature that was barely tolerable for those in it). Hobbes argued for the authority of an all powerful sovereign based on the rational interest of the governed, as compared with life without such a sovereign. In considering some initial difficulties with the Hobbesean argument, we noted that his justification was not based on the actual *wills* of the governed (as expressed in action and choice), but rather on their rational *interests* (whether or not these are expressed in choice). It is this very shift, we noted, that plagues even contemporary Hobbesean attempts to justify political authority, since they all fail to establish an important distinction between the legitimacy of authority and the rationality of obedience.

Locke's version of the social contract, by contrast, exhibits a 'will' theory of political authority, and rests on a view of human nature (and the state of nature) that considers all human beings to be capable of recognizing their own and others' natural rights. But the very reliance on actual acts of will on the part of the governed in the construction of the contract exposed Locke's view to trenchant criticisms, as no plausible standard of actual consent can realistically be met by citizens in a large society (Locke's attempt to create such a standard notwithstanding). Such problems also plague contemporary versions of Lockeanism.

Rousseau and Kant were also considered, marking a fundamental shift in thinking in the social contract tradition. No longer are political authorities justified with reference to their origins (a requirement that plagued both Hobbeseans and Lockeans), rather the fundamental role of political institutions in establishing citizen *freedom* becomes central. This led us to a consideration of contemporary social contract theory, in particular that of Rawls, where the requirement of citizen consent has been replaced by the standard of political legitimacy, the latter merely requiring a kind of idealized hypothetical consent. After considering Rawls's view in some detail, we concluded that the legitimacy of modern political authority not only requires that such authority manifests *justice* (rather than merely expediency), but also that such justice may well require robust opportunities for citizen participation in its operation, in other words democracy.

Case to consider

In the United States many groups have proclaimed themselves unbound by the laws of the federal or state governments. So-called 'separatists' claim to be free to ignore the various legal restrictions placed upon them by surrounding governmental agencies (as far as they are physically able to so ignore them). Some groups of this sort live in isolated communities, with alternative currency and internal authority structures, which, while physically within the borders of the US, understand themselves to be separate political entities.

Many of these groups are strongly motivated by overtly racist ideologies; indeed, 'white separatism' is the phrase often used to describe this movement. Members of such groups may well accept the social contract model of political legitimacy but argue that *they* (as individuals or families or groups) have not accepted the authority of the dominant political institutions. They claim that they owe no allegiance to a state authority which they reject, including the regulation of property and natural resources falling within their purview. (And therefore such groups refuse to pay taxes or submit to zoning or other land-use regulations.)

What arguments can be garnered either to bolster the case for separation (though not necessarily for the racist ideology that motivates it) or to counter such claims? If such groups cannot physically separate themselves from the political institutions that they do not choose to obey, does this mean that citizenship is, in the end, forced upon them (and, by implication, us)? Additionally, can the members of such groups claim to 'own' property and other resources without cooperatively subjecting the enjoyment of those resources to social (that is, governmental) regulation? This question leads us directly to the issues touched upon in the next chapter.

Notes on further reading

A good source on the idea of political authority is Raz (for example 1986: 23–37) as well as his earlier book-length treatment of the topic (Raz 1979). The concept of freedom has been much discussed; some standard sources can be found in Miller 1991, though see also Berlin 1969, McCallum 1967, Feinberg 1973: 4–19, Flathman 1989: 109–40, and Connolly 1983: chs. 4–5. For an historical overview of the concept, see Pelcynski and Gray 1984. The social contract tradition is examined historically in Gough 1957, Skinner 1978, Tuck 1979, and (in a critical vein) MacPherson 1962. See also the essays in Morris 1999.

Contractarianism in general is treated in Simmons 1979, Barry 1980 and 1989, and Scanlon 1998.

Hobbes's work is analyzed in a number of excellent works; for an historical treatment, see Tuck 1989, while contemporary examinations can be found in Kavka 1986, Hampton 1986, and Kraus 1993. For discussions of Locke's political views see Dunn 1969, Tully 1980 (for an historical perspective), Grant 1987, Waldron 1988: 137–252, and Simmons 1992 and 1993. Contemporary Lockeans (for the most part libertarian philosophers) include Nozick 1974, Lomasky 1987, Narveson 1988, and Mack 1983 (though see also Chapter 3 below for other references). Rousseau's views are looked at from a current perspective in Levine 1976 and 1993. Kant's work has received voluminous commentary and analysis (see readings at the end of Chapter 1 for references); for a discussion specifically of his political philosophy, see Riley 1983.

The work of Rawls discussed in this chapter (see Chapter 4 for further discussion) can be found in Rawls 1971 (revised edition 1999) and the papers in Rawls 1999a that were published prior to 1980. His work is analyzed in several places, among them are Barry 1973, the essays in Daniels 1975 and Reath et al. 1997, and in Kukathas and Pettit 1990.

CHAPTER 3

Distributive justice

- Distributive justice and equality
- Libertarianism
- Rawlsian distributive justice
- Varieties of egalitarianism
- From equality to the welfare state
- Chapter summary
- Case to consider
- Notes on further reading

In the last chapter we found that one way to defend the legitimacy of political authority was to show that the regime in question was just, that it operated according to acceptable principles, and treated citizens fairly. But what makes a society just? There are many ways to ask that question. Are people who commit crimes treated fairly in that society? Can people find redress against injuries they suffer from other citizens? Are the benefits and burdens of living in the society distributed fairly? More specifically, is the distribution of income and wealth in the society just, or are the disparities between the rich and the poor unfair? A more general version of this last question will be the focus of our discussion in this chapter, but political philosophy concerns itself with the others as well (and with related offshoots of them). Theories of justice, following Aristotle, are usually divided into theories of *retributive justice* (punishment), *corrective justice* (the payment of damages for private injuries, such as in tort law), and *distributive justice* (the regulation of social benefits, particularly economic rights and opportunities) (Aristotle 1958). We will consider the third here, as a lesson in how a generally liberal approach to political principle might extend to questions of social justice.

Principles of distributive justice amount principally to those legally enforced norms that shape the economic policies of a state, policies which determine the structure and pattern of property ownership in the society. Although I use the word 'pattern,' we should not *define* a principle of distributive justice as that which enforces some pattern of holdings over time, because, as we will shortly see, some argue that the best such principle will be one that in no way forces citizens' holdings into some favored pattern (such as equality). Similarly, the phrase 'distributive justice' could misleadingly imply that it is the state's role to *distribute* goods to people. But again, libertarian thinkers to be considered below staunchly object to that picture. In general, then, principles of distributive justice guide the structure of ownership (what rights are held by those who own goods) and the general level of wealth enjoyed by citizens, even if such levels are determined by the workings of an unrestrained market of buyers and sellers.

We will begin with the claim that justice demands (only) that equal opportunities to succeed be provided, and in this way the advantages and disadvantages gained by citizens are what they truly deserve (at least I will argue that the equal opportunity principle, in one of its forms, comes down to a claim about what people deserve). We will then consider what really is the main event: the contention by libertarians, on the one side, that justice demands only that the state protect property rights to engage in capitalist market exchanges (letting resulting inequalities in wealth and income alone), and the claims of egalitarians, on the other, who argue that justice demands the equalization of people's condition along some dimension of their lives. We will close by considering a 'compromise' that states that a government must provide for the basic needs of its citizens, but beyond that can let the (capitalist) chips fall where they may. We will raise objections to each of these approaches, ending with difficulties that will lead to consideration of some fundamental questions about the structure of liberal justice generally.

Distributive justice and equality

Aristotle first claimed that the essence of justice was that equals should be treated equally and unequals unequally (Aristotle 1958). That seemingly innocuous formal phrase can be taken apart in any number of ways, but in general it can be understood as claiming that justice requires that in so far as agents are the same in *morally relevant respects* then they should be treated the same, and in so far as they differ in those respects they should be treated differently (Feinberg 1980, Westen 1990, Raz 1986: 217–44). In the liberal paradigm we are assuming here, it is claimed that all human beings are equal in their basic moral status, that they equally deserve respect as autonomous beings. But this leaves open the question of what treatment such equal status requires, what ways such beings are 'the same' so that, following Aristotle's dictum, they should be treated the same. This shows how the crux of arguments about equality is the phrase 'morally relevant respects.' Disagreements over how much, and in what ways, equality should be promoted in a society will turn on arguments about what are the relevant respects in which people are all the same.

Typically, we understand disagreements about distributive justice as surrounding the question of how much, if at all, the state should interfere with the economic activity of its members (exchanges of goods and services) to enforce a principle of justice, though the question of distribution should be understood more broadly to include questions of the distribution of all the advantages and burdens of social life.[1] This suggests a familiar continuum between egalitarians on the left, who insist that the state should attempt to maintain equality in the pattern of holdings, and libertarians (and many conservatives) on the right, who insist that free market capitalism should be allowed to operate free of state interference, no matter what inequalities result. It might be thought, indeed, that this question comes down to the issue of whether a principle of equality should guide the social and economic policies of a state at all. But as we just noted (and others have argued), all theories of justice, at least in the liberal tradition we are working within here, are committed to a principle of equality at least at the abstract level: all citizens enjoy basic equality of moral status as reflected in the policies of the state. So even libertarians acknowledge the principle of equality in this sense (Sen 1992). Disagreements arise, however, when the question is asked 'equality of *what?*' Even if all agree that citizens should be treated equally at the abstract level, what should be used as the *measure* of that equality for purposes of distributive justice? This is the question that seriously divides theorists considered here. Egalitarians and libertarians disagree, then, about what this abstract equality entails concerning acceptable patterns of the benefits and burdens of social and economic life.

The chimerical allure of an equal opportunity principle

Common sense suggests that when people are treated differently for no discernable reason, then something is morally amiss. But what kind of 'treatment' is in question when judgments of equality are made at this level? In the operation of social institutions, what characteristic of people's lives do we regard as the vector by which their lot in life must be measured in order for us to be satisfied that they have been given equal treatment of the proper sort?

One common-sense answer is simply 'opportunity': people are treated equally by the institutions of their society when they have been afforded equal opportunity to succeed. As a base level principle, this is very attractive, for it captures what most people mean when they claim that people have been fairly or unfairly treated – they have (or have not) been given the same chances to do well. But using the principle 'everyone in society ought to enjoy equality of opportunity' as the *basic* principle of justice is problematic, at least as it stands. First, such a claim is importantly incomplete, for the term 'opportunity' can be understood in any number of ways. A principle that says that opportunities are equal when agents face the same *legal* restrictions and permissions but enjoy very different material conditions and physical abilities – defining opportunity only in terms of legal rights and privileges – is quite different from one that says that opportunities are equal only if agents enjoy both the same legal rights as well as the same resources needed to achieve their ends.

Also, it is unclear how equality of opportunity can function as a *basic* principle of justice. For consider the question: why give people merely the *opportunity* to achieve some good rather than simply providing the good itself? There are a number of answers to that question, each of which reveals a more basic principle from which equality of opportunity is actually derivative. The first is that while in an ideal world society would directly grant people precisely what they desire, real world institutions such as the government do not have sufficient *information* to give people goods directly, for they often will not know what each person thinks is valuable. So merely opportunities are provided (equally) as a substitute for providing the valuable goods directly. But this means that equality of opportunity is a second-best principle – the first best being that we should give people goods of a certain sort (such as happiness or pleasure). But this shows that giving people opportunities is not the basic social goal – having them achieve the desired state is. And as we will see, the claim that society should be organized to give people maximum pleasure or make them happy is itself quite controversial.

The other answer to the question of 'why opportunities and not outcomes' also shows the equal opportunity principle to be derivative rather than basic. That is, we do not provide goods directly to people because it is better to allow them to gain those goods by their own *free choice*. That is, opportunities allow the operation of what is truly valuable: that people's lot in life results from their own choices rather than having been provided by others. But this shows that the ground-level principle guiding our policy is not the equalization of opportunities per se but protecting the value of free choice. What the principle really says is that everyone has an equal right to exercise free choice, and protecting equality of opportunity, suitably defined, is necessary for this, so we should adopt the latter principle. We will return to this idea below.

A final construal of the equal opportunity principle also reveals it to be both derivative from a more basic idea and more controversial than it first appeared. Some think that equality of opportunity simply means facing the same legal barriers to success in life and allowing one's economic fortune to be governed completely by one's own efforts in the world of free market competition. One way this claim can be understood is that supplying equal opportunities by way of a free market with competitive prices for goods and services (along with equal legal rights) will allow social benefits to flow to those who most *deserve* them, who have worked hardest and supplied the most valuable goods to others. Therefore, distributive justice amounts to protecting equality of opportunity by granting equal opportunities to participate in capitalist economic markets and such markets ultimately provide people with the level of advantages they truly deserve.

But there are several problems with this view: first, the claim that justice demands equal opportunities is derivative from the more basic claim that people should get what they deserve. This sounds uncontroversial until one fills out what is meant by 'what one deserves.' To deserve something means one should receive some benefit or punishment based on an activity one performed or trait displayed, a benefit or punishment that is proportional to the (dis-)value of that activity or trait (Feinberg 1970, Sher 1987). But disagreements will arise over what activities will be deserving of what responses and, more seriously, what the relevant proportions are between the value of the activity/trait and the response deserved. Moreover, there is good reason to doubt that anything like a free market for goods and services actually gives people what they deserve, intuitively speaking, since what one gets in a market will depend on things other than simply how hard one works, but on such factors as how many other people happen to be around that are similar in talent and ability to you and how many people happen to want what you have to offer (factors you had nothing to do with bringing about presumably). Although effort and industriousness might well be rewarded at times in a market, so is good fortune and luck. (For a further defense of these claims, see Christman 1994: ch. 5; for an opposing view, see Arnold 1987.)

So the various ways that a principle of equal opportunity might be filled out reveals a number of controversies that dilute the initial appeal of the view, at least for many. These points will re-emerge when we consider a version of egalitarianism that includes 'opportunity' as a basic component.

Libertarianism

The lure of the principle of equality of opportunity, however, was that all justice demands of the state is to protect a certain space around the individual citizen within which she can choose to pursue whatever projects she wishes and is able to achieve them by her own efforts, short of harming others. It is not up to the state to secure a certain outcome or pattern of outcomes for its citizens, but simply protect their basic rights and leave them alone otherwise.

Libertarians argue that the extent of justified government power is limited to protecting the basic negative rights of its citizens (or those positive rights that are created by voluntary contracts among them). Notably, these rights include the right to private property, at least the right to have the property one has acquired protected, so the state is required by justice to protect the property rights of citizens along with rights to privacy, personal security, and so on.[2] These property rights are assumed to be the full package of capitalist private property rights to possess, use, exchange, and gain income from trades of property in a market, without interference, regulation or taxation (again, except to protect the negative rights of others not to be harmed). The voluntary acts of free agents acting within their rights produce just outcomes, no matter how unequal the distribution of advantages is in these outcomes or how rich or poor people become.[3]

Some libertarians claim that the most fundamental principle of their doctrine is that everyone has a right to liberty (see Narveson 2000: 306). But this is confused. For having a right to 'liberty' is, by itself, vacuous unless one knows what other rights having that liberty protects. This is true unless by 'liberty' one means being able to move about completely unimpeded by *anything*, but that is not what is generally meant here – see our discussion of 'normative' freedom in Chapter 2, note 1 above. What is meant by 'liberty' in this context is having the ability to do what one wants within one's rights. So to have a right to liberty simply means having a variety of other rights.[4] The question, then, is which ones, and why (only) these?

We asked earlier in our discussion of Locke what the basis was for viewing justice in terms of rights of this sort. We can now put that question this way: what is the characteristic of human beings such that they should be afforded this array of liberty-related rights construed as absolute in this way? A reply to this question by a famous defender of libertarianism is instructive:

> I conjecture that the answer is connected with that elusive and difficult notion: the meaning of life. A person's shaping his life in

accordance with some overall plan is his way of giving meaning to his life; only a being with the capacity to so shape his life can have or strive for meaningful life.

(Nozick 1974: 50)

The capacity to shape one's life in accordance to an overall plan is then the basis of having rights to liberty and property, rights whose stringency prevents any external (state) interference with such lives even in order to bring about good ends. But why should the capacity to shape one's life this way ground, in particular, the right to property one has acquired, but not, say, the right to be *provided* resources (from others) that one needs to live such a self-directed life, say if one were poor and lacked such basic goods? The initial libertarian answer to that question is that to recognize those latter rights would be to allow the violation of the rights of the property holders from whom the resources are taken. As Nozick says, goods do not fall like 'manna from heaven,' but are already owned by those who, according to his theory of initial acquisition, justly appropriate goods in a way not in violation of others' rights (Nozick 1974: 198). The right to property, then, is basic to the libertarian view, for otherwise, there would be no reason to bar the state from attempting to supply (poorer) people with the material necessary to live a meaningful life by limiting the capitalist property rights of the (relatively) rich, through taxation say.

The self-ownership argument for capitalist property rights

Libertarian attempts to defend the rights central to free market capitalism have a varied history, and include arguments based on utilitarian thinking.[5] The variants to be discussed here are non-utilitarian, inspired by the natural rights framework of Locke and his followers (though not tied to the details of Locke's view). In particular, the argument proceeds by claiming an unbreakable connection between the *self*-ownership that all human beings enjoy as a basic condition of freedom and the ownership of external, material goods that one has acquired. Even some socialist writers acknowledge the power of the self-ownership premise, namely that unless a person has rights over herself – her body and, to some extent, her actions and movements – then her very humanity has been denied (G. Cohen 1995: 67–91; Christman 1994: ch. 8). Libertarians have utilized this thought to argue that property rights in external goods also have this sacred status in virtue of their connection with self-ownership.

An initial problem with this strategy, though, is that *everyone* has a basic interest in using those external material goods that are necessary to carry out one's projects. If this interest is crucially connected to self-ownership (and everyone owns themselves) then both holders of property and the property-less have an equally valid claim to those goods necessary to carry out projects, even if those goods happen to be in the hands of the property-holders. Only if self-ownership is construed overly narrowly – to be understood to hold even if one has no real access to material goods – can it be claimed that unregulated capitalism (without taxation and redistribution to allow all to own some property) protects everyone's self-ownership (see G. Cohen 1995: 67–115).

However, in order to establish a link between meaningful self-ownership and material property ownership, without entailing that non-owners have claims on the goods of the owners (based on the former's self-ownership), libertarians must provide an account of material appropriation. The most well discussed defender of such a strategy is Robert Nozick, whose *Anarchy, State, and Utopia* (Nozick 1974) virtually single-handedly put libertarianism in the center of the political philosophy stage. Nozick defended what he called an 'historical' theory of entitlement (property rights) according to which all holdings which have been gained in a justifiable manner, or gained through voluntary exchange with those who acquired their holdings in a justifiable manner, are just. If property was justly acquired and freely traded, distributive justice obtains no matter what the resulting inequality of wealth and income (ibid.: ch. 7).

Initial appropriation occurs when a person interacts with previously unowned nature in some way. Locke famously used the metaphor of 'mixing one's labor' with the unowned thing to support the view that unless one subsequently gained property rights in the worked-upon object (say, it was taken away for public purposes) then one did not truly own one's labor, hence one did not own oneself (Locke 1690: ch. V). However, such rights are justified, for Locke, only if the laboring activity is not merely wasteful – that it in fact succeeds in improving the object in some way – and that others retain the opportunity to similarly appropriate comparable resources. This second qualification on the right to appropriate – that one must leave 'enough and as good . . . in common for others' (Locke 1690: 369) – has attracted the most attention in commentaries on this argument. For this consideration expresses the idea that one's natural rights extend only as far as exercising them does not harm others by appropriating goods that they need in order to direct their own lives. This is a crucial restriction, for one cannot acquire things in a way that violates the rights of others and all equally have rights to acquire unowned goods as a matter of basic liberty. The condition of having to leave 'enough and as good' fixes the baseline with which those rights (of non-appropriators) are defined.

Even stated in this simplified manner, this argument has various problems, many of which rest on the metaphor of 'mixing' one's labor with the unowned thing (see Waldron 1988:171–77, Christman 1994: 49–54, Arthur 1987). Nozick himself asks: when one builds a fence around some land, does one's labor extend to the land inside the fence or just the space under the posts? 'Why isn't mixing what I own with what I don't just a way of losing what I own instead of gaining what I don't?' (Nozick 1974: 174–75)

But Nozick ignores these difficulties because he avoids use of the labor mixing metaphor altogether. For Nozick, what matters in cases of initial appropriation is whether one is acting within one's natural right to liberty when engaging in activity such as the appropriation of goods – such activity must not violate the rights of others – and this is defined by the Lockean proviso that appropriation is legitimate only if there is enough and as good left in common for others.

But how do we define the baseline of well-being that I am entitled to relative to your (or any others') appropriative activities? The most straightforward statement of such a baseline is this: the life quality a person could have expected if the other person had not existed at all. Therefore, even if my only live option is to work on your farm, I may nevertheless be better off than if there was no farm at all, in other words, if you had not existed and acquired the farmland in the first place. In such a scenario, I cannot claim a rights violation simply because I cannot acquire the farm myself now. This is the crux of Nozick's justification of natural entitlements (Nozick 1974: 178–82).

This is a clever argument, but it is subject to a variety of powerful objections. First, the baseline against which current natural rights claims on the part of property owners (against which calls for redistribution by poorer non-owners are made) is very difficult to fix. It is completely indeterminate what the level of well-being would have been if the ancestors of present-day property owners had not acquired their holdings and left them for the rest of us. It cannot be determined, for example, how things might have turned out if *my* ancestors had acquired the property before yours did (assuming you are rich and I am relatively poor), or if some had been left for me to acquire and develop myself. While we might admit that resource development by initial appropriators and their progeny has expanded everyone's options in some way,[6] it is very much in doubt that those unable to acquire property now are still better off than they would have been in the alternative scenario, where other people acquired the goods first and instituted some alternative property scheme perhaps (G. Cohen 1986b, Arthur 1987, Christman 1994: 61–63). So by that standard, the argument proves nothing.

We must remember that property is not a simple relation of 'mine' and 'thine,' enforceable by the property owner herself, but rather a *system*, including a collective web of protection mechanisms, legal structures used for the redress of injury and the adjudication of disputes and the like, that make up an economic system (without which property 'ownership' is meaningless). Countless variations are possible, including tax and zoning systems, restrictions on use to prevent pollution, and the like, some of which will make certain groups better off and others worse off. So we cannot say with precision that a newcomer to an already established property arrangement cannot complain of being worse off than she would have been had the arrangement (and the first appropriators who set it up) not existed; for we don't know how things might have been had they or their ancestors set up an alternative system with, say, provisions for newcomers! (See Christman 1994; this is also discussed in Narveson 1988: 87–89.)

Another serious difficulty with an historical entitlement theory such as Nozick's is this: for any argument from initial acquisition to apply at all to contemporary political life, it would have to be the case that not only the original appropriation, but all subsequent transfers were untainted by injustice. But as is well known, every developed economy on Earth has in its history countless patterns of military domination, theft, murderous expansionism, imperialism, and violence. Hardly any present holdings could claim the spotless history necessary to establish a natural right to them and hence to resist calls for redistribution, especially since those calls often are made on the behalf of the descendants of those who were the victims of that violent expansion, such as Africans, indigenous populations in the West, and the like (for discussion, see Christman 1994: 63–65, and Rothbard 1978: 34f.)

Libertarianism based on liberty alone

A new twist on this argument has been developed by Narveson and others (in different forms) in a way that attempts to obviate the need (and avoid the difficulty) of reference to a proviso (see, for example, Narveson 1988: Part I, 1998). On this account, no proviso of leaving enough and as good for others is necessary since there is something morally special about beginning a project involving the use of material resources itself. What is morally special about that activity is that, once such an activity has started, another person's coming along and taking those resources used in the project is *interfering* with that project. And in so far as protecting people's liberty means prohibiting interferences with action (except in cases where that is necessary to stop aggression), the latecomer's expropriation of the material goods is an interference with liberty (ibid.: 11). Moreover, the reason this appropriation does not violate the rights of non-owners to acquire this or similar goods is that such people had no pre-existing rights to such goods in the first place: there are no rights to resources prior to establishing them by using them; assuming otherwise would (implausibly) claim that the earth is jointly owned by all (past, present, and future) inhabitants (Narveson: 1988: 85, 1998: 12).

This argument proceeds by placing the right to continue projects, once begun, at the center of the pantheon of human rights (central to freedom), while giving rights to have or take those resources necessary to live secondary importance, indeed the latter are no rights at all (Narvseson 1988: 70–71, 77–78). The only rights there are concerning property are the rights to acquire *unowned* goods and then the right to use, trade, destroy, and so on (all those rights connected with capitalist ownership) those acquired goods. Any taxation scheme transferring resources from those who possess it to those who don't have it is a violation of that right and is hence unjust (ibid.: 79–93).

The problems with this line of argument can be stated briefly: the right to continue to engage in projects once begun does not necessitate the *ownership* of the goods involved in those projects, at least not ownership in the full capitalist sense that forbids regulation and redistributive taxation. One can engage in a plethora of projects under a regime of collectively organized property rights (G. Cohen 1998: 61, Christman 1994: ch. 9). Second, the presumption that interference with a property-holder's rights is always worse than passively allowing someone to go without (without badly needed resources, say) is implausible in its most general form. There are countless instances where the relatively benign manner in which redistributive property systems 'interfere' with people's projects holds little weight compared to the tremendous good such schemes can do (potentially at least). The paradox libertarians will always face is that they claim that state regulation of property is such a deep injustice because it interferes with personal rights that are central to human dignity and autonomy, yet there is nothing (by itself) wrong with having *no* property and hence lacking the very prerogatives, powers, and rights that are meant to be so central to autonomy (or whatever it is that makes liberty so basic a right).

Consider, for example, the selectivity with which libertarians choose the rights and duties they think are basic: there are rights against fraud, but not against being lied to generally; duties to honor contracts, but not duties to keep promises generally; there is no right to mutual aid, but there are (presumably)[7] duties not to abandon one's children. One way to corral these rights into a coherent package would be to show their centrality to living an autonomous and fully human life. But doing so is disastrous for the libertarian since access to certain resources, such as food, housing, and medical care, are as central to living an autonomous and fully human life as the right to hold on to one's riches, so protecting those interests central to liberty would imply, in most cases at least, providing such basic resources (through the state) to those who lack them.

A problem inherent in libertarian thinking is the move from arguing that *some* sorts of property rights are indeed crucial for living an independent, self-controlling, and dignified life (when those rights are over oneself as well as over some material goods) to the conclusion that they all are – that capitalist property rights are inherent in the right to liberty. The right to possess and use one's property (and body), implying a right to bar others from such use without one's permission, is an example of a right central to (any plausible conception of) liberty – it connects directly with one's interest in privacy, planning and executing one's projects, engaging in social behavior, and the like. But the right to keep all of the income that would accrue to you in trades with others in a market is not (typically) so central – these merely protect the interest we have in gaining more income, a weighty interest indeed but one whose weight clearly depends on the amount of income one started with and the kinds of activities one plans to use the income for. Progressive income taxes and other 'targeted' taxes such as levies on luxury items respond directly to this point, resting on the plausible view that the cost to the richer taxpayer (in the lost income from trades) is less than the benefit to society generally.[8]

Much more can be said on this score, but let us simply conclude that the libertarian strategy of basing arguments for capitalist property rights on consideration of liberty alone, without the qualification that others have enough to enjoy those goods necessary for a decent life, is highly problematic.

Contractualist libertarianism

There have been other libertarian defenses of the claim that the basic right to liberty should be construed as necessarily including capitalist property rights. One such strategy relies on the idea of a social contract, where it is suggested that if people were to choose rationally from a methodologically acceptable starting position, they would choose principles allowing full property rights and an unconstrained market, therefore providing purportedly neutral (non-moral) foundations for the libertarian (moral) view.[9]

The basic idea is that if we assume certain general facts about human beings and the dynamics of social life, we can predict that people will agree to a regime where the widest possible liberty (freedom from 'aggression') is protected. The background assumptions that this line of argument rests upon include: all people have a basic interest in the pursuit of personal projects; all enjoy and exercise minimal rationality (in a particular sense of 'rationality'); and there exists in the world a shortage of goods and space to the extent that social cooperation is necessary (for example to solve problems of the 'Prisoner's Dilemma' type we discussed in the last chapter). Under such conditions, people will choose to participate only in those arrangements that involve non-coercive social cooperation and which respect personal liberty of the libertarian stripe, including, that is, capitalist property rights (for those with property) and no provisions to redistribute wealth (to those who do not) (Narveson 1988: Part II, 1995: especially 27f.). Indeed, the argument goes, accruing wealth through voluntary transfers is 'inherently non-conflictual' (Narveson 1995: 33). And those that do not agree to such an arrangement (because they stand to lose out, for example, or will be left to starve), don't matter, for as was the case with Hobbes, those in the minority in a decision to create a social contract are simply still in the state of nature with respect to the contractees (ibid.: 31; see also Chapter 2 above).

Now, unlike the hypothetical contract models discussed in the last chapter, this argument is meant to be based on an *actual* social contract (Narveson 1995: 25): this arrangement, it is claimed, is what it is rational (and hence morally justified) for people to agree to as things now stand in the world. But this is highly problematic. For what people will (rationally) agree to depends on their position relative to the gains and losses of that agreement given what they now have, as well as their values, motives, and desires. The 'rationality' assumed in these models is quite narrow, and involves simply the instrumental rationality we saw in Hobbes (that to be rational is to choose the best means to given ends, no matter what those ends happen to be).[10] The question of whether it will be rational (even in this sense) for me to agree to a specific bargain with you depends on the power and resources we both have prior to the bargain. If I have tremendous power, say, a talented and well-equipped army of faithful acolytes who will follow my every order (based on my irresistible demagogic power), then I will have no incentive to concede anything to you, a poor, army-less individual. Moreover, if a person finds herself with no resources at all (through natural disaster, say), she will be desperately willing to bargain away everything short of her life (perhaps) in order to secure basic resources for her and her family. In other words, the conditions under which actual rational maximizers might agree to this or that set of social conventions are completely variable. How do we decide on which scenario to begin with?

Now, if this model is meant to apply to the real world (and not hypothetically to ideally rational and equally powerful individuals), we must ask what the actual circumstances are within which people are acting. And in our world, we do not have a state of nature with free, unconstrained bargainers and relatively equal bargaining power. Rather, we have a world of tremendous power disparities (including in some places powerful warlords with armies of devoted acolytes), as well as relations of intimacy and interdependence, conditions of desperate scarcity and untold riches, and so on. Within this world, it is quite variable what kind of social system it is rational to support, and free markets with minimal government intervention is by no means the dominant possibility.

For example, if one is suitably situated, it may well be (as it seems to be for some) quite rational to simply dominate those around you with the forces at your command. Of course, one may counter with speculations about the various pluses and minuses of adopting such a bellicose posture toward others (as Narveson does in 1988: 180–81), but the point remains: the argument for the rationality of any *particular* contractual arrangement is contingent upon the relative bargaining positions of those in the actual world, positions that are underwritten by existing governments, military institutions, and legal structures. (Such arguments will also fall prey to the criticisms raised in the last chapter about basing arguments about what is *legitimate* on claims about what is, contingently, in our *interests*.)

Moreover, it is doubly variable whether the particular principles that it will be rational to adhere to will be *libertarian ones*. That all depends on whether one stands to gain or lose (again, given the wide panoply of one's motives, values, and so on) from such principles relative to the relevant alternatives. The claim that the interest in unimpeded liberty will support an interest in the libertarian principles falters on the weakness of the arguments touched on earlier linking capitalist property ownership with liberty in the relevant sense.[11]

Indeed, like all contractualist arguments, the background presuppositions of these strategies – for example that people are rational (in a particular sense) and self-interested (again in a particular sense) – are themselves *political* presuppositions. They are assumptions that carry political weight and bias the view in favor of one set of principles over another (Ripstein 1987). There are different ways that one can be said to be rational, even in the narrow sense of choosing the best means to one's given ends. (One can assume, for example, that one is rational when one chooses the best means to one's ends over the whole of one's life, or the best means given full information and choosing under ideal conditions, and so on.) And even if there was a single understanding of rationality, most people would not live up to it, so to base a justification of political principles on a contract that such rational people ought to agree to is to rest the argument on a normative premise (that people ought to be rational in this way) of just the sort at issue in political philosophy. (For an attempt to reply to argument of this sort, see Narveson 1988: 155–65.)

So we leave behind these various attempts to justify libertarian principles of distributive justice, and move on to arguments that take as a basic premise of political morality the fundamental moral equality of persons.

Rawlsian distributive justice

As was mentioned in Chapter 2, Rawls developed a theory of distributive justice that he argued should apply to the basic structure of society, one based on the idea of a hypothetical contract derived from an ideal choice situation. That use of the hypothetical contract, however, avoids the difficulties of the sort noted earlier that plague the Hobbesian use of that mechanism. For Rawls is not basing his argument on the assumption that all citizens are self-interested maximizers of their own utility, but rather on straightforwardly moral presuppositions that shape the structure of the hypothetical choice situation. Rawls argues that we should follow the principles that would be chosen under ideal conditions not because it is *rational* for us to use such a procedure (in the narrow sense of rationality), and not because doing so would maximize total overall utility, but because doing so embodies fundamental values to which, Rawls thinks, we are already committed, the values of freedom and equality. In the next chapter we will discuss the basis of that foundationalist claim. For now, however, let us trace out its implications for distributive justice.

Rawls argues that the principles of justice are those that would be chosen under fair conditions, that is, under conditions that embody the values of freedom and equality. As described in the last chapter, those conditions are modeled by the device of the 'original position' and the 'veil of ignorance.' Parties in the original position are guided by freedom and equality in the sense that they are not moved by any prior principles of justice, and they are symmetrically situated one to another. As we noted, under such conditions, and ignorant of any factors about themselves that would 'bias' the choice, such parties would choose two principles of justice: the Basic Liberties Principle and the Difference Principle. The first guarantees the protection of a certain list of fundamental liberties, while the second requires fair equality of opportunity and rights to just shares in societies' goods.

This second principle, then, has two parts: an equal opportunity component and a just shares component. Fair equality of opportunity means that all offices and positions in society should be open to all, independent of arbitrary facts about them (race, gender, natural abilities, and the like). This is usually accepted without controversy in discussions of Rawls, partly based on the intuitive power of the demand that we guarantee equal opportunity for all. But as we discussed earlier, that intuitive plausibility often masks controversy. Let us leave aside a closer examination of the equality of opportunity principle, except to ask whether such a separate principle adds significantly to the citizens' rights and prerogatives when the other principles are satisfied, when, that is, basic rights are protected (including rights against discrimination) and the person enjoys her fair share of resources. Why would we also want to say that offices and positions in society are open to all, except as a surreptitious endorsement of a meritocracy (based on the principle that positions ought to be awarded to the talented)?[12]

Focusing on the second part of the Difference Principle – the so-called 'maximin' rule – let us consider again how Rawls thinks parties in the original position would come to favor that arrangement. First, they would initially consider requiring absolute equality of shares; since they do not know where they will end up in the distribution of goods, they would want to avoid having less than others, so equality would be initially attractive. But clearly, it would also be rational to *allow* inequalities if their existence makes even the worst off in society better off than they would be under strict equality. Only fetishism about equality would prevent such a judgment (Rawls 1971: 130–35).

But why begin with equality at all? The argument is complex, but the core of it is the assumption that people in the original position will not know their natural talents – their allotment of what Rawls calls their natural primary goods. Without knowing that, they would be loathe to choose principles that would award the naturally talented; they would want social goods to be distributed in a way that did not allow those who happen to be born with natural talents (characteristics whose development becomes valued in society) to flourish while the rest of us flounder in relative deprivation. Parties in the original position, then, would treat natural talents as if they were socially owned. So the decision to set up such institutions that begin with a benchmark of equality is a decision based on the arbitrariness of the natural distribution of characteristics that, partly at least, are valued through no effort or responsible choice by the person who enjoys them. And it is not fair for a society to be set up that allows such good or bad luck to determine how people's lives will go (ibid.: 86–89, 441–49).

Rawls has been criticized for using such a fanciful and unwieldy device as the original position in order to derive principles meant to apply to real people, living here and now, in actual societies. The artificial nature of the people behind the veil of ignorance makes the principles derived in that manner inapplicable to us flesh and blood people who know our talents and feel like we deserve to reap the rewards society offers us for them (Nozick 1974: 213–31). But the method of argument Rawls uses need not be thought of as overly fanciful or otherworldly. Simply imagine that you are a relatively talented person living in a society governed by the Difference Principle (so one with taxation used to advance the position of the relatively poor) and you are moved to complain that you have to pay taxes to help the poor. The Rawlsian response to such complaints would be that part of why you are so well off in this society is that you were born under circumstances and with natural abilities that are a matter of good fortune and, when you developed them (albeit by your own efforts), others in the society happened to want to pay you for exercising them. But surely, your fortunate childhood circumstances and natural abilities were things that you simply found yourself with, so you can't claim that the whole of your riches is deserved. And separating out the part due to your efforts from the part due to your good luck is impossible. Moreover, if you tried to justify an alternative principle of distributive justice that allowed you to keep all of your riches and left the poor much worse off than in the Rawlsian society, you could only do so by reference to considerations that you would not think important if you didn't *already know* you were rich. That is, your only reason for favoring such a society is that you know you would benefit in it. If you put those reasons aside, you would be left with reasons that favor a principle of distribution that would benefit all, no matter where they ended up in the 'natural lottery' of talents. The principle would be, in other words, something akin to the Difference Principle.

This version of the core idea of Rawls's theory leaves volumes of detail out of the picture, but even this rough and ready version of the basic idea shows that the principles can be motivated without invoking what look like hard to picture scenarios or artificial entities choosing our principles for us. However, other critics of Rawls have argued that the derivation of the two principles of justice is fundamentally question-begging in that the principles that justify the premises of the argument would only be accepted if one were already well disposed to the conclusions. Support for the Difference Principle, for example, rests crucially on the design of the original position and use of the veil of ignorance, which, as we saw, demands that the justification of principles cannot rest on 'morally arbitrary' factors such as the distribution of natural talents. But what makes such things 'morally arbitrary'? Especially given that what our skills and dispositions are very much define who *we are* – they structure our identity (see, for example, Nozick 1974: 226–28, Sandel 1982: 77–81). What makes the adoption of principles based on them ruled out?

The answer is found in Rawls's claim that the original position reflects the values of freedom and equality which, in some sense, are values that 'we do in fact accept' (Rawls 1971: 19). His defense of the claim that these values – interpreted in the way his theory does – are values we already are guided by is complex and has changed (or been clarified) over the years in ways we will discuss in the next chapter. In *A Theory of Justice*, an argument based on general intuition but utilizing the standard of reflective equilibrium was proffered. That argument is along the lines of the one just given, that a basic intuitive commitment to fundamental equality implies that social institutions should not be designed to allow people's lives to flourish to a greater or lesser degree based only on the accidents of birth and surrounding circumstance. But, of course, Rawls is not an intuitionist; he is not content to rest his conclusion on that basic idea alone. The coherence of the entire theory, as well as the general acceptability of the policy implications of the conclusions (about which more in a minute), conspire to make an entire package that is acceptable because of that general coherence. Reflective equilibrium operates as the standard of theoretical acceptability. One accepts the whole ball of wax simply because of its cohesiveness and solidity.

We will return to this issue. Continuing with Rawls's theory itself, we must ask how parties in the original position are to choose principles on the basis of rational 'self-interest' when they are ignorant of their own conception of what makes life worth living and hence what their own interests are. The veil of ignorance bars from view any understanding of particular value commitments and conceptions of the good. This is based on the view that such commitments, while certainly not 'arbitrary' from one's own perspective – they define who we are – may nevertheless be arbitrary from others' points of view. In a pluralistic world, we must choose principles that those who pursue morality from a wide variety of perspectives can accept. If the representatives in the original position chose principles based on their own conceptions of the good, this would not be the case.

So, upon what ideas concerning what is good in life are the choices in the original position to be made if people there cannot choose based on their own conception of the good? The answer is 'social primary goods.' These are things that the parties in the original position can be confident that everyone in civil society will want, no matter what conceptions of the good they pursue, given the kind of people we can assume they are.[13] Such goods include: basic rights and liberties; freedom of movement and occupation; powers and prerogatives of office; income and wealth; and the social bases of self-respect (Rawls 1971: 79). All these are to be distributed according to the two principles of justice: basic liberties are provided; equality of opportunity is guaranteed; and inequalities in primary goods are allowed only if they can benefit the least favored in society. This is what rational people behind the veil of ignorance would choose for themselves, according to Rawls.

Since the basic liberties and equality of opportunity are guaranteed to all as part of the lexical priority of the Basic Liberty Principle and the equal opportunity component of the Difference Principle, the primary goods that are managed by the maxamin principle are, for the most part, income and wealth. (Recall that 'lexical priority' means that the Basic Liberty and Equal Opportunity Principles must be satisfied first, and in that order, before attempts are made to satisfy the maxamin principle.) So the economic policies of society should be arranged so that in so far as some have more than others, this is allowed only because those with less are better off in such a system than they would be in a more equal one.

The social and economic policies that would be shaped by such principles are not things discussed in any detail by Rawls, for he claims that a philosophical theory of justice of this sort is given at too high a level of abstraction to determine what ways a particular society should conform to its principles. Various local facts and contingent matters will be crucial in designing policies that meet the conditions of the two principles. The abstract principles of justice enter at the more basic stage of shaping the institutional design of society, for example its constitution. But Rawls has indicated that a democratic society with robust social programs to reduce inequalities of wealth (and more importantly guarantee a healthy basic minimum of resources for the less fortunate) would likely comply with the two principles for most modern industrialized nations. He has sometimes labeled such an exemplar a 'property owning democracy' (Rawls 1971: 242ff.). But nothing in the principles dictates that a specific system of social programs or economic policies must be adopted for justice to be done. If basic liberties and opportunities are guaranteed, and inequalities are allowed only because they maximize the lot of the worst off, the demands of justice are satisfied.

As we already noted, much critical discussion has been generated concerning this view. Some have argued, for example, that Rawls is wrong to conclude that, given the veil of ignorance, it will only be rational for people in the original position to choose the two principles of justice (in particular, the Difference Principle). Some claim that under some conditions people will choose to adopt *utilitarianism* instead: for while they may be taking a chance that society might sacrifice their own good for the greater happiness of others, it will be rational to take that chance if the total happiness will be maximized (Harsanyi 1982, cf. Barry 1973: 116–27). Rawls's reply to this argument is two-fold: parties in the original position will be 'minimally risk averse' – they will not take grand risks on the off-chance that they will result in a big payoff. (An assumption that they are not so afraid to take risks is essential for the utilitarian argument to go through (Rawls 1971: 464–74).) Secondly, Rawls rejects the possibility of choosing utilitarianism before we even get inside the original position, for he argues that such a view fails to comply with the basic values of freedom and equality (what he called the 'separateness of persons') which guide the design of the theory (ibid.: 19–24). This, of course, is a substantive moral argument (that utilitarianism is unacceptable as a grounds for a theory of justice) and so must be debated on its merits, a discussion we put to the side for now. But it indicates how heavily Rawls depends on those background values of freedom and equality (and the particular meaning he puts on them) for the structure of his view.

A second line of criticism will lead us into a discussion of the next section. This argument claims that Rawls's theory is not as internally coherent as it first appears, for the distribution of primary goods according to the Difference Principle does not, it is suggested, conform to the basic conception of equality that guides the entire view. According to that basic conception of equality, people's relative well-being should not depend on the accidents of birth but on their own freely made choices. But if primary goods, in particular income and wealth, provide the index of distributive shares for a society, some will be rendered much worse off than others based on such accidents, even if the Difference Principle is in force. This is because those who lack basic physical or mental capabilities, or who, more generally, have less ability to use the primary goods placed before them, will be worse off in the distribution even if primary goods are all 'fairly' allocated. If two people have the same income and wealth, but one needs to spend a great deal of it on goods like wheelchairs and the like, they are clearly not equal in their life prospects to those who do not. This means that even when the Difference Principle is satisfied, the distribution of goods is still unequal in these hidden ways. What this shows is that for a theory to be true to its egalitarian roots, as Rawls's wants his to be, it must correct for such differentials in ability. And in the next section we will discuss attempts to do just that (Daniels 1975, Sen 1992: 8, 26–28).

Varieties of egalitarianism

A common caricature of egalitarianism is that it defines justice as demanding *sameness* of treatment for all citizens in all ways. But while that might amount to treating people 'equally' in some deflated sense of that term, it would not be treating them 'as equals' in the sense that egalitarians insist upon (R. Dworkin 1985: 206–07). Ronald Dworkin, for example, argues that treating citizens as equals implies adopting principles that express equal concern and respect for them as persons. But to make that claim is not to justify it, and many political philosophers take a commitment to equality for granted without discussing its basis (for attempts at this, see B. Williams 1962, Vlastos 1962, Nagel 1991). And it is clear that 'equality' is one of those essentially contested concepts where what it means is as up for grabs as how important it is (see, for example, Rae, et al. 1981 and Westen 1990). For now, we will consider particular positions that have been taken on what equality in the area of the distribution of material and other goods might mean. How can people's well-being be defined and measured so that it can be determined that they are being treated as equals?

One common distinction among egalitarian principles that is useful here is that which divides calls for equality of *opportunity* and equality of *outcome*. The latter demands that mechanisms of distribution must operate so that all end up in equal positions, measured by some index of well-being.[14] The former understanding of equality eschews direct reference to how things end up, but claims that equality is realized when a certain array of opportunities are made the same for people. As we saw earlier, this principle needs filling out before it can be assessed fully, but the contrast between it and a principle of equality of outcome should nevertheless be clear.

It would seem that the most thoroughgoing egalitarianism would demand that, in the end, outcomes should be defined in terms of the overall welfare of those involved. Equality of 'welfare' refers to the state where, according to an index of welfare (where that can be defined as happiness, pleasure, or desire satisfaction), everyone's life is equally prosperous. This follows in a utilitarian vein but substitutes for the requirement of maximizing utility (welfare) the call to equalize it. By way of redistribution in some form, states are achieved where all are equally well off as measured by this welfarist metric (for discussion see R. Dworkin 2000: 11–64, G. Cohen 1989, Arneson 1989).

The claim behind this view is that all differences in talent and good fortune should be corrected for so that everyone, no matter what their unchosen backgrounds and natural abilities, ends up equally well off in society as measured by their level of happiness. A more pristine egalitarian outcome could hardly be imagined. But there are problems with this picture arising from within the egalitarian perspective itself. (And there are several criticisms that would come from those who don't accept calls for equality of this sort at all, such as libertarian thinkers – see, for example, Narveson 1984.) The first is that many aspects of one's state that produce relative losses in welfare result from informed, voluntary choice, where people's personal decisions result in their particular level of welfare. Critics point out that the laudable egalitarian aim of correcting for arbitrary deficits in well-being is overstepped by the goal of equality of welfare in that equalizing happiness without regard for the responsibility people might have for their own lots in life goes beyond correcting for bad luck and undeserved misfortune. Those who choose to lay around and contribute nothing to their own or others' happiness get as much attention from the welfare-egalitarian distributive mechanism as do the hard working and the industrious (who exert effort to make themselves happy). A related problem surrounds the phenomenon of 'expensive tastes' – preferences that demand high levels of resources to satisfy. On the equality of welfare plan, those who voluntarily adopt tastes for very expensive goods receive extra resources in order to make them as happy as everyone else; in this way the equalization of happiness (welfare) pays too little attention to the costs that people's welfare needs have on surrounding others (R. Dworkin 2000: 48–59, G. Cohen 1989: 912–16).

A further criticism of equality of welfare concerns the nature of 'welfare' itself, whether that is construed as happiness, pleasure, or desire satisfaction. On the one hand, many people have desires concerning *other* people, what we might call 'external preferences,' the satisfaction of which makes them feel better (promotes their welfare). This includes such things as the desire that people around one not engage in homosexual intimacy, practice a certain religion, perform certain sex acts, and so on. If we followed equality of welfare, we would then have to distribute goods in a way that takes those kinds of preference into account. But, on the other hand, do we really think that distributive justice must satisfy such preferences, especially if it means taking resources from others in order to do so? Equality of welfare seems to imply, implausibly, that we must distribute goods in order to satisfy such preferences to achieve properly equal outcomes (R. Dworkin 2000: 25–28). A more general version of this criticism will point to issues that we will discuss in the next chapter.

So welfare, in the narrow sense borrowed from utilitarianism, is not a neutral or accurate measure of well-being for everyone, so egalitarianism may be ill served by using it as a metric of just outcomes. Based on these considerations, some philosophers have turned to equality of *resources* as a proper index of when people have been treated truly as equals. One such is Ronald Dworkin, who argues that equality would be reached if people each had a bundle of resources that they would not want to trade with anyone else's bundle, independent of how much happiness they happen to receive from those goods (R. Dworkin 2000: 65–120). Equality demands, he claims, that people be allotted resources – wealth and income, say – that are equal in the sense of being what people would trade for in a completely free market starting from equal stakes. He models such an outcome by use of an idealized auction, where all goods can be bid on (from stores of initially equal trading currency) until no more exchanges are desired, where no one 'envies' the bundle of another. The actual well-being or flourishing each person achieves is not the focus of distributive equality, only the resource bundle they have at their disposal (R. Dworkin 2000: 67–68).

This, in a way, is a more general version of Rawls's view of fair shares of primary goods. Primary goods (especially income and wealth) are special instances of resources. For both Rawls and Dworkin, distributive justice must be concerned not with the actual state of being achieved by a person but the access she has to valuable goods with which she can decide what life plan to pursue. In this way, the problems that plagued the use of welfare as the egalitarian metric are avoided, in that those who have chosen risky lifestyles (and lost), cultivated expensive tastes, or harbor external desires, do not lay claim to extra shares on the basis of losses of well-being stemming from those factors.

What about the problem that plagued Rawls's theory, though, that those with different skill levels – handicaps and extra talents – will be unequal even if their resource bundles are the same (and neither envies that of the other)? Dworkin claims that insurance should be provided for all those suffering from deficits in natural talents (handicaps) and subsidized by general taxation. The rate of the insurance is determined as the average of what all in the population would pay to indemnify themselves against having such handicaps. Then those with special needs are given extra resources as payment – collecting on the insurance as it were (R. Dworkin 2000: 73–83).

With this scheme, Dworkin is trying to draw a line between those aspects of a person's quality of life that the rest of us should be concerned with – through the functions of the state and based on a fundamental commitment to equality – and the aspects of life that are the person's responsibility alone. Natural endowments are not our own responsibility – we did not choose them – but our effort and ambitions are. Dworkin claims, then, that the egalitarian distribution should correct for differences in natural endowments, but not for differences stemming from varying levels of ambition and effort. Also, the shares that a just distribution affords to everyone should be measured in a way that is responsive to the costs others suffer by not having those goods, what are called their opportunity costs. The idea of an auction tries to do that. At the level of policy, these principles would direct that economic markets should be allowed to distribute goods in the population but social welfare and redistributive policies must also be in place to correct for the inevitable differences in skills, starting points, and unchosen disadvantages people experience.

A problem that has been raised about this view, however, is that various disadvantages could be suffered by people even if they possess an envy-free resource bundle and are insured against all handicaps. First, the insurance-based response to handicaps might be flawed in that averaging the rates at which people would insure themselves against various impairments does not cover those who subsequently suffer *rare* forms of disability, something which the average person would not try to guard against. Second, Dworkin's distinction between the person's circumstances – that which the state should respond to by equalizing – and her 'personality' – that which is left to the person to develop as she wills – is not a fair way to draw the social division of labor in correcting for distributive injustice. For many people will have tastes, values, and preferences which were in no way *chosen* by them but which may well be expensive to satisfy or be costly in other ways. Someone might say, for example, that she can't help that she was born liking only spring water and being nauseated by tap water – this is not a handicap but is something that causes her to spend more of her resources than others have to for drinking water. The distinction between what is the state's concern and what is the person's should not be drawn in the way Dworkin does between personality and circumstances (resources), but rather, and more deeply, between what the person has chosen and what she finds herself with. In this way, those expensive tastes for which the person bears no responsibility would still be something the egalitarian state would correct for, even if they would not have been insured against in the hypothetical way Dworkin outlines.[15]

One solution to these difficulties is to broaden even further the metric by which we measure people's status in life (which egalitarianism is devoted to equalizing). Since resources are but means to whatever ends people wish to put them, perhaps the more basic measure of the success of a person's life is simply her opportunities to achieve desired states (whatever those are). Indeed, some have suggested that welfare, in the sense discussed and rejected earlier, is what people can be said to aim at – happiness or desire satisfaction. But rather than securing equal levels of welfare directly, as equality of welfare attempted to do, the state should equalize everyone's 'opportunity for welfare.'[16] In this way, if a person chooses to squander her opportunities (by developing expensive tastes and the like), the egalitarian state ignores this and leaves such choices up to the person, acknowledging the importance of well-being as well as responsibility.

But this still inherits the difficulties we noted about gearing any calculation of a life's quality as a function of the pleasure or happiness it contains. Even if opportunities for welfare are granted rather than the welfare itself, the quality of a person's life is still measured by the narrow gauge of the amount of personal welfare it contains or is likely to contain. People are not pleasure machines, and so distributive mechanisms that orient distributions around the chances people have to pursue welfare (whether that is understood as pleasure or desire satisfaction or the like) misjudge the quality of those lives (R. Dworkin 2000: 291–6).

What these views have in common is a position that in many ways represents an egalitarian nod to right-wing critics who claim that egalitarianism pays too little heed to the responsibility people have and should bear for their own lot in life, even when that lot compares unfavorably to other citizens. These egalitarian views attempt to build sensitivity to personal responsibility into the metric for equality, claiming, as do both Dworkin and defenders of equality of opportunity for welfare, that only those deficits in well-being that are the result of unchosen factors – conditions for which the person in question cannot bear responsibility – are remunerated in the egalitarian redistribution. But a problem arises concerning the *determination* of such responsibility. How in principle can society (the state) determine when a person is responsible for her ill-fare and when that is due to environmental factors, elements of her upbringing or early education, or other conditions for which she is not responsible, and when she brought it on herself? Explanations for people's actions are necessarily complex. What general theory of responsibility should be adopted which neutrally determines what actions are the person's own and what were forced upon her by unchosen conditions? (For discussion, see Arneson 1997, 1999b.)

Second, responsibility for an outcome turns, to some degree, on the options one faced in making choices that resulted in that outcome. Extreme necessity, where the only alternative to choosing something is that one would suffer unbearable harm, generally defeats one's responsibility (for discussion of these issues in a legal context, see Ripstein 1999; for views on moral responsibility, see the essays in Fischer 1986). But how can a liberal state (committed to neutrality of its principles) determine when choices that result in bad outcomes are the result of 'necessity' and when they are a self-imposed harm the costs of which the person must bear herself?

Finally, even if the persons can be said to be responsible, in some sense, for her deficit in well-being, should society stand by idly if that deficit is so severe that it completely debilitates her (preventing her functioning as an active citizen), or even brings about her death? Some theorists have claimed that losses of certain basic abilities merit egalitarian attention no matter what the source of those losses are, since such disabilities remove the person from the category of active citizens which all egalitarian theories are committed to protecting (Anderson 1999). This leads us to the next conception of equality of condition to be considered.

Perhaps, however, this is a step in the right direction, for it could be claimed that what the distribution of resources in a society really should aim to secure for people is their *freedom*, where that is understood not merely as negative freedom (and so an array of opportunities) but freedom in a more positive sense which includes the ability to make one's choices effective. The way to describe such freedom is that people pursue various functions (what they do and the ways they try to be) that define the success of their lives. Having the capabilities to achieve those valued functionings, then, is what should be afforded people in equal amounts and in ways that correct for natural deficiencies (handicaps). This is the view of the economist and philosopher Amartya Sen (Sen 1992).

Sen argues that certain basic capabilities – adequate nourishment, mobility, the conditions of self-respect, ability to take part in one's community, and so on – allow people to achieve the valued states (both of activity and of character) that define true freedom.[17] Those who suffer from deficient capacities (to effectively utilize resources or primary goods) will be afforded extra resources to establish these basic capabilities, and the market will be constrained and corrected (through tax and transfer schemes, social welfare programs, and the like) to eliminate inequalities in capabilities among the population. If a person then wastes the abilities that are granted, that is not the state's concern and hence personal responsibility is again respected.

The debate on these issues continues, with various alterations of these indices being proposed, positions defended, and new views developed (Arneson 2000a, R. Dworkin 2000: 285–303). What these debates come down to, however, is the question of how to measure the quality of a person's life in a way that maps on to the equal moral status she deserves, as well as properly divides the areas of that life quality that are her own responsibility from those areas that should be corrected if justice is to be done (see the essays in Nussbaum and Glover 1995 for discussion). One thing that might be noted at this point is that the descriptors used to specify criteria for the quality of a life (resources, income, wealth, opportunities) all show a marked tendency toward *individualism* in the conception of good lives. Hence, the value of personal, familial, and communal *relations* get no weight unless they are cashed out in terms of resources and specific goods. Cultural heritage, reflected perhaps in public monuments and celebrations, shared activities, and other such collective goods, may get ignored in theories of this sort that see the individual participants in voluntary exchanges as the paradigm citizen. This suggests that an element of distributive equality that needs further emphasis is the ability of people to participate in democratic institutions that, in turn, decide on the promotion of such collective and relational goods. (For discussion of such an alternative, see Anderson 1999).

One final word should be added concerning these formulations of the egalitarian ideal. Some committed to true equality for citizens balk at this entire approach to distributive justice, one that measures equality in terms of the outcomes that individuals can achieve independent of the good or bad luck they encounter. For example, it has been argued that a truly egalitarian society demands not that each person has a certain amount relative to others, but that the power and authority relations among citizens do not involve oppression, domination, discrimination, or unequal status (see Young 1990a; for discussion of a similar idea in a different context, see Pettit 1997). What philosophers of this sort press is that the fundamental moral equality from which we begin in these discussions is meaningful only when social relations are structured in a way that respects this; and how much a person owns is only one narrow aspect of that social existence.

Moreover, what is fundamental in securing equality is that people enjoy the same status as active participants in the social and political life of their community, that they have the resources and opportunities to actively participate (either directly or through representatives) in the collective choices made in their communities which concern their own lives and pursuits. That is, equality at the most basic level demands a fully functioning *democracy*, where people are equally able to effectively express their wills in the ongoing deliberations that determine not only the distribution of resources, but the kinds of resources that the society will try to provide, some of which will be collective and communal (such as parks, public symbols, artworks, and the like). As we saw at the close of the last chapter, legitimacy is conferred on governments (according to one line of argument) only when robust democratic institutions are set up that allow citizens to participate (directly or indirectly) in those social processes that, in turn, construct and determine their lives. In this way equality is connected directly to the demands of freedom when the latter is construed as 'self-government.' (For discussion of similar ideas, see Anderson 1999, Christiano 1996, J. Cohen 1986, Gould 1988).

From equality to the welfare state

Many philosophers, however, do not think that distributive justice demands anything close to the equality of condition that the egalitarians we just described insist upon. Yet they also think that leaving people's fates to the cruel happenstance of capitalist markets is equally mistaken. They argue, then, that the basic conditions necessary for a decent life must indeed be secured for people, conditions defined perhaps by the requirements of an autonomous existence, but that further attempts to *equalize* their well-being are misguided and not required for justice (Raz 1986: ch. 9, Frankfurt 1987, 2000).

Under such a conception of justice, capitalist markets for goods and labor would be allowed to operate, generating the inequalities of wealth and social status that are the inevitable outcome of such mechanisms. In this way, the inequalities of natural talents and initial endowments that the strict egalitarians wanted to reverse would be left uncorrected. However, it is acknowledged by these theorists that the market itself will not supply many of the basic goods that the particularly disadvantaged citizens will need to function in society, especially those who find themselves in ill health, homeless, or without marketable skills. Various social welfare programs (whether administered at the national level or with more localized arrangements) will be necessary, then, to relieve the egregious suffering of the poor, bringing them up to a level of basic functioning. But inequalities of wealth and resources beyond that will be of no concern.

The view that justice demands merely providing citizens with basic needs but not the further equalization of well-being can be called the 'sufficiency view,' since it claims that the state must ensure that all have a minimally sufficient level of basic goods but that this requirement exhausts the demands of distributive justice. Such views are sometimes defended by way of negative arguments directed at more stringent egalitarian programs of the sort we have been discussing (including that of Rawls). Indeed, when discussing those programs we considered internal criticisms – ones arising from other egalitarian viewpoints – but put to the side head-on attacks from anti-egalitarians. A brief discussion of such external criticisms might now be in order, then.

One line of criticism of strong egalitarian views on the distribution of goods is that they seem to yield counterintuitive judgments in certain cases. Imagine, for example, that there were ten people who needed a certain drug to stay alive but there was only enough of the drug to save five of them. The critic claims that egalitarianism demands not that we give the drug to some five people from the group (randomly selected perhaps), for this produces unequal outcomes; rather the egalitarian must demand that we allow all ten to die for this is the only way to treat them all equally. And surely this is wrongheaded (Frankfurt 1987, Raz 1986: 227).

However, these types of criticism show a possible misunderstanding of the basis of egalitarian theories of justice. As we saw in the case of Dworkin and Rawls, the fundamental principle of equality is that all have equal moral *status* – they must be treated with equal concern and respect in Dworkin's version – which means that people's condition should not be the result of arbitrary and unchosen factors. It is not that outcomes where equal well-being is enjoyed are aimed at for their own sake; rather, they are aimed at because the need to do so is derived from this more basic principle of equal status.[18] For this reason, it would not be implied that we should throw away the medicine rather than give it to only some of the sick people. Choosing five people at random would be *required* in fact by the principle saying that in so far as one advances the well-being of citizens (giving them the medicine in this case) one must do so in a way that shows equal regard for them. Indeed, if we did not have use of a comparative, egalitarian, principle of this sort, it would be unclear why we should give the medicine to a *randomly chosen* set of five people. If our only principle were the satisfaction of needs, it would be permissible to choose our *favorite* five people, or the five tallest individuals, or make a choice based on race or gender. The strongly intuitive idea that when doling out scarce resources to satisfy basic needs one must choose impartially is itself an egalitarian (that is, comparative) principle, one which the 'sufficiency' theorists have no theoretical resources to support.

Defenders of the sufficiency view often claim that the real pull of justice is the relief of great suffering, not the equalization of states of well-being (Frankfurt 1987, Raz 1986: 239–40). For if there was not poverty, if all in the population were at a fairly high level of income and well-being, the demand that inequalities among them should nevertheless be eradicated would have no force. The intuitive pull of egalitarian claims would have no force if all basic needs were met – we hardly see the need for equality of condition when that claim is made on behalf of the rich against the *very* rich.

But this criticism neglects the ways in which economic inequalities both represent and cause other disadvantages in one's standing as a citizen of the state. Even if one were very well off financially, it may well be unfair (barring some justification for it) that one's neighbor had even more resources and hence enjoyed the greater social status, political influence, standing in the community, and the like that often comes along with greater resources.[19]

On the other side, egalitarians can claim that defenders of the sufficiency view really are egalitarians in disguise, but that the metric of well-being they use is simply the satisfaction of *basic needs* rather than a more robust index (such as welfare or resources or primary goods). The welfare state, egalitarians claim, succeeds (when it does) at making people equal in enjoying the basic goods necessary for a minimally decent life, as Sen argued should be the case, but it fails to adequately take into account all the *other* ways that people can be rendered unequal which are just as arbitrary and often as harmful as inequalities at the basic level. Defenders of the sufficiency view must defend their claim, then, that basic needs are the *only* dimension in which citizens of an otherwise just polity must be made equal.

One final remark on welfare state approaches to distributive justice: Claiming that capitalist markets can be allowed as the principal distributive mechanism in a society, yet using tax and other state revenue sources for social programs and welfare state institutions to relieve poverty, may well cause a tension in the manner in which the state commands legitimacy. That is, public support of the state and acceptance of capitalist markets (and the inequalities resulting from them) is based on a public conception of independence and individual responsibility that can be at variance with assumptions concerning responsibility implicit in the welfare state, since the latter distributes basic goods independent of effort, work, and choice (Habermas 1975, Taylor 1985: 248–88). Recent moves in Western industrial nations to dismantle centrally organized welfare state programs may be understood as a response to this tension (cf. Christman 1998). As we saw, egalitarians struggle with attempts to combine a principle of equality – eradicating disadvantages due to arbitrary factors – and respect for responsible choice – leaving disadvantages due to free choice as they lie. Such attempts mirror the concern that the use of markets assume a merit- or effort-based mechanism for the distribution of goods, while redistributive programs to correct inequalities eschew attention to merit (see Anderson 1999). This tension plagues both egalitarian and welfare state approaches in ways that have yet to be fully resolved.

This leads us back to the question of the *basis* of the equality to which these theorists are committed. Even if we settled on the proper understanding of *how* it is to treat citizens equally, it has been left unaddressed *why* they should be treated equally in the first place. This precept of political morality in the modern age – that all 'men are created equal' – is such a commonplace where natural hierarchies and caste systems have been abandoned that it seems unnecessary to provide a justification for it. This basic commitment to (some kind of) equality defines, for some, the modern, liberal approach to political life. We shall now turn, then, to the question of whether this liberal project can live up to its ideal of respecting the equal status of all its citizens, given the deep and complex differences among those citizens, especially differences concerning their self-understanding, value commitments, and motivations.

Chapter summary

Here we faced head on the question of what makes a society just, considering in particular the question of the justice of the distribution of material goods. Noting that such questions turn centrally on interpretations of citizen equality, we considered the idea that merely supplying equality of *opportunity* for all citizen's sufficed for justice, but we noted the incompleteness (or emptiness) of such a principle standing alone. In considering the libertarian view that distributive justice demands no more than the protection of existing property rights of citizens (without interference or involuntary taxation, thus establishing capitalist free markets as the economic engine of the society), we discussed arguments that such a view cannot plausibly support its central claim that only *property rights* deserve such a sacrosanct position in accounts of distributive justice (to the exclusion of other more positive rights to basic material goods for example). We considered, in addition, a recent attempt to justify libertarianism on the basis of a social contract among rational self-interested agents, but saw that this faced the same difficulties raised in the last chapter against Hobbesean arguments for state authority based on such (effectively hypothetical) contracts.

Rawls's view was again considered, this time focusing on his 'Difference Principle' which demands that inequalities of income and wealth in a society are only justified if they serve to benefit the worst off group. It was noted, however, that Rawls's use of 'primary goods' as an index of distributive justice in a society was overly narrow, and covered up other sources of inequality that (equal amounts) of primary goods would not reflect. This led to consideration of a variety of egalitarian views which utilize contrasting measures of equality. It is roundly rejected that the ultimate measure of equal shares should be 'welfare' (individual utility or happiness) by itself, since this takes no account of the personal responsibility that people for the most part have for their particular level of happiness.

But a more promising metric that we considered was equality of resources, defined as equal shares of whatever bundles of resources are available to the population given what others desire (that is, given what others would pay for those resources). But this view faced a problem similar to the use of primary goods, in that people who suffer from handicaps (through no fault of their own) will not be remunerated in the right ways when only external resources are used to measure their condition. We concluded by consideration of Amartya Sen's model of equality of basic capabilities (as a reflection of people's real freedom) and remarked that the disagreements about the proper measure of material equality rests ultimately on complex philosophical questions about the quality of life, questions that go to the heart of liberal political philosophy.

Finally, we considered views that defined distributive equality in terms of guaranteeing all citizens certain minimal levels of goods and services (amounting to a kind of welfare state), but not extending to equality of material positions more generally. We raised questions about this limited 'sufficiency' view in that such a view fails to live up to the basic commitment to equality of status that liberal theory is built upon (and these views claim to embrace). We ended with the suggestion that distributive justice, in the end, might best be thought of as concerning social *relations* (of power, status, and capabilities) rather than merely comparisons of wealth and income. And once again, this suggestion led to the point that institutions of democracy were essential to justice in ways not directly acknowledged by the theorists considered here.

Case to consider

In the United States in 1996, the federal program to provide minimum food and income benefits to poor single parents with children was dismantled in favor of granting funds to states who would administer new programs. These new programs placed total time limits on eligibility for benefits – five years in most cases – and required that most recipients find paid employment within a set time period in order to receive benefits. (The program to give benefits to poor men or women without children was never very generous, but this was also discontinued in its previous form.) Advocates of this change argued that only if able-bodied people were willing to support themselves through paid employment were they deserving of tax-subsidized income support. Those who, through their own self-destructive behavior or unwillingness to work, were unable to support themselves should not be given subsidies from those who do work. Moreover, working for a wage was a more effective and respectable way to move out of poverty and into an independent lifestyle than accepting government 'handouts.'

Critics of these changes argued that most of the people previously eligible for benefits (as well as many who were not helped by the old program) were in the state of poverty through no fault of their own; many poor people already worked for a wage, albeit an inadequate one, and it is exceedingly difficult to tell if a person is trying 'hard enough' to find work and escape from poverty. Most pockets of poverty are entrenched and well established, so that educational and employment opportunities are not available in the area. And placing a time limit on benefits when it may take longer than five years to escape from poor conditions (for some) was inhumane.

To what degree if any should the state use taxation and redistribution to alleviate poverty and eliminate the inequalities of wealth and opportunity that one finds in advanced industrialized nations? (A related question concerns international obligations to reduce inequalities in rich and poor nations.) Given the vast differences between the life prospects of the well born and those of the poor, and given the dire conditions of poverty that can be found in such societies (facts both sides acknowledge), what are the demands of justice concerning such a state of affairs? Is inequality of wealth and life prospects an intrinsically evil condition that just regimes should always attempt to eradicate? Or are inequalities and poverty merely the unfortunate results of competition and natural differences (in skill for example) that social institutions cannot be concerned to correct?

Notes on further reading

For recent treatments of the justice in general, see Kymlicka 1992, Gaus 1999, and Sterba 1986. The general principle of equality in the context of political theory is considered in Rae et al. 1981, Temkin 1993, Westen 1990, Rakowski 1991, Nagel 1991 and Sen 1992, with an historical overview in Johnston 2000. The principle of equality of opportunity is examined in the essays in Paul et al. 1987 and Bowie 1988.

References for the libertarian approach to justice were listed above (Chapter 2), though see also Vallentyne 2000b for a variant of the standard libertarian approach; for further consideration of Nozick's views, see the essays in Paul 1981. For a critical perspective, see G. Cohen 1986a, 1986b, Miller 1989, and the essays in Vallentyne 2000a. Locke's views on property are treated in several volumes, for example in Waldron 1988: 137–203, 390–422, Munzer 1990: ch. 10, and Sreenivasan 1995.

Rawls's works were discussed in Chapter 2, though concerning questions of distributive justice in particular, see Martin 1985, Barry 1989: 213–44, and Kymlicka 1990: 50–55. Rawls's conception of 'primary goods' is discussed and expanded in Rawls 1982. Concerning the metric for equal shares in an egalitarian distribution, see G. Cohen 1989, R. Dworkin 2000: Part I; for recent developments, see Arneson 2000a. Critical approaches to egalitarianism are taken up in Raz 1986: ch. 9, Frankfurt 1987 and 2000, and Kekes 1997: 88–119. Amartya Sen's views are developed in Sen 1992 and applied in several of the essays in Nussbaum and Sen 1993 and Nussbaum and Glover 1995.

The 'sufficiency' approach to distributive justice is developed most extensively in Raz 1986, but for considerations of issues germane to welfare state liberalism see also Moon 1993: 121–45 and the essays in Ware and Goodin 1990.

CHAPTER 4

Toleration, pluralism, and the foundations of liberalism

- The canons of liberalism
- The perfectionist challenge
- Utilitarian liberalism: Perfectionism in disguise?
- The response of political liberalism
- Liberalism, public discourse, and democracy
- Chapter summary
- Case to consider
- Notes on further reading

In the last two chapters we have worked within the liberal paradigm of political thought in order to locate the grounds of political theory and to determine principles of distributive justice. Here, we delve deeper to look at the fundamental architecture of liberalism itself and ask if such a framework for political theory, which rests on the values of autonomy and equality, can in general be justified. In particular, we begin the task (taken up in earnest in Part II) of subjecting the basic components of liberalism to critical scrutiny. In this chapter we will ask whether liberal principles take sufficiently into account the objective validity of values grounded in general facts about human beings, values which, when properly articulated, ground legitimate state policies promoting them which go beyond the neutrality toward conceptions of the good that liberalism requires. In this way, we will be inquiring into the limits of liberal toleration and its commitment to neutrality concerning moral values. Before turning to these critical questions, let us spell out a bit more clearly the basic framework of the liberal approach to political philosophy we have been discussing.

The canons of liberalism

Speaking in loose and general terms, a liberal society is one that is, or attempts to be, an *open* society, a free and tolerant environment where the widest possible range of pursuits are allowed, consistent with equal such opportunities for everyone. Laws are structured and society is organized according to the principles of toleration (by way of respect for autonomy) and equality, where state action attempts to maintain a basic neutrality concerning the different ways of life taken up by its members and restricts behavior only when it is necessary to protect the equal status of all citizens. But one person's openness is another person's constraint, and it becomes practically as well as theoretically daunting to consistently set out the basic principles of such a society.

Historically, of course, liberalism has meant many things and there is no presumption here that the basic outlines of liberal theory put forward capture all of those positions. But there certainly are dominant strains of thought in the tradition underwritten by liberal political philosophy that provided the philosophical support for modern constitutional democracies put in place in opposition to hierarchical monarchies in medieval and Renaissance Europe. As we saw in Chapter 2, popular sovereignty is one such idea, where political authority is understood as legitimate only when the citizens governed by it in some way are the source of that authority, rather than divine mandate or the natural order of the universe.

In rejecting a metaphysically ordered hierarchy of values, liberalism also introduces the idea of *pluralism*, the claim that there exists a plurality of valid conceptions of the good. No single overriding value and no fixed ordering of values can be determined to be objectively valid for all agents, on this view. Different pursuits, such as increasing one's own happiness, promoting world peace, expressing praise and devotion to a religious leader, celebrating aesthetic beauty, and so on, might be determined to be valid for some person or group; but such a determination cannot be set out independently of the judgment of the people in those groups themselves – the universe, so to speak, is not ordered with its values in place for all to simply discover and live by.

This is not to say that liberalism is committed either to skepticism – that no moral values can ever be known to be valid at all – or to subjective relativism – that all values are grounded in the varying perspectives of different persons at different times according to their subjective viewpoint. I will discuss skepticism below. Liberalism is not committed to what I am calling subjective relativism, since, while it does deny the validity of values apart from human endorsement of them, it does not rest on the view that a person's subjectively endorsing a value is sufficient for its validity. That would make the validity of all value claims *solely* a function of individual choice. Rather, liberalism assumes that values gain their legitimacy *in part* through people's endorsement. This is called its 'constructivism.'

Notice that we keep getting back to the basic importance of individual judgment, both in legitimating authority and determining what is valuable. This, I think, should be put forward as the basic organizing idea of liberalism: the fundamental value of an individual's rationally and autonomously pursuing or embracing those things she judges to be worthwhile. One way to put the basic principle of liberalism, then, is the claim for the equal moral status of all persons conceived as autonomous beings (ones who rationally and autonomously pursue things they judge to be worthwhile). Justice is formulated in a way that expresses this respect, where people are considered ultimately able to reflect upon and embrace (or reject or revise) conceptions of value for themselves. Now this is not to say what the ultimate grounds are for this value – whether it is a universal value for all rational agents, a political postulate posited to gain social stability, or a common value for constitutional democracies in a certain age (or some other justification). It is merely the base-level value for liberalism of the sort we are discussing here (for discussion, see Larmore 1987, Gray 1993). But the overall approach to social justice that liberalism embodies can be seen to rest on the ultimate valuation of persons as having a basic interest in pursuing their own conceptions of what is valuable, and doing so 'from the inside' as it were (Kymlicka 1989: 10–12). This concept of the person will be the focus of much controversy as we proceed, but for now we can see it as the center of the liberal theoretical framework (Kymlicka 1989, Waldron 1993, R. Dworkin 2000, Galston 1991, Macedo 1990, Moon 1993).

Connected with this idea is the (notorious, for some) *individualism* of liberal philosophy. But we should be as clear and non-committal about this as we can: liberal philosophy is committed to the protection of interests at the individual level, the person's interest in leading an autonomous life, however that is conceptualized (and there is much debate about that). That is not to say that liberal philosophy insists that people should lead lives separated from history, commitments, traditions, and communities, but only that their interest in either embracing or, if they wish, rejecting such membership is of fundamental importance. (In the next chapter, the controversial nature of this brand of individualism will be our main concern.)

Since justice, on the liberal view, amounts to the protection of people's abilities to lead autonomous lives, the considerations of securing the rules of justice, the right, is of more basic importance than promoting any specific conception of what is valuable for people, the good. Only if people's abilities to pursue the good by their own lights – their autonomy – is protected by the rules of justice can the state concern itself with the promotion of people's good; never can it do so in violation of that basic respect for autonomy. The rules of justice, the prohibitions and permissions that regulate social interaction, are to be 'secured' and 'protected,' while the *good* – what is valuable, fulfilling, virtuous and worthwhile in human life – is something said to be 'promoted.' The liberal view being stated here is that such moral factors can be conceptually separated and securing the first is more basic than promoting the second.

It must be noted, however, that some defenders of liberalism reject the idea that the priority of the right over the good is definitive of liberalism in its most plausible versions (Kymlicka, 1989: 21–43). For Will Kymlicka, *all* defensible political views recommend that states should be organized to help citizens live good lives, and hence all place regard for the good at the center of their frameworks. What is distinctive of liberalism is merely the particular conception of what makes a 'good life,' namely that it is a life in pursuit of valuable ends endorsed by the person pursuing them 'from the inside.' In our terminology, this amounts to claiming that the state should promote the good of its citizens by promoting their ability to live autonomous lives in pursuit of (what they take to be) objective values.

This issue could be seen as merely terminological, in that the claim that equality of moral status is fundamental to liberalism is equivalent to stating, with Kymlicka, that promoting (equally) the ability of citizens to live good lives is fundamental. In fact, however, the difference goes deeper, for the account of liberalism that stresses the priority of right claims that the state should *respect* the equal status of persons in *their* pursuit of the good; this is different from claiming that the state should *promote* that good. The first insists that social *relations* among people (who are pursuing their own values) is the primary focus of justice and not the content of the lives those people lead. To say that the state should promote the good of its citizens in this latter sense will be labeled 'perfectionist' here, and hence treated as a challenge to liberalism (see pp. 103 ff. below).

The liberal state, in its purest form, then, is anti-paternalistic and anti-perfectionist. It is anti-paternalistic in that it does not interfere with a rational autonomous person's pursuit of what she thinks good (for her) even if such interference is thought to promote the person's good from a more objective point of view. Its anti-perfectionism is merely a generalization of this stance, in that the liberal state does not promote the good overall for its citizens in any way that violates respect for the autonomous lives of those citizens.

Liberalism and neutrality

When we think of an open society, we think of one where certain rights and freedoms are protected and where government power is, in certain areas at least, curtailed. The right to practice one's own religion, to participate in political associations and social groups, to speak freely about various topics, to enjoy a realm of privacy, are all basic components of an environment one would call free and open. The position that underlies these sorts of rights is the view that the state should not be structured so as to promote any *particular* religious view, political outlook, or conception of value for citizens – such matters are up to the citizens themselves. That view can be expressed by saying that the state should remain *neutral* toward citizens' own conceptions of the good life.

This attempt at neutrality is a way for liberal states to enact a distinction between public and private life. A right to privacy, for example, is thought to be basic in a free society, but what general characterization can we give of the distinction between what is public and what is properly private? The liberal answer (in its most unrefined form) is this: actions that have an impact on just social relations – those activities that violate or threaten to violate acceptable rules of social interaction – are the proper subject of political control, the public. Those actions which do not carry such a threat but involve an individual or group's pursuit of what is thought as valuable – activities that are involved in one's conception of the good – are out of bounds of public control, they are private. So the distinction between public and private is an application of the liberal insistence on the priority of the right (rules of just social relations) over the good (the promotion of some conception of value for citizens). And the neutrality of the state is merely an extension of this position: the state should be neutral concerning all citizens' conception of the good life.[1]

In discussions of liberalism in recent decades the commitment to state neutrality has been closely connected with the liberal principle of *toleration*, where an obligation is thought to exist to 'tolerate' diverse lifestyles, value systems, and modes of individual expression (see Mendus 1989). But neutrality and toleration are different attitudes, and hence would describe different stances toward policy if embodied in state action. For to be neutral is to hold no position on the issue in question, or at least to let one's position play no role in action affecting two, perhaps opposed, parties. But toleration implies that one is 'putting up with' or 'allowing, despite one's disagreement with,' some lifestyle or behavior pattern. Toleration, then, includes a negative appraisal of what is being tolerated, to some extent or other (ibid.: 8).

A third possibility, one that liberals sometimes actually embrace but at other times are criticized for avoiding, is the *celebration* of diversity. It is one thing to merely *tolerate* that which is different, it is another to be *neutral* toward it, but it is still another to positively *value* diverse values and lifestyles. So celebration is at the positive end of the spectrum defining the valuation of different lifestyles, while neutrality is in the middle and toleration stands at the opposite end. We will leave to the side for the moment which view liberalism must include.

So just what kind of neutrality is liberal theory attempting to defend, and why? An immediate distinction that should be made in this context is between what has been called 'neutrality of aim' and 'neutrality of outcome' (Raz 1986: 111–17). For it is one thing to remain neutral in the kinds of reasons one advances for a particular policy, but it is another to try to guarantee neutrality of all of the consequences of the implementation of that policy. The latter neutrality is never really defended by liberal theorists, as it would mean trying to guarantee equality of outcome for all those affected by a policy. Indeed, this principle would be incoherent as a fundamental requirement for the justification of all principles since people's desires conflict, so no policy's effects are ever neutral in this way. Therefore, the neutrality to which liberalism seems to be committed is neutrality of aim – neutrality concerning the reasons given for the principles guiding state policies. That is to say, the state or its operatives (designers of its constitution, legislators, those in political office) should not advance policies that are justified in a way that makes reference to some particular set of values or aims, ones which may well be (reasonably) rejected by many in the population.

But exactly whom should this rule apply to and what activities does it cover? First, does it only apply at the level of constitutional design, such that the justification of overall governmental functions and citizens' basic rights makes no reference to contested values? Or does it extend to legislation of all sorts, implying that decisions to build roads or provide for the national defense must be defended with reference only to neutral considerations? Certainly, it seems too strong to extend the neutrality principle to those running for office, since various groups which define themselves with reference to social goals and values put forward candidates in elections to advance their cause. But if people can be non-neutral in the electoral realm, how does it make sense to gag them later in the legislative assembly? If they are not to be so limited in the structure of their justifications there, then neutrality seems only to apply to the arena of constitutional design. But is that the kind of neutrality liberalism demands?

To answer any of these questions one must ask more than merely what neutrality *means* (Raz 1986: 113, Montefiore 1975: 5, Waldron 1993: 143–67). In this context especially, one must look deeper and ask why the state should be neutral in the first place. What more basic principle does the neutrality to which the liberal state is committed rest upon? There are three possibilities that I will briefly explore here, each of which has gained prominence in the tradition of liberal thinking. They are: 'skepticism,' 'the priority of right,' and 'the demands of legitimacy.' What we will see is that the first will not successfully ground liberal neutrality, but the second and third will comprise two complementary aspects of the basic architecture of liberal theory.

One line of defense of state neutrality is the claim that conceptions of the good do not admit of truth or falsity, or at least their validity cannot be known objectively. This kind of moral skepticism comes in many versions, some of which are more acceptable than others. A radical version would claim that no grounds for normative claims can ever be provided, that they are never true (or false) but are merely expressions of emotion, say. Liberal tolerance would not fare well if it rested on this kind of skepticism, though, since such skepticism surely would plague the principles of liberalism themselves. If no moral propositions are uniquely valid, then the claim that society ought to allow maximum liberty for its citizens, or protect their basic rights, and the like, is equally groundless (Mendus 1989: 75–82).

Weaker versions of skepticism might be considered, though. One could argue, for example, that while value claims are not groundless, they nevertheless cannot be justified in a timeless manner, impervious to new considerations, altered perspectives, and new information. This really amounts to a commitment to 'fallibility' rather than skepticism, for one might hold that even views that turn out to be true are, in principle, vulnerable to new findings and alternative interpretations; this does not imply that we must be complete skeptics with regard to their truth, only that we are always open to countervailing considerations. Where value questions are concerned, one might insist that since experiences over a lifetime will have a profound effect on what turns out to be a value for a person, such value commitments will always be subject to possible revision. At the same time, however, considerations of stability, enduring commitment, reliability, and the like speak against assuming that values always *must be* questioned and revised in order to be valid. The question arises, then: what conception of the person and her value commitments are we assuming in pressing for neutrality based on fallibility of values? We will face this question again below. What the issue comes down to, as we will see, is whether values can be considered valid for a population independent of the actual social deliberation about those values that might take place in considering them. One need not be a skeptic to claim that the justification of a value claim will, in practice, require some public discussion and deliberation. But rules of justice of the sort liberal theory insists on (reflecting equality of moral status and supporting various rights of free expression and participation in such discussions) will be necessary to structure these activities. And the neutrality that is at issue here will apply to those arenas themselves.

The second family of reasons supporting neutrality refers back to what we earlier described as the liberal commitment to the priority of justice over the directive to promote any particular conceptions of the good. This is not to claim that value commitment cannot be valid or that statements about the good cannot be 'true,' but rather that it is more important to regulate just social relations than it is to promote even 'valid' values.

The priority of right is not a self-justifying, free-standing principle. Rather, it rests on the idea that principles of justice must express the fundamental equality of the moral status of persons of the sort mentioned above. This is the view that all people (described in a certain way, say as rational and autonomous) stand in fundamentally equal relation to each other where the basic organization of society is concerned. No person or type of person has, shall we say, 'metaphysical' priority over any other, as might have been believed in the Middle Ages (in Europe) where the 'great chain of being' marked out a complete order of moral importance for the universe, as explained in Chapter 2. Modernist liberalism assumes, at least abstractly, that no such ordering can be accepted and that the lives of all humans have equal moral standing. Political structures must then reflect that equality (see R. Dworkin 1990).

The other basic element of liberal thinking we mentioned is a commitment to moral pluralism, namely the claim that there are multiple conceptions of value that are, from some perspective or other, equally valid. In other words, even if some values are objectively supported, pluralism acknowledges that no *single* core value, such as human happiness or religious salvation, defines all that is good in the world. Similarly, pluralism implies that no single *ordering* of values is objectively fixed. Pluralism is not subjectivism, however: we can admit (though we need not) that some values are objectively grounded independent of human choice; but the claim is nevertheless made that even if there are such values, there are more than one of them, their priority and order of combination cannot be objectively determined, and all cannot simply be reduced to a single (more abstract) core value.

Let us see now how moral equality plus pluralism implies the priority of right: if all people are granted equal moral standing in the organizing structure of a society, and there are multiple conceptions of value each of which are valid from some point of view or other, then justice demands that principles governing social relations – the right – take priority over the need to promote any one value or set of values. For to do otherwise would be to champion the aspirations of one set of people – those that adhere to those promoted values – over another – those that don't – and this denies the second group the equal standing they deserve (as autonomous pursuers of value). So seeing people as equal and admitting their various, and sometimes conflicting (but equally valid), value commitments requires that we set up society according to principles of justice that are, in a minimal sense at least, neutral concerning the value commitments of those citizens. Promoting a conception of the good that a person does not share shows less than full respect for that person's capacity to judge such matters herself (cf. R. Dworkin 2000: 237–303).

But the idea that equal respect for persons' capacity to judge value questions for themselves is the basis for neutrality shows that such neutrality rests on a prior commitment to respecting the autonomy of citizens, for 'autonomy' simply refers to the capacities to judge value questions for oneself, independent of external forces and manipulations. Therefore, neutrality based on equality is really neutrality based on the value of autonomy for citizens.

Before considering problems with this strategy, let us turn to the third set of reasons supporting liberal neutrality (keeping in mind, of course, how much these strategies overlap). Reminding ourselves again of the background commitments to moral equality and pluralism, let us look at the way that principles of justice for a society must in some way be *justified* for the population that will live under them. Basic to a liberal society is the claim that policies and laws that regulate peoples' lives must in some way be acceptable to them, otherwise such policies would be oppressive and blindly coercive. This is the position that we ended with in our discussion of the grounds of state authority in Chapter 2, that such authority is grounded in the justice of the state and justice requires that some measure of popular endorsement of the central powers of a state be secured.

What this approach to political justification rests on, then, is respect for (again) the autonomy of people living in that society. For autonomy embodies the capacity to guide one's life only by those values and principles one embraces as one's own, perhaps after critically reflecting on them. The 'liberal principle of legitimacy,' then, is this: political power and authority is justified only when the principles supporting that authority can be accepted as legitimate by those persons living under them. The connection between this principle and the liberal stand on neutrality is that only if the state is guided by principles that are justified without reference to disputed conceptions of value (that is, they obey the norm of neutrality) can such principles gain the acceptance demanded by the legitimacy requirement (Rawls 1993: 137).

But who are the people we are imagining that are judging such principles as legitimate or not, and what standards are they using? Clearly, such a group cannot reflect just any attitude or standpoint that might be found in a population, for some people simply have mistaken beliefs, or are unable to make competent decisions about such things (either because they are too young or severely impaired); and some people have as a basic value commitment precisely that they *not* live under common principles with others (certain racists for example). So the principle of legitimacy rests on rather substantive assumptions about the people involved and the reasons they might give to accept or reject a principle.

So in considering the equality-based and legitimacy-based defenses of neutrality, we see the way in which liberalism rests on the value of autonomy. What this means, though, is that the liberal commitment to neutrality is ultimately based on standards and principles that are not themselves neutral – they embody political, and perhaps moral, presumptions about which there could be principled debate. After all, not everyone thinks autonomy is the ultimate value (especially for some of the ways in which it is defined). The question is, then, what is ultimately the basis of liberalism, and hence our reasons for having a free, open society of the sort we are imagining? Is it a set of universal, objective values that are simply put forward and defended on philosophical grounds, such as the value of autonomy? We will first consider a group of thinkers who answer 'yes' to this question, but use that answer to challenge the liberal commitment to neutrality. Then we will turn to a different strategy for defending the liberal state, one based on the very nature of political life itself.

The perfectionist challenge

An alternative to liberal neutrality concerning what it is proper for governments to do in the promotion of values for a population is 'perfectionism.' Perfectionism generally refers to the view that human life can be appraised in terms of certain 'excellences,' progress toward which marks greater comparative value of a particular life. Such views come in a variety of forms and commonly follow Aristotle in thinking that the essential characteristics of humans – their rationality or capacity for practical wisdom for example – carry with them standards of flourishing (virtues) that could, in principle, be used to evaluate a given human life. Extending that view to social and political relations would imply that social institutions should be constructed to promote humans' development of those virtues. (See our discussion of 'virtue ethics' in Chapter 1.)

Modern perfectionist doctrines need not rest on such a sweeping, metaphysical vision about the teleological order of the universe, as Aristotle did, but can simply rely on the more modest view that human beings are structured in such a way that certain traits or capacities happen to be basic to their leading good lives. Such views rest on a conception of 'human nature,' either expressed as a structural account of the essence of human existence, thought, and action (Hurka 1993, Nussbaum 1993), or as a generalization of what virtually all humans pursue virtually all the time (Sher 1997). Some of these theorists are self-consciously 'liberal' in their perfectionism, in that they put forward a conception of the good which includes *autonomy* as one of its elements (Raz 1986, Wall 1998). What generally marks off a perfectionist doctrine, however, is that the specification of the good for human beings (according to which flourishing or excellence can be measured) is meant to be valid independent of human desires for, and judgments of, that good. Although we will consider below an exception to this, for the most part perfectionists claim that there are objective, desire-independent goods for people that political authorities have an obligation to promote.

By contrast, the tradition I have been describing as the liberal paradigm sees justice as the *first virtue* of social institutions. Only if the institutions that order relations among citizens are just (fair, equal, and respectful of autonomy) is the political arrangement in question acceptable. On the other hand, perfectionists claim that the first virtue of political institutions is the promotion of good lives for their citizens, which may include a guarantee of justice among them but only as part of the package, not the basic element. Whatever the components of good lives turn out to be, these theories imply, state power should aim at promoting them and discouraging destructive factors.

Perfectionism as a political philosophy proceeds in two steps. The first is a critique of liberal neutrality, and the second is the presentation of a replacement political view which places the promotion of the human good at its center. The first tack takes various forms, but the general line can be spelled out this way: liberal neutrality rests in large part, as we saw in the last section, on the importance attributed to individual autonomy, either as the dimension of humanity that grounds the equality of moral status we are all owed or as the model of the person who grants legitimacy to state power. In either case, the question arises whether protection of individual autonomy is an *absolute* restraint on the promotion of other social goods or whether it is merely one (very important) good among others. In either case, perfectionists argue, liberal neutrality will not find unwavering support in this reference to the value of autonomy.

On the one hand, strict neutrality would not be called for if autonomy were merely one value among others, to be balanced and promoted along with those others. For there will likely be cases where such alternative values will outweigh the importance of autonomy and justify promoting particular conceptions of the good despite limitations on autonomy this might entail. (A policy prohibiting the use of all dangerous narcotics, for example, would be justified on the grounds that protecting the health of citizens outweighs the limitation of their autonomy that such prohibitions involve.) This is not a strictly neutral stance. Therefore, seeing autonomy as an overridable value will not be forceful enough to support liberal neutrality (Sher 1997: 45–105, Hurka 1993: 158–60).

However, rather than claiming that respect for autonomy is simply one overridable value among others, liberals could argue that autonomy is simply a constitutive element of a person's commitment to any *other* value. The claim is that value commitments are valid for a person only if that person autonomously embraces that value for herself. Only if a person rationally and reflectively identifies with the value being promoted – health, happiness, or prosperity for instance – could such a value apply to her life in the first place. Values do not simply stand alone, independent of human beings seeing them as such; and values *for a person* (something being good for you) are not valid independently of your autonomously accepting them as valuable. And if this is true, then no state could actively promote a conception of the good life unless the citizens affected could autonomously embrace the good in question, and that restriction would be enough to require the neutrality we are considering here.

Perfectionists counter by claiming that such a conception of value is itself controversial (Hurka 1993: 148–52, Sher 1997: 58–60, Sumner 1996: 174–83, cf. Griffin 1986: 135–36). They question the claim that pursuits must be rationally endorsed by the person in order for them to have value, or that such non-autonomous values will always get less weight than some reflectively endorsed pursuit. Would having as one's life ambition counting the blades of grass on one's lawn, even if autonomously chosen, have more value than being induced, non-autonomously, to enlighten oneself by the great artworks of the world?

Is reflective endorsement really a necessary condition for all values for a person? In later sections we will encounter arguments that answer yes (qualifiedly) to that question, and hence draw the line around liberalism at this point. The form these arguments will take, picking up an earlier discussion, will be molded by the liberal principle of legitimacy that the uses of state power are legitimate only if those subject to it could not reasonably reject it.

So much for the critical component of the perfectionist project. The positive doctrine it advances is composed of a view about the human good and a parallel argument that a state's policies should be guided by the aim of advancing that good for its citizens. Now, one immediate difficulty most people will have with perfectionism is that it seems to imply that the state would be allowed to *coerce* its citizens to pursue some version of human excellence. However, there is nothing intrinsic to the perfectionist doctrine that requires this, and there is much reason to think that the use of coercive means to improve a person's life will be fundamentally counterproductive. Some goods are by their nature immune to external imposition, it might be claimed; to embrace and embody them at all, one must do so voluntarily. Religious belief and devotion may be an example, as it was for Locke (see Chapter 2 above). People tend to resent and resist forceful measures to make their lives better. Besides, there are countless non-coercive alternatives (the educational system, public promotion of good habits, making bad habits costly, and the like) which can be used to promote the good without the use of force (Hurka 1993: 147–60).[2]

Perfectionism, then, must take a specific position on the nature of value and our knowledge of those values when it claims that states can promote the good along with protecting rules of justice. A quick distinction on this score, however, is in order. On the one hand, perfectionists can claim that the set of desire-independent (that is, objective) values for a citizenry is valid relative to the particular cultural and social grouping that defines that citizenry. On this view, the values in question are meant to emerge out of the particular history and mode of social life peculiar to that collectivity. On the other hand, the perfectionist doctrine can put forward values and ideals that are allegedly valid for *any* culture or community. Such perfectionism rests on a thoroughly general conception of human nature such that certain values apply to all people everywhere.

We will deal with the claim that there are definitive values for a community below (later in this chapter and in Chapter 5). For the present, let us merely comment that a perfectionist view that rests on community-based values must insist that such values can be determined for that community without the free, open, and tolerant social practices of the sort liberalism demands. That is, they must claim that the pursuit of such values by the state can *override* the neutrality that liberal theory requires (otherwise the view would not be significantly distinct from liberalism). The other perfectionist view, then, is the universalist claim that, as a matter of 'human nature,' there are certain values that define a flourishing human existence, for all people in all places. The challenge for this sort of perfectionism is to produce a set of objective values that are described specifically enough to determine particular social policies. But it is notoriously difficult to specify a view of 'human nature' that does not already have value assumptions buried in the account, value assumptions that are controversial from some reasonable point of view. Consider such basic human goods as physical health and long life: there are certainly people who have led what they consider flourishing lives while sacrificing such things. Consider artists, writers, and musicians who have pursued physically self-destructive lifestyles but ones which (from her or his point of view) were intrinsically related to the thing that gave their lives meaning and value (the creation of works of art). Some musicians, writers, and artists seem to have produced valuable bodies of work while destroying themselves in the process (consider musicians such as Charlie Parker or Gerry Garcia, a painter like Jackson Pollack, or writers such as Malcolm Lowry, Charles Bukofsky, or William Burroughs). The claim that such individuals should have forsaken whatever inspiration or energy they (seem to have) received from their unhealthy habits is certainly not self-evidently true (though in each particular case the question of whether they could have led as creative a life while being healthier is an open one). Such people may well object strenuously if a state imposed a set of perfectionist values that forced or strongly induced them to forsake all unhealthy or dangerous activities.

It could be noted that this is simply a question of priorities: perfectionists claim that good health is one value among others whose importance must be determined in particular contexts. But unless a precise ordering of values comprising a good life could be given philosophically (and convincingly), then it is left to each person to decide what relative weight to give to competing values. But such individual determination of value for a person is exactly what liberalism protects!

In addition, the inference from statements concerning the 'essence' of human beings to conclusions about objective values faces the age-old difficulty of supporting value claims with descriptive premises. Now, we might reject the strict view, associated with David Hume, that statements of fact and statements of value can always be logically separated and that no inference from one to the other is possible (as we discussed in Chapter 1). Nevertheless, any *particular* inference from descriptions of basic human organic structure to conclusions about objective human values or the nature of human flourishing are always vulnerable to the objection that the account of human nature used as the premise in the argument contains value assumptions of the very sort they are meant to support, namely specific accounts of the human good (for discussion of this objection, see Hurka 1993: 33–36, 48–50).

One challenge raised by these various perfectionist positions still looms: if individual citizens order their own lives in terms of what they take to be objective values, and base their allegiance to political authority on those values, then why must the organs of the state restrict the justification of policies to considerations that make no mention of such values? In other words, why must the state be barred from referring to objective values in its justification of policies when its citizens refer precisely to such values in their own reasons for following those policies?

Before considering this challenge further, let us take a slight detour to consider a possible implication of liberal neutrality, as we have conceived it, that has profound ramifications for the theoretical traditions out of which liberal theory emerges. In particular, it may well be that if liberalism must embrace a strong principle of neutrality about promoting values, then there cannot be a *utilitarian* defense of liberalism.

Utilitarian liberalism: Perfectionism in disguise?

Throughout the nineteenth and twentieth centuries in various places, theorists have relied on utilitarianism to defend conceptions of justice that contained all the central components of liberalism – the protection of individual freedoms, respect for diversity of values and lifestyles, and a rejection of hierarchical (inegalitarian) conceptions of moral worth and social rank.[3] The most developed such defense is found in the work of John Stuart Mill. Though Mill's brand of utilitarianism was complex, he claimed that the doctrine of 'liberty' (that the only reason government or society could justifiably interfere with the liberty of an individual was to prevent harm to others) in no way rested on appeals to natural rights or considerations of intrinsic justice, but rather relied solely on considerations of utility (Mill [1859] 1975).

As explained in Chapter 1, utilitarianism is a general moral theory that evaluates acts, rules, institutions, and so on in terms of the relative utility contained in the outcomes produced by those acts, rules, and institutions. So the 'right' – what one ought to do or how institutions ought to be constructed – is determined according to the 'good' – the maximization of utility. Of course, 'utility' or 'welfare' can be defined in a number of ways as we saw earlier, as simply pleasure and the absence of pain, happiness, desire-satisfaction, and so on. For all such definitions, the individual's own state is the locus of attention, not external goods that someone might regard as valuable in themselves independent of the utility for people they may bring about (such as the beauty of the natural environment or the preservation of a culture).

And there is a grand tradition of applying utilitarian thinking to the defense of liberal reforms and liberal forms of government. But as we have defined it, liberalism is committed to pluralism about conceptions of value and the good life, a pluralism that, along with the emphasis on moral equality, implies neutrality in the justification of social policy. The degree to which utilitarianism is a liberal theory, then, is a function of how 'neutral' the promotion of utility turns out to be.

Utilitarian liberalism amounts to the view that treating people as moral equals, protecting basic liberties, respecting the pluralism of points of view in a population, and so on is justified because doing so maximally promotes the utility of citizens. That is, the basic components of liberal doctrine, along with the various policies that tend to arise from those components (such as limited paternalism, protection of free expression, freedom of religion, and so on), are justified based on the prediction that such things will result in the most utility for all affected (for a sophisticated defense of such a claim, see Hardin 1988).

But there are some general reasons for skepticism concerning whether the promotion of utility is consistent with the equal regard for all citizens' views of the good to which liberalism is committed. First, many people pursue value systems that are grounded in the importance of things other than *their own* happiness. Devotion to a religious tradition, for example, might rest on praise for and obedience to a divinity, where the fulfillment or happiness arising from such commitments is not part of what makes those activities good in the person's judgment. In such a tradition, a person's good would not be defined by how much happiness she experienced; so promoting her good would similarly be misguided if defined by that standard.

Utilitarians might respond that we need not understand 'utility' as 'pleasure' or 'happiness', but rather as merely the satisfaction of whatever the person's desires are, perhaps qualified by the requirement that they be fully informed desires (Arneson 1989). But even defined this way, utilitarianism still rests on a contentious conception of what is good in life. For many people do not think that even the satisfaction of their own *desires* is what adds value to their life, at least not as much as other things might, such as how successful the person's children are or whether a cure for cancer is found. As we noted, many people pursue what they take to be *impersonal* values – worthwhile pursuits that gain their prominence independently of how they affect the people themselves. In fact, some have argued that a fundamental aspect of the modern human condition is the search for values outside of ourselves, grounded in considerations unconnected to our subjective desires and pleasures (Taylor 1989b).[4]

Also, utility is a measure of *individual* well-being – one's welfare (utility) is defined apart from one's association with others, participation in a culture or tradition, or the like, except in so far as such participation leads instrumentally to one's own good. But many people define the value of their lives according to whether some *group* flourishes (such as a family, a culture or a cause), not whether they are made better off individually, as singular members of that group. Further, utilitarianism does not regard *persons as such* as valuable (and hence not as equally valuable), despite the traditional utilitarian slogan that 'everyone counts for one and no one counts for more than one.' That phrase means the fact that all that really matters in the utilitarian moral calculus is utility itself; people themselves are only regarded as of moral worth as 'vessels' of utility, so to speak. If the principle of equality central to liberalism is characterized as the view that all *persons* – understood as rational and able to pursue their own conceptions of the good – are equally morally worthy, then utilitarianism again diverges from liberalism; for liberalism regards the happiness (utility) of human beings as valuable only in so far as they themselves, as reflective pursuers of ends, regard it as valuable. If they don't, then utility gets no weight. This directly contradicts utilitarianism. (A related consideration lies behind Rawls's and Nozick's claim that utilitarianism should be rejected because it fails to give proper importance to 'the separateness of persons' – Nozick 1974: 33, Rawls 1971: 24.)

Many theorists will not be happy with the conclusion that utilitarianism cannot supply the basis for an acceptable liberal view of justice, for there are many examples of utilitarian liberal thinkers throughout the ages. But at least at this level of analysis, it appears that utilitarianism rests on too specific and controversial a conception of what is valuable in life to provide the sole support for liberal principles. (It is for this and related reasons that the focus of debate in recent political thought has been on the Kantianism of liberal political theory.)

Let us continue, then, with the consideration of attempts to justify liberalism in a way that responds to the fact of pluralism – that citizens of a complex modern society will hold different, and fundamentally conflicting, value perspectives – and the challenge of perfectionism – that it is paradoxical to claim that political principles should not rest on an objective conception of value when the citizens ruled by those principles will often be guided by their own concern for objective values. The principal attempt to reply to these challenges in recent years has been that of John Rawls, in his second incarnation.

The response of political liberalism

As we discussed in Chapter 1, John Rawls developed a highly influential theory of justice in the liberal tradition in his 1971 book *A Theory of Justice*. According to this view, justice applies to the basic institutions of society and manifests a hypothetical agreement among free and equal persons, choosing principles without the influence of factors that are 'arbitrary from a moral point of view.' The original position and the veil of ignorance were devices that represented this thought experiment, where fair principles were chosen by otherwise self-interested representatives who were placed in a position of ignorance of any particularities of their own situation, knowledge which would serve to distort the fairness of their choices. From such a situation, the principles of justice were derived, namely the Basic Liberty Principle and the Difference Principle.

As originally understood, this was a 'foundational' political theory, one which rested on fundamental moral commitments in the tradition of Kant and the social contract theorists of the seventeenth and eighteenth centuries. Under such an interpretation, 'justice as fairness' (as the theory is called) represents a specific moral view, though one justified by the procedure of 'reflective equilibrium' described earlier. This can be seen by realizing that the principles of justice which emerge from the original position in Rawls's view are derived only because certain prior moral assumptions lay behind the construction of the choice situation itself (as we saw in our earlier discussion of Rawls). These moral assumptions, then, manifest the foundational moral view upon which justice as fairness rests (Barry 1973: 10–18, 1989: 213–54).

But in so far as people who would be governed by such principles would themselves hold widely divergent moral viewpoints, not all of them Kantian certainly, such a foundational conception of justice would conflict with the moral commitments of those to whom it applies. So just as utilitarianism was seen as representing a controversial moral doctrine in conflict with liberalism's commitment to neutrality, Rawls's theory of justice as fairness was also seen as representing a contentious, indeed parochial, moral viewpoint in tension with the undeniable pluralism of the modern moral world. (This critique will be discussed in greater detail in the next chapter.)

In response to this realization, as well as other related criticisms of his original theory, Rawls published *Political Liberalism* in 1993, putting forward an alternative understanding of 'justice as fairness.' Rawls now argues that rather than resting on a foundational, morally grounded, conception of justice, justice as fairness was simply a 'free-standing' conception around which a diverse population could form an 'overlapping consensus,' even though their own individual moral outlooks were very different and in conflict with that of others in the population (Rawls 1993). Rawls himself saw the need for this reformulation, for without this new understanding, justice as fairness could never achieve the general stability and social cohesion that he claimed for it (Rawls 1971: Part III). In the revised view, an acceptable conception of justice must arise out of specific historical situation, informed by the dominant moral and political ideas of the age. In the case of 'justice as fairness,' the social tradition in question is the legacy of constitutional democracies in the West that emerged in Europe after the Protestant Reformation and the wars of religion. The conflicts that precipitated these wars showed, Rawls points out, that no single moral or religious outlook could reign over a large society without the imposition of unacceptable levels of oppressive force. The pluralism that marks the modern age (in the areas of the globe referred to here) is a permanent fact of social life, a deep and abiding condition that no amount of ideological or moral persuasion can eradicate. Therefore, the problem of modern (liberal) society is this: 'How is it possible that there may exist over time a stable and just society of free and equal citizens profoundly divided by reasonable religious, philosophical, and moral doctrines?' (Rawls 1993: xxv).

Notice how Rawls refers to 'reasonable' religious, philosophical, and moral doctrines. What he means is that while such doctrines are 'comprehensive' in that they provide for their adherents pervasive value systems that order the entirety of their lives and values, their adherents nevertheless acknowledge that others hold different, conflicting, value schemes that will not themselves ever be subsumed by their own. Devotees of reasonable comprehensive moral doctrines, then, acknowledge the pluralism of which they are a part. In this realization, however, people take on the 'burdens of judgment' in that they realize that no full justification of the political principles that govern the society can arise solely from a single comprehensive moral viewpoint, even their own, and that other such contrasting viewpoints co-exist in the society and correspondingly ground others' political obligations (to the same central principles).

A second thing to note about modern societies, on this view, is that they are assumed to be populated by 'free and equal citizens' (Rawls 1993: 19, 30). But if we are avoiding foundational moral commitments here, how can we begin by insisting that such basic values as freedom and equality are already built into our system of justice? Wouldn't that demand a prior moral argument of a foundationalist kind, the sort we are trying to avoid here? (Recall that this question arose in our discussion of Rawls's view in Chapter 2.) Rawls's answer is that the principles of freedom and equality, abstractly stated, are simply the central parts of the legacy of modern constitutional democracies to which a theory such as 'justice as fairness' is meant to apply. This is a historical development that, like the reasonable pluralism that unfolded at the same time, is a contingent aspect of modern life in the West. A theory of justice, then, must acknowledge that development, and the commitments to freedom and equality it entails, and construct a more concrete interpretation of those ideas that could be accepted from the diverse points of view marked by reasonable pluralism.

This contrasts sharply with the Kantian foundationalism that appeared to characterize the earlier view (as well as other versions of liberalism, many still being defended as such). In the foundationalist version, all people, by virtue of the structure of practical reason and the nature of political life, are committed to the basic values of autonomy (free reflective choice) and the principle of equality built upon it. The concept of the person used to derive principles of liberty, equality of opportunity, and economic fairness is allegedly a concept with which all human beings by nature will identify. But in the 'political' version of liberalism, those ideas are merely taken on as part of a *heritage* – the mode of social life that dominates 'our' age – and the concept of the person utilized to model principles is not meant to reflect any actual people's self-understandings. Rather, it is merely used as a 'device of representation,' a projection that we all can see as valid from our diverse moral perspectives, valid, that is, for the purposes of generating principles of justice which will garner legitimacy from these diverse points of view (Rawls 1993: 24ff.). What we want is a set of principles that will provide political stability for an irreduceably pluralistic population which reflects respect for freedom and equality, values we inherit as part of our heritage; and justice as fairness and the devices used to derive its principles is merely one prominent example of such a set of principles.[5]

The 'concept of the person' alluded to here deserves special attention (and will occupy us again in later chapters). The person who is imagined choosing principles of justice from behind the veil of ignorance, as well as the citizen of the well-ordered society governed by those principles, is considered as a being with two basic moral 'powers,' a capacity for a sense of justice and a capacity for a conception of the good (ibid.: 18–20). Such a person has a highest order interest in exercising those capacities and in seeing herself as able to form and revise value conceptions which then become self-authenticating sources of valid claims on others. This may not square with a person's actual self-understanding, however, as she may well see herself as *unable* to abstract from her self-defining commitments (her religious devotion for example). But this is not required by the theory, as it proposes this picture of the person only as a model for the derivation of principles in order to achieve an overlapping consensus amidst a reasonable pluralism of moral viewpoints (ibid.: 29–34).

Similarly, the original position (along with the veil of ignorance) are also devices of representation and are not meant to mirror a choice situation in which we can easily place ourselves. We are not meant, for example, to be able to abstract from our actual gender, race, place in society, and connection to our natural talents and conceptions of the good (as the earlier version of the view seemed to demand of us). We are merely to see that such 'institutional' identities can represent us in our attempt to live with radically different fellow citizens under principles that can claim allegiance from us all (ibid.: 30).

The realization that one cannot expect one's own moral outlook to provide the basis for a public conception of justice for a pluralistic society is a crucial element in the political conception of liberalism. It underlies, for example, the idea of 'public reason' that Rawls puts forward as a set of constraints on the manner that principles guiding social policies can be justified. For in keeping with the realization of pluralism, public reason demands political justifications that can be shared by those with a wide variety of comprehensive moral views (justifications of the basic provisions of the constitution, say). For this reason, elements of public dialogue that make crucial reference to particular moralities (not shared generally) must be bracketed. This bracketing need not exclude *all* moral considerations, nor must it rule out reference to conceptions of the good altogether. Indeed, Rawls argues that some reference to value conceptions will be made as part of the justification of justice as fairness (Rawls 1993: 173–211). But these claims will merely be that it is *reasonable* to value certain things (such as the value of rationality, the primary goods used to evaluate a person's place in the distributive scheme, and the good of political society itself). One need not view such values as paramount in one's own moral conception but only acknowledge the reasonable value of those things, a value that must be postulated for an overlapping consensus around basic political principles to be established (Rawls 1993, 1999b).

Rawls's theory is complex and subtle and this brief summary merely brings out certain key points. One issue that is especially important for our purposes is the relation that is meant to obtain between a citizen's personal moral view and the political principles that reign in a liberal society. Rawls says at one point that the individual's moral outlook and the principles of justice merely must be *compatible*, since most people's set of moral values is not detailed and comprehensive enough to make clear all possible links to political principles (such as the priority of liberty or equality of opportunity) (Rawls 1993: 160). At other times, however, he claims that people's comprehensive moral doctrines must serve to 'affirm' the liberal view (ibid.: 147). As long as the different moral outlooks that predominate in a society congeal around a single constitutional framework guided by a publicly justified set of political principles, and these moral outlooks help to support and affirm such principles, liberal justice is secured.

But has Rawls really responded to what we called the perfectionist problem with liberalism, that while political principles must be justified neutrally, citizens' own commitments to those principles rest on their own particular values, ones that they view as objectively valid? Rawls insists that commitment to shared political principles cannot merely be a matter of strategic importance to the different groups, for that would amount to adopting a mere *modus vivendi*. It must be that the shared principles are 'affirmed on moral grounds' (Rawls 1993: 147), though these grounds will be different for the various systems and moral frameworks adhered to. This means that the groups will not withdraw their support for the political principles even if their moral view eventually becomes dominant in the society (ibid.: 148).

It is also essential, however, that individuals see the shared political values as *more important* than the different moral doctrines they hold, for in cases of conflict – when certain justice provisions run counter to their moral or religious beliefs – they must accede to the requirements of justice as part of the shared political view. The strength of commitment to any such political principles, then, will depend on the degree to which such principles rest comfortably on the foundational elements of the moral view in question.

The issue of abortion provides a striking case (Sandel 1982: 197–99, 1996: 20–21, 100–03; cf. Rawls 1993: 243 n. 32). A Catholic may affirm the principles of protecting privacy and the right to one's body from within her own religious world view. But her religious commitment to the sanctity of life from the moment of conception is also affirmed in this way; indeed, it is more fundamental than a right to privacy or bodily control from this person's point of view. So in so far as liberal principles might include a right to abortion (if they do), why would this Catholic have any remaining reason to follow them?

The answer to this question may lie in the degree to which the comprehensive doctrines found in a population are 'reasonable' in Rawls's special sense. For it is not merely that each person affirms the constitution from their own private moral perspective; they must also do this in constant recognition of the plurality of moral perspectives found in society. They must recognize that any commitment they have to a moral view is understood in light of different commitments by different people living around them, and there is no escape from this pervasive social confrontation. (Secession is not an option.) But this gives rise to two important issues: is the variety of moral, religious, cultural, and philosophical viewpoints to be found in modern society too great and too full of conflict to support a common consensus about basic constitutional principles? Or, are people's recognition of what they take to be objective moral values so firm that they will withdraw support from provisions of a political regime that fail to reflect those values?

Rawls's view, then, can be tugged on from two diametrically opposed directions. On the one hand, it can be argued that the view is not political *enough*, in that the pluralism that exists in modern societies runs far deeper than Rawls acknowledges, to the extent that only a strategic compromise – a *modus vivendi* – can be established from different viewpoints around a single constitutional framework. On this view, justice as fairness (or some similar doctrine) may well find general acceptance, but that will be a result of bargaining and strategic positioning rather than moral commitment (Gray 1993, Larmore 1996). In the other direction are the perfectionists, who continue to claim that individual citizens will have no reason to place their commitment to public political principles above private moral commitments when the two conflict, especially in so far as those individual moral commitments are seen to rest on objective values. Again, why should citizens feel committed to political principles based on value-neutral, publicly shared, considerations (obeying the constraints of public reason) when their own motivations for conforming to those principles lie in their (private) comprehensive value systems, ones they take to be *true*?

This brings us full circle to the problem of legitimacy of liberal principles for a diverse population discussed at the end of Chapter 2. The legitimacy of political authority is taken to rest on the reasonable acceptability of that authority by those ruled by it. The problems this view faces raised by the twin perspectives of radical pluralism and perfectionism, stated briefly, are these: (a) if the self-conceptions, value systems, religious commitments, and so on, of the citizens ruled by political authorities are as diverse as it appears in modern societies, then no clearly defined set of principles could be justified philosophically for such citizens, except as a result of mere bargaining and strategic engagement (a mere *modus vivendi*); and (b) there is no reason to rule out the philosophical possibility that some values are objectively valid for all human beings and hence supported by reason, the claim made by perfectionists; this is an especially powerful consideration when we realize that most in the population guide their lives by what *they* take to be objective values (Arneson 2000b). The challenge for the liberal paradigm is to navigate a course between these positions.

Liberalism, public discourse, and democracy

One thinker who has directly confronted the relation between legitimacy and the interchange of conflicting conceptions of value in modern societies is Jürgen Habermas, who, along with Rawls, has emerged as one of the most important political theorists of recent decades. Habermas's wide-ranging views can only be touched upon here, as they involve multiple components and a fundamentally interdisciplinary method of political philosophy (including sociology, psychology, and linguistic analysis) (see Habermas 1996b, 1998, White 1988, Rasmussen 1990).

For Habermas, normativity – the expression of evaluations of states of affairs – must be seen as a linguistic practice that is 'cognitive,' but not 'foundationalist.' That is, expression of normative judgments (such as moral claims) involve reason-based judgments and are not merely the expression of emotion (as some philosophers had previously claimed). Such judgments can be 'valid' in a way parallel to the way scientific and descriptive judgments can be true. But such judgments cannot be said to be valid by way of their relation to some set of undeniable foundational principles that all rational creatures must accept (*à la* the 'first philosophy' described in Chapter 1). Their validity is established in *practice*, particularly by the linguistic practices of participants in normative discourse.[6]

Habermas claims that interpersonal communication that is not merely expressive (as in an artistic performance) or purely strategic (trying to get someone to do something whether or not she agrees with the reason for doing it) generally involves certain presuppositions concerning the validity of the claims being made and the sincerity of those making them, among other things (Habermas 1998).[7] A norm that a person expresses or relies on, on this view, is valid when all affected can accept the consequences that its general observance can be anticipated to have for the satisfaction of everyone's interests (Habermas 1990: 65–6). That is the formal principle of validity. But this means that normative validity occurs not as a philosophical monologue based on theoretical reflection, but as an actual dialogue among a plurality of people confronting each other in social space. This is in contrast to Rawls's view, where hypothetical 'model conceptions' and 'devices of representation,' such as the original position and the veil of ignorance, were used in a quasi-fictitious way to establish the validity of principles of justice. For Habermas, such principles must be worked out in actual practice in the public sphere of open discourse and not in a philosopher's abstract reflections.

In this way, Habermas's views imply that principles of justice are inextricably tied to the institutions of *democracy*. While Rawls sees justice as closely tied to the operation of public reason, and hence provides a framework for a working democracy, Habermas insists that democratic deliberation and activities in the public sphere *define* principles of justice. Now those conditions that make reasoned discourse even possible must be established as a matter of right (freedoms of speech, association, political participation, and the like). All other constitutional and political provisions are matters to be determined in communicative deliberation among the governed. So there exists a certain foundational demand for basic freedoms in Habermas's view. But these are justified by their place in the system of public communication and not on some universal metaphysical grounds. And he also insists that all substantive provisions of justice must be subject to ongoing discursive validation (Habermas 1996b).

This view responds to the challenge of perfectionism simply by supplying a theory of normativity which rejects such perfectionism. Since norms and values are justified, for Habermas, by way of a dialogic interchange constrained by norms implicit in communication itself, it cannot be held that values exist objectively and independent of collective deliberation. But this also represents an opposition to the radical pluralists (including some which we will encounter later, in Chapter 7 for example). For the communicative rationality by which values are grounded, for Habermas, cannot be merely a strategic stance taken with those who stand in my way. Prevailing in such a competition could not provide me with the right kind of reason to act on my own value commitments, or so he would claim (see Habermas 1995: 294–326).

This exchange of views has led us to see the close connection between the justification of the basic freedoms in a society – the Bill of Rights in its constitution, say – and the necessity of a fully functioning democracy. Theories of democracy are wide ranging, grounding arguments for its design in considerations of freedom, equality, or the need to aggregate individual citizens' preferences (see, for example, Christiano 1996, Habermas 1996b, Held 1987). What we have discovered here, if the arguments of Habermas and Rawls are to be followed in broad outline, is that the operations of democratic institutions may well be necessary as part of the determination of the principles of justice themselves. But in these contexts, democracy must be understood in a very broad sense, more than merely a mechanism for voting; for democracy is part of the social process that establishes the public agreement which constitutes the legitimacy of the principles in question. Such an institution must include, then, an overlapping network of public spaces and other mechanisms that allow the free flow of information and opinion, including all forms of electronic media and mass communication. The wide dissemination of people's opinions and the facts they rely on are necessary for any manner of public acceptance or convergence upon social policy to take place. Democracy is simply the name for this complex network of exchange.

But in all these discussions, certain assumptions were being made about the kind of person who is to live under the principles in question and whose point of view was presumed in the procedures for justifying principles. Indeed, all views about social life implicitly or explicitly posit a 'conception of the person' both in their description of the dynamics of that life as well as the assumptions they make about how the norms guiding it are to be justified. As we saw above, the claim that just principles must be accepted as legitimate by those living under them assumes a kind of being who makes such judgments of legitimacy. The precise conception of the autonomous person, then, will be crucial in the determination of the plausibility of principles of justice. For example, the picture of the disembodied, pared down, reflecting self assumed in some standard models of autonomy controversially leaves out elements of our personality that some claim are crucial in the determination of whether principles guiding our lives oppress us or liberate us. In the next chapter, we will consider this sort of challenge, and this will begin a more thoroughgoing, and in some cases more radical, critique of the liberal paradigm that forms the second half of this book. Many of the issues we have touched upon will re-emerge in those discussions.

Chapter summary

The liberal commitment to the priority of enforcing the rules of justice over promoting the good for citizens came under scrutiny here from two opposing directions, one based on an insistence on value pluralism (more extensive than that which is recognized by liberalism) and the other on perfectionism (of a sort ruled out by traditional liberalism). After spelling out the basic contours of liberal philosophy, including its commitment to value pluralism, the fundamental value of autonomy, the priority of the right over the good, and equality, we considered the way in which liberalism is committed to a principle of neutrality. The liberal state is structured so that government policies cannot be justified with reference to controversial conceptions of the good, and in this way remains neutral toward its citizens' moral commitments. The priority placed on enforcing the right over promoting the good (and hence liberal toleration of diversity) was shown to follow from the basic liberal commitments to the equal value of autonomy and acknowledgment of pluralism, for state promotion of some controversial value conception in effect shows greater respect for some citizens than others and hence violates equality.

In next raising the question of whether liberalism rests on objective values itself (despite being committed to neutrality in enforcing justice), we considered the perfectionist challenge to liberalism. This view insists that liberal principles must rely on values that are taken to be objective and true, and not merely a reasonable compromise among equally valid viewpoints. For the arguments supporting liberal neutrality based on respect for autonomy all fail, perfectionists claim; and, moreover, there are certain identifiable objective values that can be understood to be based on human nature, or at least are things that are almost universally valued by human beings. We cast doubt, however, on various perfectionist attempts to ground particular values objectively, worrying about the contentious nature of any particular example of such a value (even leading a long life), and we also raised questions about the derivation of value claims from 'factual' accounts of human nature. We then discussed utilitarian liberalism and concluded that justifying liberal principles on the basis of the maximization of utility was indeed a version of perfectionism, and so subject to whatever criticisms could be raised against that view.

Rawls's attempt to defend liberal principles as purely 'political,' rather than on foundational moral grounds, was examined. We saw, however, that this view faces the same double-edged challenge – from pluralists who claim that a political doctrine of this sort could not be affirmed from all of the various reasonable moral viewpoints found in modern society, and from perfectionists who claim that a merely political justification of liberalism fails to give proper weight to objective values (and citizens' commitments to them). We then turned to the work of Jürgen Habermas and constructed an argument for the claim that only if political principles gain their support through actual deliberation and public discourse will legitimacy be secured for liberal principles. In this way, it was claimed that institutions of democracy play a constitutive role in the justification of political principles for a liberal society. And we noted the relevance of all these discussions to the conception of the person at the center of liberalism, and specifically the understanding of autonomy used in them.

Case to consider

Motivated by a call to promote the physical health of its population, a certain state passes legislation that makes cigarette smoking illegal. The production, manufacture, and sale of tobacco products (used for smoking) is similarly outlawed. Implementation of this restriction will be phased in to allow smokers to quit and those in the tobacco industry to restructure their agricultural and manufacturing activity away from smoking related uses. The goal, however, is to make the entire nation 'smoke free' by a certain target date.

Opponents of the measure claim, first, that such restrictions will never work; just as with prohibition and restrictions on narcotics, such restrictions will only create black markets that make everyone worse off. More fundamentally, they argue that individual citizens should be allowed to choose to engage in risky activities as long as others around them (or who are dependent on them) are not harmed. But defenders of the legislation say that they were elected on a platform of making the nation more healthy (we can assume that they did so campaign), that this provision was announced as its major goal, and hence a majority of voting citizens favor the elimination of smoking as a matter of public health (and not merely because of its external harms to non-smokers, but because of the health of smokers themselves).

To what degree might the arguments of the opponents of this legislation be grounded in liberal claims about the priority of respecting autonomy over promoting the good? Correspondingly, in what ways are the arguments of the legislators pushing the ban on smoking based on perfectionist principles? Considering the arguments discussed above, who has the strongest position?

Notes on further reading

Discussions of the basic components of liberalism can be found in Larmore 1987 and 1996, Kymlicka 1990, Johnston 1994, Beiner 1997, R. Dworkin 1977, 1985 and 2000, and the essays in MacLean and Mills 1983 and Arneson 1992. Recent defenses of liberalism include Macedo 1990, Galston 1991, Waldron 1993 and 1999, Moon 1993, and Kymlicka 1995 (cf. also Gaus 1996). Toleration is examined in Mendus 1989 and Greenawalt 1988 and 1995. The question of the nature and basis of the principle of neutrality in liberalism is considered in Waldron 1993: 143–67 and Sher 1997: 20–44.

The perfectionist challenge to liberalism is effectively summarized and powerfully defended in Hurka 1993 and Sher 1997, while perfectionist versions of liberalism itself are defended in Raz 1986 and Wall 1998. Defenses of utilitarian liberalism can be found in Hardin 1988 and discussed in Kymlicka 1990: 9–49.

Rawls's *Political Liberalism* (Rawls 1993) has generated numerous commentaries (though see also Rawls 1999b for further clarification and development of his views). The essays in Davion and Wolf 2000 are especially helpful as a source here. Rawls's views are criticized in interesting ways in, among other places, Habermas 1998: 49–104 and Sandel [1982] 1999; 184–218 (as well as in the perfectionist literature just cited: see, for example, Wall 1998: 63–123).

Theories of democracy are surveyed in Held 1987 and critically discussed in Christiano 1996 and Dryzek 2000; but for alternative perspectives, see also J. Cohen 1996, Fraser 1997: 11–40, 69–98, Mouffe 2000, and Young 2000, as well as the essays in Benhabib 1996a and Paul, et al. 2000.

PART II

Critique of the liberal paradigm
Challenges and departures

CHAPTER 5

Conservatism, communitarianism, and the social conception of the self

- Conservatism
- Communitarianism
- Liberalism, freedom, and culture
- Chapter summary
- Case to consider
- Notes on further reading

Liberalism is the approach to political philosophy that places individual autonomy at center stage, so that under the rubric of liberalism, justice is defined as that set of principles that would be accepted as legitimate by autonomous citizens. And such principles of justice must be enforced prior to the promotion of controversial conceptions of value, lest the autonomy of those citizens in determining what is valuable be ignored. In this way, equality of moral status – the equal value of autonomous persons – is fundamental to liberalism as we have developed it here. The priority of justice and equal respect for autonomy will be the linchpins of the liberal paradigm we will be critically discussing in this and the following chapters.

Our concern in this chapter will be whether the liberal approach to political philosophy rests on a problematic conception of the person (as autonomous and independent), one which illegitimately ignores the importance of communal values and community stability as well as the deeply social nature of the self and its principles. In a related manner, we will look at claims that liberalism unfairly tilts away from a more traditional, conservative approach to social values and political principles. In both cases, the underlying accusation against liberalism is that its presuppositions do not live up to the neutral universality it claims for itself; rather than expressing an overall approach to justice that people of different ideological persuasions, value commitments, and moral orientations can all work within, liberalism will be accused of being just one more parochial value system among others, and one which many in modern society reject.

Conservatism

As explained in the Introduction, the liberalism we are considering here should be taken to represent a general approach to justice in the modern era, a theoretical view which underlies constitutional democracy and popular sovereignty in general, and not a particular political agenda or set of policies. The reason for this is that we were trying to develop a more abstract view about political power and justice *generally* that speaks to both 'liberal' and 'conservative' policies, in the narrow senses of those words. Liberalism in this broad sense certainly is in opposition to various forms of political fundamentalism, fascism, and despotism, but it is not meant to oppose (most of) what goes by the name 'conservative' in the policy debates of the current day.

Some theorists, however claim that this is inaccurate, that liberalism in our broad sense represents a theoretical framework that actually *does* contrast with what could be called a theoretically 'conservative' view, one that more congenially supports many policy initiatives that conservatives (in the narrow sense) advance. Now we certainly want to maintain a distinction between disagreements on matters of policy and more abstract philosophical disputes about the nature of justice (and freedom, equality, and so on). And for ease of exposition, we can use 'conservative policies'and 'liberal policies' to refer to those initiatives aimed at particular problems for specific societies (whether to expand the military or revoke the use of the death penalty, for example), reserving 'conservatism' and 'liberalism' for the more general philosophical stances.

There is, I think, a philosophical position that can be called 'conservative' that is significantly different from the liberal paradigm we have been discussing, and it may be true that such a philosophical view supports more strongly conservative policies of the usual sort, such as demanding strict, retributive penal systems, a strong military, promoting certain pronounced moral ideals ('family values'), strongly supporting certain traditional religious practices, and the like.[1] Though we will not discuss the relation between conservative philosophy and conservative policy, we will consider this more abstract conservatism in order to draw a contrast with the liberal paradigm we have been developing.

The bases of such a conservatism can be found in the philosophical work of thinkers such as David Hume (1985), Edmund Burke (1968), Hastings Rashdall (1924), Michael Oakeshott (1991), Robert Nisbet (1986), and more recently John Kekes (1998). Some of these thinkers present these views as more of a turn of mind or an 'attitude' rather than a codified political view (Oakeshott 1991).[2] But for conservatism to offer itself as a rival to liberalism, it must be more than an attitude, for attitudes are simply dispositions that various people may or may not have, not general considerations that provide others without the attitude with reasons to adopt it. (Though, of course, a claim that a dominant view does not pay sufficient *respect* to some specific attitude is a valid criticism of that view, so we will have to take note of that separately.)

But more than an attitude, conservatism can be understood as a philosophical view about the purposes and limits of government power. The mark of a conservative philosophy, of course, is that it aims to protect traditional values and pays great heed to history and established practice. Correspondingly, it is wary of attempts at 'progressive' change in order to restore or establish a new, allegedly more just, social arrangement, since such changes often have the effect of destroying those traditional practices without sufficient basis for the belief that things will be better, overall, with the change. So, in short, conservatives are traditionalists.

Conservatism also is *perfectionist*, however, in our sense of that term. This is because it views the point of state power as the promotion of the good for its citizens.[3] The aim of political institutions, on this view, is to establish (and more importantly to protect) the conditions necessary for citizens to lead flourishing lives. Just social relations may be one aspect of such lives, but it is one among others, including such things as citizens' enjoyment of good health, shelter and rest, companionship, self-respect, and so on. Certain social conditions are necessary for these goods, then – things such as freedom, equality, a healthy environment, justice, peace, order, security, toleration, adequate levels of education, and the like (Kekes 1998: 22). On this view, most of the population can lead fulfilling lives even when some face conditions of injustice, at least to a degree. This is what distinguishes conservatism from liberalism most starkly: liberals insist that justice, defined with reference to equality and autonomy, is the primary virtue of a decent society and a condition that is necessary for citizens to lead worthwhile lives.

Expanding on this last point, conservatives view autonomy as one possible element of a good life, but one which may well be forsaken (to some degree) in localities where adherence to traditional practices gives greater weight to obedience and authority than individualized autonomy. If autonomy is conceived simply as the capacity to make unforced choices based on open alternatives which agents evaluate for themselves (see Kekes 1997: 16–20, Raz 1986: 369–78), then the liberal claim that autonomy is a fundamental necessary condition of good lives is wrongheaded (or at least controversial and hence non-neutral). For some lives are embedded in traditions or authority structures that do not afford individuals with this power of independent choice, and therefore if such lives are indeed worthwhile (and conservatives claim that, in principle, they can be), autonomy is not always crucial for a worthwhile life. (This argument turns on the precise conceptualization of autonomy to which liberalism is committed, a topic to be discussed further below.)

These elements of good lives, however, are very general and abstract. Conservatives of the sort we are discussing go on to insist that any specific interpretation of what those values should mean for a particular society, and any ranking of their importance in cases of (inevitable) conflict among them, cannot be determined by *a priori* philosophical reflection outside of established social practices themselves. For conservatives insist that the more specific determination of the components of good lives in a society must be based fundamentally on the traditions and established practices of that society, at least those that have shown themselves over time to have succeeded in providing decent lives for the majority of its citizens. Conservatives, then, refer to the *past* to answer all questions about the future, and they regard the danger of destroying what is good about a society as always more worrisome than correcting what is bad, at least correcting it according to untried and nontraditional practices.

Because of this required reference to established practice in defining value for a society, conservatism implies that establishing and maintaining social stability against both internal and external threats is a fundamental state concern.[4] Social reform in the name of securing justice for some part of the population, then, is less important in the conservative view than retaining the orderly practices that make the pursuit of values possible for the general population. Though the exact recommendation concerning what policies to pursue in this regard will be, for most conservatives, a matter of community discretion, again based on the lessons of past practice.[5]

The distinction between conservatism and liberalism, at this level of abstraction, is deep but surprisingly subtle. After all, there are many similar claims made from both perspectives. Both view values as ultimately plural and not given by a single philosophical theory of the good (since conservatives may well accept that what is good varies from one society to another). And both are willing to countenance the promotion of values that all in a society freely judge to be worthwhile. Liberals, however, justify the pursuit of such values by government authority, not based on the abstract validity of the value claims themselves, but on the autonomous endorsement of those values by those whose lives are shaped by their promotion. Autonomous judgment is at the root of all confirmation of values, for the liberal theorist. While the conservative insists that being grounded in the dominant practices of a community is what establishes the validity of conceptions of value. Autonomous endorsement is not directly relevant.

Admittedly, it will not always be clear what the dominant values of a community *are* that make the overall stability of its way of life possible. Indeed, in all political conflicts there will be disagreements both about how to interpret the value foundations of an established practice as well as how to rank conflicting priorities when they are well defined. This point also shows the contrast between liberals and conservatives, since liberalism claims that the procedure for deciding such (inevitable) conflicts must be *just*, and hence must involve equal respect for the autonomous judgments of all participating in the debate. Conservatives, and perfectionists more generally, claim that 'just' procedures for collective deliberation are not always required, and certainly not normatively basic. What conservatives claim is that those with authority as established leaders of a community will be best positioned to interpret the historical record (Kekes 1998: 40). Procedures that require equal participation, fully democratic processes, and the like may well be unnecessary.

But why should persons already in power be best suited to determine what is truly worthwhile for citizens in a diverse community? Such a procedure virtually guarantees that inequalities of power and status will be maintained, no matter what the justification for them, since conflict about their legitimacy will be adjudicated by those who, virtually by definition, are positioned so as to favor the status quo (the already powerful). Societies that have been seen as relatively flourishing always contain sectors that have not shared fully in that flourishing: oppressed minorities, (often) women, the poor, and groups who were conquered when the dominant groups gained power. The values guiding such a society will be seen in one way by the dominant group – as prizing stability, peace, overall happiness for most citizens, and so on – while in quite another by those not sharing power – as distorted, illusory, unjust, and so on.

However, even when the values being successfully pursued in a decent society are well enough understood, the question will always arise whether further reform is needed to correct whatever shortcomings remain, including most often problems of injustice. Conservatives hold that established practice must always be the ground to determine what course of action to take – whether to pursue reform at all, and if so how vigorously and in what manner. But this is simply one side of a debate whose opposition will be those who claim that overwhelming evidence exists that past practices are corrupt and new initiatives must be tried. In other words, the conservative 'attitude' that sees established practices as more reliable than untested but progressive proposals is simply one side of the debate in question, namely whether the society is truly promoting the good for its citizens. The claim that defenders of historical traditions must always carry the day in such an argument is simply an article of faith, a dogmatic position unsupported by general philosophical (or indeed empirical) evidence. What we are left with in the end is merely the conservative 'attitude' with which we began, a disposition that some hold but surely not a principled position that will convince those with another view.

But this still leaves us with the other elements of the conservative view that contrasts with liberalism and which should be investigated more thoroughly, namely the view that states should indeed promote shared communal values in the first place, and that those who define their value commitments with reference to communal ties and traditional practices are not adequately represented in the liberal philosophy. These and related claims will be taken up in the remainder of the chapter as we discuss the position that for many years was thought of as the major opponent of liberalism in political philosophy.

Communitarianism

Throughout the 1980s in the Anglo-American philosophical world, the debate between communitarianism and liberalism held center stage in much of political philosophy. Spurred by Michael Sandel's critique of Rawls (Sandel 1982), and important books by Charles Taylor (1979), Michael Walzer (1983), and Alasdair MacIntyre (1984), the communitarian critique of liberalism was one of the central concerns of political theory for a full decade and beyond (for an overview, see Delaney 1994). The challenge of communitarianism, as with other lines of thought we are considering, proceeds in two parts: a critique of the liberal paradigm; and an offer of an alternative view. As we will see, the first is more powerful and fully worked out than the second, but both provide profound questions for the tradition of Enlightenment liberalism.

The critique of liberalism offered by communitarians develops at several levels: against the liberal conception of the person, concerning the liberal account of value commitment, and regarding the social effects of the implementation of liberal principles. Let us touch on each of these in some detail.

The communitarian critique of the liberal self

Communitarianism is certainly not the first, or only, view to challenge the alleged hyper-individualism of liberal theory – Marxists, for example, have done so for quite some time (see, for example, MacPherson 1962). As has been discussed, liberalism rests on the proposition that political power is justified only when it is acceptable to citizens considered as rational autonomous agents; such agents are imagined to be choosing to accept such power on the basis of values and commitments they have chosen or judge to be valid, independent of any 'external' factors, such as their society, history, culture, or other people. Such connections are simply contingent aspects of their identity, understood as objects of choice rather than elements that constitute one's very being. As a result of such a framework, the interests considered basic in a free society are things like freedom of speech, assembly, mobility, and the like, or more generally, freedom to enjoy the autonomy by which such agents are defined. So the autonomous agent is both the model of the person judging the acceptability of political principles as well as the agent whose interests those principles are designed to protect. The critique of liberalism mounted by communitarians, then, draws a bead on this specific target.

Speaking in general terms first, communitarians reject the conception of the autonomous person with capacities to reflect upon and possibly reject any particular aspect of herself or her place in society as a model upon which to build political principles. On the communitarian alternative, selves are fundamentally *social* both in their metaphysical constitution and their psychology (though we have been speaking of these claims in psychological terms).[6] On the communitarian view, agents engage in thinking and acting not in a detached reflective mode, but as fully embedded personalities defined and shaped by a social milieu. In contrast to the liberal ideal of free agency according to which persons engage in activities only as a result of reflectively choosing them, communitarians stress the way in which all action is *defined* by ongoing practices and social institutions (for discussion, see MacIntyre 1981: 203–25). One steps back and reflects on some aspect of one's social life only when ongoing modes of action and reflection have been interrupted or break down (Bell 1993: 39). Therefore, a key component of the positive communitarian framework will be the protection and promotion of goods defined by ongoing practices.

The way in which ongoing practices provide the normative framework within which reflection takes place (rather than present themselves as objects of it) can be seen by consideration of *language* (Bell 1993: 156–69, Rorty 1989: 3–22, Taylor 1991: 33ff.). Though we might stop to reflect on certain aspects of the language(s) we use; for the most part, the norms that govern our mode of thinking, communication, and self-expression function as unchosen structuring devices within which all these acts of reflection take place. Such norms are not simply options we can choose to ignore, nor are they 'facts' about the world that can be discovered, they are rules that *constitute* the thinking and acting (and self-conceptions) that make up our world. And language is a social practice, which, along with other social practices, provides the building blocks of our thinking rather than the object of our reflections.

Relatedly, value commitments should not be seen as grounded in autonomous, reflective choice. Rather, they are often the unchosen horizons within which particular choices are made and aims are defined. Foundational values, for many, are simply given to us as a background framework within which we can pursue our projects. Such 'strong valuations' are not merely options that can be weighed in moments of rational reflection but provide frameworks that organize our thoughts about values more generally (Taylor 1979: 157–59, 1989b: 4, Sandel 1996: 14–15). Moreover, many fulfilling pursuits and value orientations do not involve reflective choice and open options; they simply involve playing out the defining value orientations within which one finds oneself and according to which one presses on in life. The idea that only the life-pursuing aims that one sat back and chose independently like items on a smorgasbord blinds us to the myriad pursuits structured by unchosen factors and traditional commitments. And it also occludes those aspects of all our lives that are never questioned or reflected upon but accepted as given (Bell 1993: 34–43, Christman 2001). As I discuss below, some people view questioning one's basic faith or value commitments as a *wrong*, indicative of weakness and lack of resolve.

To see these points from a different angle, let us look once again at Rawls's original position and the way it functions in the formulation of his theory of justice (see Chapter 2). For Rawls, principles of justice are those that would be chosen by agents understood as ignorant of any contingent facts about themselves that are 'arbitrary from a moral point of view.' Indeed, such agents choose principles without reference to their own conception of value and the good. This implies, then, that the identities by virtue of which political principles are justified are not conceived with any reference to the values people hold. Such values, this model implies, are simply the object of reflective choice – left up to the person when she begins her life in the well-ordered society – not what *defines* her as a person and so not what helps determine principles of justice. Communitarians, however, claim that models of such 'unencumbered' selves do not resonate with the self-images of actual people, who see their commitments to certain values and their place in a tradition not as something to be shed like an old coat when judged to be obsolete, but rather the stuff that makes them who they are. Attempts to justify principles of justice that abstract from that fact are simply wrongheaded, they claim (Sandel 1982: 15–65).

Now, this critique can be expressed as a metaphysical claim – namely that as a matter of ontological status, persons must be understood as 'constituted' by relations with others or be committed to values, without which they would cease to be who they are. Indeed, this is usually the manner in which such claims are made and how they are taken (Sandel 1982: 62, Gutmann 1985: 309). But this leaves the critique open to an easy reply, for as a general, ontological claim about the essential nature of persons, it is surely as controversial as the liberal view it is opposing. For it is not obviously incoherent to understand 'persons' as beings who can reflect upon and choose all of their values, at least in a piecemeal manner.[7] We certainly can point to many individuals that undergo radical change in their lives and remain (by all the usual accounts) the same person (Waldron 1992: 762, cf. Kymlicka 1995: 85).

But the communitarian challenge should better be understood as a contingent claim about social psychology, that *some* or *many* people – or all people *sometimes* – understand aspects of themselves as so deeply constitutive of their identity that they cannot be assumed to be able to question those aspects at all. This assumption, then, conflicts with their own understanding of themselves and so should not be used as a basis for political principles. That is, if some or many of us cannot realistically stand back from some of our most basic, self-defining commitments, then political principles justified in a manner that assumes we can, and which generates policy priorities that assume we have a highest order interest to do so, do not neutrally represent all of our self-perceptions and interests. Such a contingent, social-psychological basis for an alternative conception of the self is sufficient to support the view that liberalism merely represents a parochial standpoint rather than the neutral framework fairly representative of all of people that it has claimed to be.

So according to the communitarian picture of moral personality, reflection on values and connections takes place, but often as a matter of self-*discovery* rather than self-*creation*. On this view, people do not (or do not always) review their commitments and connections in order to validate or to reject them; rather, they look into themselves and at their relations with surrounding others to try to better understand what constitutes their own identity, what connections lie at the root of their moral being and provide the basis of their judgments. The alternative liberal model would understand these reflections as a process of decision and choice: should I remain a Catholic or consider another faith? Should I reject the values of my culture? Do I really connect with my community any more? On the communitarian view, however, such questions cannot reasonably be asked in that manner but would take the form: '*As a Catholic*, do I continue to feel as deeply about my faith? Is my culture or community going in the right direction?' One discovers aspects of oneself and perhaps questions aspects of the larger movements and value systems of which one is a part, but one does not ask whether or not to *be* a part of them (MacIntyre 1984: 220).

Liberal theorists reply, however, that this is not a realistic general picture of moral personality, even taken as a psychological claim. They insist, for example, that '[n]o matter how deeply implicated we find ourselves in a social practice or tradition, we feel capable of questioning whether the practice is a valuable one – a questioning which isn't meaningful on [the communitarian] account (how can it *not* be valuable for me since the good for me just *is* coming to a greater self-awareness of those attachments and practices I find myself in?).' (Kymlicka 1989: 54) Granting the obvious fact that we cannot choose or reflect upon all our commitments at once, nor did we create such commitments and connections out of nothing, it is nevertheless always possible, liberal theorists claim, to subject those commitments to piecemeal review and to reject them if we judge them inadequate. And more importantly, it is a fundamental *interest* of all human beings to have the capacity to undertake such review, to live in institutional settings (systems of law) that allow such reflection, and be able to communicate with and move freely about networks of others as part of this process of questioning and review (cf. Macedo 1990, Galston 1991).[8]

But this is to miss the most powerful aspect of the communitarian challenge. For such critics of liberalism need not claim, as a general thesis of human psychology, that *all* deep commitments are unrevisable in this way or that all people experience such self-constituting connections. All that needs to be claimed is that for a significant number of people, or for most of us relative to some of our connections, such revision is not psychologically possible; and hence seeing the power to engage in such reflective revision as the fundamental interest of all citizens misrepresents the values of many segments of the population (Christman 2001).

So the liberal ideal of the autonomous self seems to presuppose powers of self-revision not experienced as possible or valuable by some (or all of us some of the time). This raises the question, though, that if autonomy is both what is presupposed and protected by liberal principles, what do we mean by 'autonomy' here: does it require that we have the power to reflect upon and revise under any circumstance our connections and commitments? If so, the communitarian challenge remains in play. The challenge for liberalism will be to develop an altered conception of autonomy – one which captures the fundamental commitments of the liberal approach to justice, but which does not imply Herculean powers of self-alteration of the sort communitarians object to. We will return to this question later in the discussion.

The social self and value commitments

These controversies can be approached from a slightly different angle. What is really at stake in these debates over the psychology of identity concerns whether the liberal model of the autonomous self paints an acceptable picture of people's motivations, and hence their basic interests. For the basic tenets of liberalism imply that any value a person has, including ones that are seen as the basis of moral obligation, is valid because (in part at least) it was *judged acceptable* to her. That is, liberalism rejects the strong perfectionist claim discussed in the last chapter that values can be valid for a person independent of that person's choice or reasoned embrace of those values. Communitarians often counter, however, that many values hold for people quite irrespective of the individual's own decisions about their status; they *impose* themselves upon the person, as it were, and organize her life externally. Of course, the person may recognize the importance of the value, but her seeing it as such is not a constitutive condition of its validity.

Consider how such things as a relationship with another person, a family member, an ethnic heritage, or a religion have value for a person. It is often not that one looks around, considers the options and *chooses* any of these things. Rather one *finds oneself* in the midst of them and comes to see their virtues, thereby discovering aspects of the (already established) situation that were in no way chosen, but which have come to define one's outlook and value orientation (see, for example, Bell 1993: 5–6). Liberals, of course, acknowledge this, but insist that the ability to reflectively embrace or reject these commitments is nevertheless possible and desirable for the person, and this partially constitutes the basis of the value in question. But communitarians reply that the source of the value of these connections, traditions, and belief systems is decidedly not the choice of the person involved; rather it is the intrinsic nature of the thing itself; reflection merely reveals this to the person.

In addition, communitarians point out the cost of designing social institutions in a way that (wrongly, they say) puts primary value on the powers of reflective choice. Some traditions, for example, see faith as a *virtue* and view doubt and questioning of one's commitments as a moral failing. One need not endorse this view of commitment oneself to see it functioning in the psychological make up of some of us and to argue that liberalism fails to reach its ideal of neutral regard for all personal value systems by not acknowledging this. For as long as such groups exist and are not clearly irrational or deluded, then a liberal emphasis on mobility, choice, and review of all value commitments will not express basic respect for this orientation, and hence will fall short of this neutrality.

These criticisms once again highlight the liberal commitment to what has been called 'constructivism' in moral theory (Rawls 1999a: 303–58). That is, the validity of values on the liberal view is partially secured by the fact that individuals themselves rationally grasp or embrace the value in question; things are worthwhile for a person only if they are 'endorsed' by her (R. Dworkin 2000: 217–18). What communitarians are claiming is that the ground of values can reside completely in the existence and flourishing of traditional practices which partially constitute the entire value orientation of the person. Someone's community can, they say, be the source of what is good for a person independent of her choosing to embrace or endorse that value.

This brings up what some have described as the vacuousness of the liberal conception of human freedom, that liberal philosophy values freedom (or autonomy) not because of what it allows the person to accomplish – finding true values grounded in factors external to her – but for its own sake, as a formal condition of choice (Taylor 1985). But individuals as such cannot meaningfully be said to value freedom of choice *fundamentally*; for that is merely valuing the means to, or on some views a component of, what is truly valuable – the object of such choice. When a person pursues a project, embraces a value system, or embarks on a life path, she does not do so simply as a way of valuing the capacity to choose freely *per se*, rather she is guided by the aims of the project (value system, life path, etc.), the value of which informs and structures decisions. It is simply paradoxical to claim ultimate value for a capacity. Capacities are, by definition, capacities *for* something.

Of course, liberals can reply that states shaped by liberal justice can certainly advance people's values indirectly, through the creation of settings and spaces that people can use to achieve their aims themselves (Kymlicka 1990: 209–10). But the paradox remains: liberal justice sees as a first priority the protection of what for citizens themselves is merely a means to what is truly valuable, the freedom to pursue worthwhile goals but not the goals themselves. As we saw in the last chapter when discussing perfectionism, liberalism seems to entail the unsettling view that state action is justified with reference to justice or the right, while the motives of those living under those policies are aimed toward the pursuit of the good. And when there exists a shared conception of such goods that people use to orient their own pursuits, it is problematic to claim that the state should nevertheless avoid getting involved in promoting that good for fear of violating its basic neutrality.

A similar point arises concerning human motivation and the connection between individual value commitment and political obligation. For according to liberalism, people's reasons to conform to the principles of justice cannot involve any particular conception of the value of social life (since they cannot involve any particular conception of the good generally). Justice is prior to the good in that the rules of just social relations do not rest upon or presuppose any particular set of motivations or value systems on the part of those living under them. This implies, then, that citizens' motivations to conform to social justice principles do not involve any shared values or conception of the good life. Political legitimacy of state institutions is established merely in so far as such institutions are regarded as just (as we saw in Chapter 2).

But communitarians (and others) argue that public support of such institutions, specifically when they require day-to-day sacrifices of one's own narrow self-interest for the sake of social programs required by justice, will be lacking unless the guiding principles of such institutions are grounded in a conception of value citizens actually hold. When principles of justice demand personal sacrifices on some people's part such as taxation to reduce inequalities or provide welfare benefits to the poor, or to support educational programs to ensure equality of opportunity, and the like, they will lack the requisite citizen support unless they are seen to advance shared conceptions of the good (Taylor 1985: 248–88, Sandel 1982: 66–103). Communitarians argue that liberal principles rest on such an individually oriented conception of political obligation that this measure of social solidarity and communal support will always be lacking.

In this way, communitarians claim that liberal individualism is, or will eventually be, self-defeating, unable to maintain itself as a viable political order over time. But liberals have a reply: they can argue that such civic unity can indeed be part of the goals of a liberal state, just as such states are not enjoined from promoting *generally shared* conceptions of the good as long as doing so does not take priority over ensuring justice. However, the promotion of social unity in this way, they argue, should not be accomplished by *political* means, not by the coercive power of the state (Kymlicka 1989: 81–95, 1990: 223). They argue that only informal, voluntary social organizations such as civic groups, religious congregations, and the like can shape communal ties in a way that fosters required degrees of social connectedness, but do not use the state's police power in doing so.

But this reply may not adequately respond to the challenge raised here. On the one hand, to insist that the promotion of civic unity and shared endeavors should be a non-political, and so in a way 'private,' activity is to underestimate the necessity of these practices and connections for people's pursuit of their values. For in an area where such ties are either not established or disintegrate, the effectiveness of the principles of justice to that degree breaks down. (Recall that the communitarian argument pointed to the need for shared civic identity focused on the promotion of community values for the stability that enforcing rules of justice requires.) It then becomes a matter of justice, not merely expediency, to foster the social cohesion necessary for principles of right to have effect. Moreover, the line between public and private here is an exceptionally blurry one, as state power is used in many ways to indirectly foster the collective activity of groups and the general public which, in turn, creates this kind of civic feeling. Public parks, city plazas, public television and radio, monuments and museums, neighborhood murals, meetings spaces, and countless other supplementary resources are generally provided by political institutions (that is, paid for by public money) and are essential for the successful carrying out of the collective activity we are considering. Political acts – legislative provisions and the use of public funding – are necessary to support these communal actions; without such state action, this activity would almost certainly devolve (a tendency we will say more about in a moment), so in so far as they are necessary to support just institutions, then state action (direct or indirect) is necessary for their existence. The good of supporting these sorts of group activities in support of common aims goes hand in hand with enforcing justice, rather than occupying a lower priority in the ordering of political provisions.

In further criticizing liberal presuppositions about values, communitarians stress the way in which many values cannot even be *understood* as attached to individuals or individual interests alone. That is, some values are essentially social, in that they are meaningful only as part of a collective activity and communal pursuit. The interests they express, then, are not individual interests, but the interests of groups (as such). Consider public monuments and patriotic symbols. Whatever value such objects have, it is a value contingent upon a *collective* participation in their meaning. Indeed, when such symbols are controversial, it is precisely because of the intended collective expression. In recent debates over the use of Confederate symbols in the flags of some southern US states, for instance, the issue was controversial just *because* such symbols ostensibly expressed common values, and many in the population felt alienated from such symbols for this very reason, specifically the implicit association between such iconography and the legacy of slavery. Such a controversy would never arise if these symbols were merely meant to express the values of some self-selected individuals acting on their own. Therefore, in so far as liberalism is built upon the interests of individuals *per se* – interests relating to autonomy in particular – then such theories denigrate those values that cannot be expressed in individualist terms.

But this brings us back to the question of what exactly we mean by 'autonomy' in the liberal pantheon of basic political values. Does the autonomy that liberalism presupposes and promotes, and in reference to which it defines basic human interests, require that all values are individually defined, that detached reflection on values and commitments is always possible or desirable, or that people must view their own powers to reflect on values as more basic than the pursuit of the values themselves? While we cannot spell out a full view of such a concept here, we have been alluding to the idea that autonomy merely requires that a person have the capacity to rationally reflect upon single aspects of the self in a piecemeal fashion, and that such reflection need not have actually taken place in each instance for the person to be autonomous, but merely that it be possible. Autonomy then requires that, were a person to review any particular commitment, personal trait, or aspect of her value orientation, she would not reject or repudiate that factor. This does not imply that these elements of her existence are individually defined or the product of her own prior choices, merely that she would not feel deeply alienated from them were she to reflect.

Seeing liberal autonomy in terms of such hypothetical self-reflection takes the sting out of examples of unreflective, but fulfilling lives presented by communitarians. For a person to live a good life but not be autonomous in the manner here proposed, she would have to be pursuing values that she not only has not reflected upon, but which she would *repudiate or reject were she to do so*. But it is hard to see why we should accept a view that claims that social structures which induce subjects to maintain ties that they would reject upon reflection ought to be protected. Liberals could plausibly argue that social conditions that induce people to live within such value systems amount to a kind of oppression.

Liberalism and the breakdown of communities

One line of critique communitarians have mounted that does not directly come down to the contested models of moral psychology we have been discussing concerns the *effects* of liberal justice on the social life of communities living under it. In various ways, critics of liberalism have claimed that the priority placed on justice, conceived in terms of individual rights to autonomy, have tended to *produce* patterns of social existence that tend to erode crucial elements of a fulfilling life, where the factors that people themselves would name as essential to a successful and happy life are made more difficult to maintain. Those factors include such things as long-term family ties, stable communities, active social and civic life, long-standing connections with neighbors and (geographically proximate) extended family, and the like. But the patterns of existence that result from the emphasis on individual rights prized in liberalism involve mobility, change, review of connectedness, rejection of problematic relationships, openness to alternative lifestyles, and so on. These critics point out, not that these latter tendencies are somehow intrinsically evil, but that according to what people themselves say about what they want in life, the patterns listed in the second group make impossible the enjoyment of the factors in the first, and hence make more difficult the very fulfillment that liberal justice was meant to allow (Bellah et al. 1985, Putnam 2000).

The charge raised here is more a question of sociology rather than philosophy.[9] It concerns the social patterns that tend to arise when legal, political, and civic emphasis is placed on the rights of autonomy rather than the good of connectedness. This pattern can be seen in the very language of liberal principle, for what liberal justice protects as a first priority is liberty, specifically the freedom to review and reject any conditions or networks one finds oneself in, and to move to other forms of social life that seem more in keeping with one's values. The *right to exit* is foremost in the pantheon of liberal privileges (Kymlicka 1995: 37). The challenge being discussed here does not denigrate the importance of those freedoms – clearly, being denied the right to exit from stifling relations is the very definition of oppression – but it claims that putting the primary emphasis on such rights and building social and legal institutions that enshrine this emphasis has definite costs. These costs are ones that liberal philosophy not only underestimates, but in some of its guises cannot even acknowledge.

To be more specific, liberalism insists that the right to reflectively review all value commitments and personal ties is fundamental to a just society. Hence, social institutions are constructed so that such rights are given first priority. This has produced a society in which *exercising* such rights has naturally come to be prized. But reviewing and rejecting commitments whenever they seem unsatisfying produces a life that is devoid of the very constituents of a fulfilling existence (at least for many), the enjoyment of long-standing and self-justifying ties to others, characterized by loyalty, reliability, unquestioned support, and stability. In short, liberal politics produces liberal culture, which, in turn, produces hyper-mobile, individualized populations who change their lives often, concentrate on the individual self-fulfillment they enjoy at various stages in their lives, and forget the very things that (they will come to realize) make life worth living. (I speak here in terms of voluntary choice, but critics point out that the very opportunities afforded to people in liberal cultures, especially concerning professional aspirations and employment prospects, are strongly geared toward *inducing* these lifestyle patterns.)

This line of critique, however, relies on the precarious claim that protection of liberal rights as a basic component of justice *inevitably* leads to the social pattern of atomistic, isolated lives described here. Certainly, there is evidence (in the US for instance) that certain sorts of communities have eroded, but it is not clear that new types of communal ties may develop in different forms (through the Internet for example) or that people may insist on reversing this individualist trend through non-political means (see Kymlicka 1995: 88–89). More importantly, the connection between liberal values and large-scale social trends certainly has much to do with commercial and economic factors associated with global capitalism, factors which reward labor mobilization, re-orientation of professions, and consumer-oriented values. Globalization of economic production and the consequent decentralization of productive processes (along with the increased centralization of economic power) is likely to bear a large share of the responsibility for the breakdown of communities and the hyper-mobility of individuals. And while liberal principles bear a traditional connection with private property and free market capitalism, we saw in the last chapter that there is by no means a necessary connection between them. So unless the case can be made that the priority of right and the value of the autonomous person has some inherent connection to the patterns of globalized capitalism that have put such pressure on communities, this line of criticism will remain incomplete. (Though we will further consider arguments that insist that consideration of material and economic forces should be fundamental to political philosophy in Chapter 7 below.)

Communitarianism as a positive alternative to liberalism

Most of the writing in the communitarian vein is critical, attempting to show that various aspects and presuppositions of liberal theory are problematic, in particular the conception of the autonomous person at its roots. Far less has been said about communitarianism as a positive doctrine, one specific enough to mark its contrasts with liberalism as well as guide social policy (for critical discussion see Kymlicka 1990:

230–32). But we can construct in broad outlines the communitarian approach to political life and mention some of the responses to it that liberal defenders may voice. This can be added to our consideration of conservatism discussed earlier which, as should be clear in the end, is a variation of communitarianism.

A central aspect of the positive program of communitarianism concerns the ways that communities should govern themselves, in particular the manner that collective deliberation operates and the grounds upon which it is justified. On the liberal view, collective deliberation is necessary to establish and maintain legitimacy of the authority structure of the state (as we saw in Chapters 2 and 4). On a communitarian view, deliberation is not the source of legitimacy of the values of the community, but a means of discovering these values. Public discussion and deliberation is an activity that aims at revealing the implicit shared meanings that (already) constitute the moral frameworks of citizens (Bell 1993: 126–27). Engaging in such activity, directly or through representatives, manifests the freedom of citizens as social beings and it requires (according to some communitarians) a host of virtues and skills that society must instill in its members through robust civic education (Sandel 1996: 126–27).

There are many variations of this picture and several details in its structure that must be put to the side here. The fundamental point is that mechanisms of collective choice are needed in order to find, interpret, and prioritize the values that define the community. Those values comprise 'the good' for that community, so the principal difference between this view and liberalism is a reversal of the priority of right; for communitarians, the purpose of collective decision making is to identify the common good and consider ways to best promote it (Sandel, 1982: x, 1996: 26–27). In this light, democracy embodies the ideals of classical 'civic republicanism' of the ancient world, where participation in the collective self-government of one's society in pursuit of the common good was a manifestation of virtue and freedom (Sandel, 1996; for a contrasting understanding of republicanism, see Pettit 1997).

A quick side note about the idea of 'the common good.' This can be understood, to one degree or another, objectively or relativistically, as we mentioned earlier.[10] The common good for a people can mean the aggregated desires of that population – the values they accept for themselves at a time. This is a highly relativistic and, at the collective level, subjectivist understanding of the values underlying political life. But communitarians need not be subjectivist in this way; they can claim rather that the good for a population is, objectively, what is best for them given various background facts about their society and its history and the social nature of its people. This is one way to understand Rousseau's idea of the General Will, for example (Rousseau 1760/1987; for discussion see Bell 1993: 55–89). This is relativistic but not subjectivist, and this will be the understanding of the communitarian vision we will assume here.

But two questions arise concerning communities and democracy that raise serious issues about the communitarian vision. One involves the procedure for such collective deliberation and the other concerns its ultimate justification. First, what guarantee is there, if any, that the methods of collective discovery of the common good for a community will actually involve all of the citizens and do so in a relatively egalitarian manner. Certainly there are countless examples of closely knit communities that come to decisions by way of strictly hierarchical procedures, ones that systematically exclude segments of the population and thereby relegate them to secondary status (the Catholic Church is one example). We saw above how the conservative strand of this sort of thinking embraces this implication, and this was grounds for criticism of it. But must communitarians generally endorse whatever collective process a particular community uses to discover and interpret its values, no matter how exclusionary, unequal, and oppressive it turns out to be?

The second question flows from this one: if the ultimate aim of collective deliberation on the communitarian view is the discovery of shared meanings (the common good for that population), is there any vantage point to criticize those values themselves, including the values implicit in the traditional procedures the society uses to make decisions? We certainly know of many communities who shared what we would judge to be despotic and unjust values (the murderous racism of the antebellum south, the horrible anti-semitism of Nazi Germany, and the like). Do communitarians have the resources to critically appraise those cohesive communities that are constructed on the basis of oppressive values (see Bell 1993: 74–78)? Or are communitarian theorists committed to the processes of equal participation, basic rights, and fair procedures that liberalism enshrines as part of any community's process of collective choice that is worthy of support? If so, such theories are not based unqualifiedly on the value of a search for the good prior to protection of rights, but rather on an endorsement of fair and just social relations in a common process of searching for shared values. The distance this second position stands from liberalism, then, diminishes to a vanishing point.

A common line of argument in communitarian thinking is that there exists no Archimedean point from which a person or a society can judge the good, no position behind a veil of ignorance which defines our true nature. Societies as well as individuals always judge values from a position 'always already' (in the Heideggerian phrase) ensconced in a thick network of background values and shared norms. For this reason, they argue, collective choice in a society is always a process of interpreting and revealing those shared ideals (Bell 1993: 67). But it is one thing to point out that all judgements are set against a backdrop of unspoken value assumptions, taken for granted but operative in shaping the substance of what is in fact decided consciously, but it is another to say that such factors *justify* the values they shape. Were we to turn our attention to the factors that lead us to consider a question a certain way or orient our thinking, and we judge such a factor (and its effect on us) *negatively*, would we still have to say that, nevertheless, 'that's just the way things are around here and we'll have to accept it'? No, we would say that any factor relevant to a decision *were it to be reviewed* must be subject to general endorsement or embrace by those shaped by it for such a factor not to be labeled oppressive. This is the lesson of the revised conception of autonomy suggested above: it is not that countless factors beyond our conscious awareness don't shape our thinking, it is rather that all such elements are subject to at least hypothetical review according to (other) accepted standards of value.

So the communitarian alternative to liberalism turns on the claim that consideration of the good for a person or a community takes precedence over the specification of what is just for her or them. But liberals reply that no ideal of the good is self-justifying, certainly not independently of collective human judgement about its merits; and they go on to insist that part of what grounds values is precisely this human judgement about them. At least this is true for what we have called 'constructivist' liberals, those who insist that values are grounded in part by human reflection and judgment.[11]

Communitarians, in rejecting this idea, take one of two positions, one pointing to the conservatism discussed earlier and the other to the perfectionism we considered in Chapter 4. On the one hand, they may claim that the ultimate ground of values for a community, after these are duly discovered and interpreted, is the fact that such values form and undergird the traditional practices of that society – they simply, though at a deep level, are what make up the historical structure of a given society and are justified because that is what forms the individual consciousness of the citizens of that community (Bell 1993: 55–89). On the other hand, communitarians can step beyond this position and claim that the 'common good' for a society is grounded in what can be seen as objective values, ideals that are valid not merely because that society always has accepted them as such, but rather because of the 'moral worth or intrinsic good' of the ends themselves (Sandel 1982: xi). This second position is perfectionist (and many may claim that it is thereby no longer identifiably communitarian) and hence subject to the analysis we gave earlier of that view.

One final issue must be raised in the consideration of the communitarian alternative to liberalism, an issue that will occupy much of our thought (in different form) in the next section: just how should we identify our 'community'? Most of us live in highly mobile and multi-layered social worlds, with connections to our family, local community, our race and its heritage, collections of people organized around a common goal, groups defined by sexual orientation, and countless other overlapping collectivities. Communitarians tend to focus on civic groupings, small groups of physically located individuals engaging in common practices and living under shared norms. But if the linchpin of social groupings is the set of factors that 'constitute' our value orientation and consciousness, clearly, the influence of this local group may well pale in comparison to the connections we feel with other, physically dispersed people and causes. At times being Jewish may mean more to a person than being a member of a local school district, while at others the reverse may be true. Communitarian thinking becomes vague and unhelpful when trying to answer the question of how to define the 'community' about which they theorize. And for this and related reasons, critics have been quick to point out the problem of 'scale' in the communitarian program: how could their views ever be applied to the large complex and multicultural populations that make up even the relatively smaller political units that operate in modern society (for discussion see Kymlicka 1989: 57–58 and Sandel 1996: 338–49)?

Liberalism, freedom, and culture

The insight of communitarianism is that the pursuit of human goods and a fulfilled life is clearly not an individual matter, but takes place and depends on a network of social relations in which the person is deeply entwined. Culture refers to that array of practices, rituals, language, and symbolic structures that constitute meaningful pursuits for many people. The conception of value that structures and guides a life is often made meaningful by its place in a historically grounded network of symbolic understanding. One's identity, in fact, is often constituted by relations with such cultures (at least in the case of what Kymlicka calls 'societal cultures' – see Kymlicka 1995: 75, and Margalit and Raz 1990).

The question that arises for traditional liberalism, then, is whether the value it places on individual freedom (autonomy) – and the rights and privileges considered basic to that freedom – is compatible with the protection of cultures and cultural practices which, for many, are essential to the enjoyment of that very freedom. People value freedom because it makes possible the pursuit of goals and activities whose meaning depends on a network of cultural practices and traditions; the continued existence of such cultural practices depends on social support (or at least special exemptions from general social rules that typically do take account of culture). The question, then, is whether the liberal commitment to the priority of the right prohibits the protection of specific cultures for fear of violating neutrality and equal respect for autonomy. This question has been at the center of a large and important literature on the relation between liberalism (in particular its conception of autonomy) and multicultural societies (Kymlicka 1995, Tamir 1993, Sterba 2001: 77–104).

Autonomy cannot simply mean being left to oneself, for self-government implies being moved by forces that one in some way embraces (or does not stringently resist), and lacking a supportive environment with which one minimally identifies would not count as being so moved. Imagine, for example, being kidnapped and dropped in the middle of a completely foreign culture, where the social practices, rituals, symbolic expressions, religious and general way of life was totally alien. Even if all one's basic, individual rights were protected – speech, association, religious practices – one would certainly not feel that one was being moved by forces one could embrace. The feeling of alienation and dislocation would be acute. This illustrates the deep connection between being a truly self-governing agent and being able to pursue values – especially collectively constituted and culturally grounded values – that are meaningful. Cultures give meaning to values one pursues (Kymlicka 1995: 75).

Liberal theorists have attempted to respond to this by adapting their conceptions of autonomy to take into account the importance of culture to self-identity (Kymlicka 1995, Raz 1986, Tamir 1993). For two related reasons, protection of (some) cultures is essential for the exercise of the autonomy basic to liberalism. The first is that a wide array of diverse cultural practices in modern societies provides a rich panoply of value options from which to choose, and in so far as autonomy requires open choices, autonomy requires protection of diversity of culture (Raz 1986: 390–99). However, this alone would not be sufficient to support the continued existence of *one's own* culture (for it only requires that there be a diversity of cultures generally). The second reason for requiring the support of culture in virtue of its connection with autonomy picks up on our earlier point about meaningful options: continued existence of cultural practices is necessary for one's living one's life 'from the inside' (R. Dworkin 2000: 217–18, Kymlicka 1995: 86), pursuing values which one endorses and embraces. In some cases, the erosion or disappearance of ways of life would mean that one lost this ability.

Therefore, there is room in the liberal framework for supporting the continued existence of certain identity-defining cultures. Such policies would include perhaps (following Kymlicka 1995) granting special group-related rights concerning representation on governing bodies and special exemptions from general rules (such as allowing members of Native American tribes to possess and consume peyote as part of religious practices). The argument for any particular policy of this sort would be that it is necessary to ensure the health and survival of cultures that provide for their members deep and meaningful modes of living and value orientations.[12]

There are limitations in utilizing such arguments for the protection of cultures and communities, and some will not think that this sufficiently insulates liberalism from the community-based critiques being developed here. For example, the justifications of policies outlined just now ties the value of culture to particularly *liberal* values – individual autonomy – rather than the intrinsic value of the culture itself. Many members of, for example, religious societies do not regard the protection of their way of life as merely a part of a valuable autonomous life, but rather something required by morality itself, as a directive from God perhaps.

But this shows that liberal theory must also pay attention to its own commitment to value pluralism (and constructivism), as discussed earlier. No particular cultural practice or value system can be given priority in the justification of policies for a multicultural and pluralistic society without implying secondary social status for those who do not embrace that practice or system, according to liberalism. The commitment to the equal moral status of all persons would rule out any government policy that rested upon the promotion of contested values or particularized ways of life, even those which its followers considered the only true path to fulfillment. At the national level, at least, liberalism is, then, committed to respect for the autonomy of the individual even if, in doing so, it allows and supports the existence of sub-cultures that those individuals rely on for the autonomous pursuit of their values.

This points once again to the problem that liberal politics will always have with balancing a commitment to justice of a sort that can gain general legitimacy from the population with recognizing the wide diversity of moral outlooks found there. This is the issue to which we will now turn. In particular, we need to ask whether our approach to justice and politics has up to now been sufficiently sensitive to the varieties of human beings found in modern societies, to their differences and multiple self-identities.

Chapter summary

The focus of this chapter generally is the individualist conception of the autonomous person at the heart of liberalism. This conception was placed under scrutiny by considering alternative theoretical approaches that placed social *groups* at the center of analysis, in a way not reducible to individual members of these groups. We first considered 'conservatism' as a view put forward in contrast to liberalism at the theoretical level (and not merely as a set of policies that might be justified from within traditional liberalism). Conservatism amounts to a theoretical stance that posits the goal of political institutions to be the promotion of the general well-being of the citizens living under them. Such institutions succeed in this task when traditional values definitive of the way of life in a given community are protected from erosion or threat, both from within and externally. Values which define the health of such societies will surely include just social relations but, in contrast to liberalism, securing justice will not necessarily be the primary goal of political structures. Rather, such institutions should protect valued ways of life as interpreted by persons of prominence and experience, based on past success and established practice. We raised serious questions about this philosophy, however, in casting doubt on the presumption that prominent members of the society will be neutral judges in matters of interpreting the society's dominant values (as well as its history) and challenging the presumption that past practice is as reliable a guide to successful social forms as reform-minded speculations about alternative (more fully just) modes of social life.

Next, we considered communitarianism, a view motivated by a direct attack on the individualist conception of the person in liberalism. Communitarians argue that both in the model of the person assumed in the derivation of liberal principles and in the conception of the actual citizen whose interests such principles protect, liberal theory assumes a problematic view about the unencumbered nature of the self. Rather, persons should be understood as socially constituted and their interests defined with crucial reference to their place in ongoing, historically entrenched communities and social practices. We considered in some detail the communitarian critique of the liberal self and the conception of value based upon it, but concluded that in both cases the challenges raised turned on the precise conception of autonomy presupposed in liberal theory.

But communitarians also point out that independent of the theoretical commitments of liberalism, societies governed by liberal structures tend to experience the breakdown of communities and the atomization of social life. People in societies where basic individual rights (justice) are given priority over promoting socially defined projects and ideals tend to act as competitive individuals without constitutive social ties, producing an erosion of social practices, stable communities, and collective pursuits. The reply was given, though, that these patterns are as much the result of economic trends under an increasingly globalized capitalism, a system that has no intrinsic link with most versions of liberalism (and is positively resisted by egalitarian liberals). Finally, we examined communitarianism as a distinct program for political institutions and found that serious problems arose, in particular concerning the procedures that would be adopted for locating the defining characteristics of the community and interpreting its values, in so far as communitarianism was to remain distinct from the conservativism considered earlier, the perfectionism examined in Chapter 4, and liberalism itself.

But can liberals give a plausible account of how cultural and communal connections *are* fundamentally valuable for people? Are the critical challenges raised by communitarians still valid, namely that the liberal conception of the self remains overly individualistic and detached from cultural connections and communal ties? We considered attempts to show a close connection between the freedom that is protected in liberal societies and the survival of certain cultural practices. We concluded that, once again, the plausibility of these attempts turned on the flexibility of the conception of autonomy upon which they relied. If autonomy could be understood as the capacity to reflect upon and embrace those values which form one's character and motivate one's behavior, and the connection between such embracing of one's values and the existence of cultures is made, then the link between the protection of autonomy and the protection of cultural practices can be established. Though this does not relieve liberalism of the difficulty of balancing the need to articulate well-defined principles for just and stable political institutions and recognizing the broad pluralism of values and perspectives found among those governed by them.

Case to consider

The US Supreme Court, in *Wisconsin* v. *Yoder* ruled that the Old Order Amish of Wisconsin could gain an exemption from that state's mandatory education laws (which required attendance at formal schools up to the age of sixteen) based on the claim that such education conflicted with the traditional values of that religious community. Consider a parallel (hypothetical) case where a traditional religious group which lives in a certain self-contained geographical area has as part of its traditional value system a prohibition on the education of *girls and women* (and a corresponding social hierarchy of men over women). The males in this society make all of its decisions and the girls are trained to become homemakers, cooks, and domestic workers. The women do not protest this arrangement, at least not openly. The group claims that this arrangement is part of its traditional social structure dating back hundreds of years. They further claim that the values of obedience, religious devotion, protection of community ways, and strict adherence to established law define the good for them and orient their thinking about common values.

Consider that such a group now argues that its members should receive an exemption from mandatory education provisions in that they insist that girls should not receive higher than an eighth grade education (the group has no similar provision for boys). This, they argue, is crucial to their common way of life, and the forced public education of girls of their community will directly conflict with their pursuit of the common good, organized in this traditional way.

Can such an exemption be justified on communitarian grounds? Does the possibility of such a justification provide a counterintuitive implication for communitarian arguments? Independent of how the laws of the larger society should be enforced, how should we approach the question of what is just or good for this community? Does it make sense to say that since it is unjustly organized (if you think it is) it is not really pursuing its own good? If it is pursuing its good, given its traditional self-understanding, does it make sense to say that it is unjust?

Notes on further reading

Writers developing a conservative political philosophy of particular interest are Nisbet 1986, Oakshott 1991, and Kekes 1998 as well as the readings in Kirk 1982. (Those defending the new 'natural law' approach are listed in n. 5 above.) Communitarianism has been much discussed. The famous progenitors of the view (though not all of whom embrace the label) are: Taylor 1979 (though compare 1989a), Sandel 1982 (2nd edition, 1999, which has an important Preface and Epilogue commenting on recent developments in the controversy over liberalism and communitarianism), Walzer 1983, MacIntyre 1984, Bell 1993, and Sandel 1996. See also Walzer 1990, Mulhall and Swift 1992, and the essays in Avineri and de-Shalit 1992, Paul et al. 1996, and Etzioni

1999. The sociological critique of liberal individualism can be found in Bellah et al. 1985, and Putnam 2000.

The liberal commentary on the communitarian challenge is interestingly developed, for example, in Guttman 1985, Buchanan 1989, Taylor 1995 (especially chs 7 and 13), and Kymlicka 1989 and 1990: 47–134. For analysis of this debate that focuses especially on the concept of liberal individualism, see Crittenden 1992 and Pettit 1993. Liberal attempts to incorporate considerations of culture and multiculturalism can be found in Margalit and Raz 1990, Tamir 1993 and especially Kymlicka 1995 (for commentary on Kymlicka, see Kukathas 1997). For a recent overview of this literature, see Kymlicka 1998 (and the essays in that volume to which that article is an introduction).

CHAPTER 6

Race, gender, and the politics of identity

- Ideal theory and ongoing injustice
- Critical race theory
- Gender, sex, and the challenge of feminism
- Identity, injustice, and democracy
- Chapter summary
- Case to consider
- Notes on further reading

In this chapter and the next, we consider movements in political philosophy that demand not only new content in political theory, but radically new methods as well. And as with many other issues covered in this book, the topics examined here each deserve much fuller treatment than merely a portion of a chapter; indeed, many of these subjects plausibly call for a restructuring of political thought so as to make that subject a centerpiece of it, rather than simply one more topic on a list to be considered.

Here we examine the challenges to the liberal model of political theory raised by considerations of race and racism and gender and sexism. These foci of discussion represent some of the most trenchant and tumultuous challenges to traditional political philosophy (indeed, philosophy generally) that have been raised in recent decades. Together, these topics will also lead us to once again take a closer look at the liberal conception of the person and to reconsider the particular social, psychological, and metaphysical assumptions made there in constructing normative principles applicable to contemporary societies. First, we will consider a challenge to the general methodology of liberal theorizing motivated by considerations of race and gender (and other aspects of social identity), namely the claim that political theory must attend to historical and ongoing *injustice* in constructing theories of (among other things) justice. We then move to considerations of race and racism and then to feminism. Many themes touched upon here will return in slightly different form in the next chapter, and in fact many strands in the movements discussed here fall under the rubrics discussed there (Marxism and post-modernism).

Ideal theory and ongoing injustice

Western political theory in the Enlightenment tradition has generated principles and ideals typically meant to apply universally, and to any and all social situations. Such principles are justified without essential reference to the details of the social settings to which they are to apply. Since they are based on impartial reason and apply to humanity *as such*, there is allegedly no need to qualify their scope with reference to particularities of time and place. (Though of course all actual theories in this tradition betrayed this ideal and made highly specific qualifications about the kinds of places and people to which they were meant to apply.) In this same vein, a fundamental assumption behind such theories is that whatever *injustices* exist or have existed in the actual world, they are irrelevant to the nature and justification of political principles themselves.

However, the critiques to be discussed in the present chapter claim that ignoring the identifiable patterns of oppression and injustice that have plagued the worlds to which principles of justice apply not only artificially truncates the normative scope of those principles, but also distorts their meaning when they are put into practice. In areas where racial injustice has been rampant, for example, principles that are justified with no reference to that injustice as a background assumption in their justification will not adequately respond to that phenomenon when utilized in the world. In fact, the use of principles of this sort will predictably serve merely to protect the status quo and galvanize those ongoing injustices themselves.[1]

For example, the arguments we surveyed in Chapter 2 concerning the grounds of political authority focused on the social contract as a means of justifying political power in a society. But the historical conditions in the Western world under which political power *has been* solidified, and in which the social contract theories of Hobbes, Locke, Rousseau, and Kant were in fact developed, involved the systematic exclusion of large groups of people from equal citizenship and political power. Moreover, it has been argued by some that the very *point* of the social contract model was to justify the exclusion of those groups and to solidify the power of expansionist European states by assuming a conception, 'man,' which really referred only to Europeans (Mills 1997; cf. also Pateman 1988). Indeed, all of the major social contract theorists held views explicitly excluding the indigenous peoples of colonized areas and (for most theorists) women from the category of citizens (Eze 1997). In fact, the establishment of a general consensus that all segments of the (adult, sane) population should be afforded completely equal rights and opportunities is a *very* recent phenonemon.[2] It is argued, then, that the tradition of justifying state power by reference to a collective contract cannot be properly understood outside of the historical context in which those theories were developed, a context that has included the violent expansion of European power at the expense of indigenous peoples and the fervent oppression of certain members of those societies themselves.

But merely because the particular philosophers who developed social contract theory held racist and sexist views does not imply that social contract theory itself (or more generally, liberal theories of justice) do so. For such theories are simply *silent* about the particularities of identity which define the agents to which they apply, implying that the rights and obligations specified in them apply equally to *all* persons regardless of race, gender, sexual orientation, physical ability, and the like. But do they succeed in this implied universality? Does failure to mention particular aspects of identity in specifying those who fall under the theory imply that the view applies to all people *neutrally*? It depends. Such theories would indeed imply the exclusion of certain groups if the experience and interests of the members of those groups are not captured adequately by the assumptions behind the theories' principles. In the case of race, for example, it could be claimed that members of different races have fundamentally different outlooks and characteristics that cannot be reduced to a single, neutral, set of dispositions, interests, and personal traits. To make no mention of racial difference is to adopt, unconsciously perhaps, a white male perspective as the norm.

But to claim that there are inherent differences in interests and characteristics among the races seems highly contentious, even racist, a question we will take up below. Can the claim that seemingly neutral theories actually exclude members of minorities (say) be sustained without relying on such 'essentialist' claims? It can if what is being asserted is that certain groups carry with them the experience and history of systematic oppression, even attempted annihilation, that fundamentally frames their interests and perspective in social interaction, not as a matter of 'natural essence' but merely as a consequence of social facts. Therefore, if political principles based on 'neutral' models of personhood posit basic interests that ignore such experiences and interests, then these models do indeed represent a surreptitiously biased theoretical perspective. What must be examined in considering this line of critique are the various ways in which the experience of oppression shapes people's fundamental interests, and hence is glossed over in the allegedly impartial theoretical perspectives of dominant views.

Relatedly, theories of justice tend to specify conceptual conditions of what a society (generically described) would look like were it completely just. But such theories include no provisions, generally, concerning how to make a *non*-ideal (unjust) society live up to or adopt those conditions. The charge being examined here is that applying ideal principles to non-ideal circumstances will imply, for the most part, simply ignoring those injustices and their effects.

It is as if we were trying to decide the fairest rules for a footrace while ignoring the fact that when the competition begins, half the participants will already be twenty yards behind. Our rules will likely contain stipulations that all runners must be even at the starting line, but will say nothing about how we must *repair* the situation where they are not. Principles of justice are phrased as the obligation to *respect* the freedom and equality of citizens, not typically how to *institute* freedom and equality when not in evidence.

As we saw in Rawls's theory of justice (in its initial version especially), the ideal of impartiality in the derivation of political principles was modeled with the use of an original position where particular facts about one's identity and place in society were barred from view. The only facts about society that one could assume in deriving such impartial principles were those that are 'uncontroversial' and widely shared (Rawls 1971: 119). Moreover, Rawls claimed that theories of justice were best seen as 'strict compliance theories,' where it could be assumed that the well ordered society to which they were to apply was characterized by general compliance with the principles (ibid.: 7–8, 215–16). This implies, then, that the derivation of principles of justice does not include reference to past or ongoing injustices evident in the societies to which they will apply.

But, of course, societies in the modern world are marked by horrendous patterns of injustice and oppression (patterns which only the most eccentric historian or social observer would deny). What ways, then, might applying such ideally derived and 'impartial' principles ignore or distort the interests of those victims of injustice that live in the societies governed by those principles? One example might be the particular basic liberties that would be chosen as fundamental to the pursuit of a life plan. (Recall that for Rawls, the first principle of justice is that equal basic liberties must be protected, though he left it somewhat open what *particular* liberties will be considered basic in a given society.) If agents in the original position knew that racial discrimination and prejudice was rampant in the society they were considering principles for (based perhaps on a history of colonial policies or slavery), something like 'freedom from racial discrimination' may well be among those basic freedoms or clearly derivable from them. Without that assumption, freedoms of the sort that protect those untouched by such discrimination and injustice (such as freedom of religion, association, and speech) may get priority. What an impartial appraisal of the basic interests of those who populate our society will produce will vary depending on what is assumed about general patterns of behavior in that society (Mills 1997: 17).

This line of critique gains more power when the pattern of injustice in a society has produced inequalities – in wealth, status, education, and so on – which extend past the period when overt discrimination remains in practice or in some way exists independent of it. In such societies, principles of equal status which guarantee the same political and social rights for all (against discrimination for example) will not contain provisions which directly address the inequalities that have resulted from past discrimination. Of course, egalitarian liberalism, of the sort discussed in Chapter 3, would imply that any inequalities of wealth or status which do not result from voluntary choices of the less favored should be corrected. But those principles do not pick out any particular inequalities as deserving of special attention.[3]

A similar point has been pressed about liberal theory from a feminist point of view, where it is argued that facts about social structures, such as the typical roles men and women play in raising children and living in families, are problematically ignored in liberal theories of justice. It is pointed out that the traditional family structure manifests identifiable injustice itself, where unequal burdens for household labor and child care (which results in disparate abilities to live independently and pursue other professional pursuits) are borne by women (Okin 1989). In so far, then, that principles of justice make no mention of such patterns of inequality in actual social practices, they fail to properly evaluate the social situations to which they are meant to apply.

Also, how do the shape and meaning of the principles of justice we derive change if it is acknowledged that the society in question is marked by pervasive discrimination at the informal, social, and 'private' level? In other words, does the society count as well ordered or just if all formal and public laws against discrimination are obeyed, but people systematically and predictably treat certain classes of people with disdain, ridicule, and derision in every other aspect of social relations? Imagine that in decisions about with whom to socialize, with whom to become intimate, whom to go to extra efforts to encourage and help in their endeavors, and countless other aspects of civil society not explicitly covered by laws against unequal treatment, members of the dominant group in the society uniformly ignore, avoid, deride, or shun those outside of that group. Do we describe such a society as 'just' when all of the public rules of behavior are obeyed but in every other aspect of life people are treated unequally? (Cf. Cochran 1999: 59–61, and L. Thomas 1999.)

Finally, attention to ongoing practices of injustice and discrimination (and inequalities of wealth and status that correspond to such practices) raise methodological questions about the degree to which political philosophy must remain a purely normative enterprise, and the degree to which normative theorizing can be fully distinguished from descriptive and interpretive theory. An alternative view, one motivated by sensitivity to ongoing struggles for justice, would combine normative theorizing with attempts to understand the complex dynamics of social interaction and institutional structure that make up modern social life. Such a descriptive and interpretive enterprise would take place at a higher level of abstraction than the 'positive' social science disciplines of economics, political science, sociology, and history (at least in their most purely explanatory forms), but it would include attempts to interpret the mechanisms of political life as well as provide abstract principles in order to evaluate them (Mills 2000: 445; Hampton 1997: xiii–xv). Such a model for political philosophy would then place considerations of racism, sexism, discrimination, and the like at center stage, integrating attempts at gaining a deeper understanding of these phenomena with deriving principles used to evaluate them. Analysis of how injustice occurs would be mixed inextricably with accounts of what injustice means.

Critical race theory

What is racism, what is race?[4]

Racism and ethnic prejudice is a ubiquitous, some would say fundamental, aspect of the modern world (Outlaw 1999: 58–64). The legacy of colonial expansion by European powers, the violent subjugation of indigenous peoples, the forced importation of slaves to the Americas (especially to the United States), and the influx of post-colonial people into 'first' world countries, have made for a pattern of inequality and discrimination that pervades Western society. Ongoing prejudice, discrimination, social exclusion, and inequality of opportunity mark everyday life in modern societies. These behaviors and conditions are fueled by, and oriented around, racial classification and hierarchies.

Racism is a set of beliefs, dispositions, and behavioral tendencies that express or are motivated by negative attitudes toward the members of certain groups, called races, who are 'marked' (physically) as different. To be racist, therefore, is to act toward people in ways predicated on their (and one's own) race. Such actions need not be conscious or intended as racist – they may well merely reflect an unexamined disposition that a person rarely stops to consider. Of course racism is often overt and intentional: countless numbers of those in the majority population espouse specific derogatory attitudes toward minority races, attitudes that issue in action. So racism can be either overt and conscious or subtle and unreflective; but in all cases, actions that are motivated by negative attitudes toward people because of their race qualify for this label.[5]

But despite the ubiquity of these attitudes, actually defining 'race' turns out to be rather difficult (and controversial), since there is no generally accepted scientific or biological classification of people according to race that we can turn to for an answer. The genetic differences between, say, a white American and a black American are relatively minuscule and not significantly larger than the average genetic difference between any two people chosen at random. There is no 'racial gene' that marks off people of different racial categories (Appiah and Gutmann 1996: 68, 69 n. 53).

Though, clearly, race is a socially, politically (and personally!) important category. We can say generally that races are those groupings of human beings into categories specified with reference to morphology and genetics, that typically (these days) include such groups as 'white,' 'black,' 'Asian,' and so on.[6] Such bodily characteristics – the lightness or darkness of skin, the texture and curliness of hair, facial features, and the like – have been used to differentiate people of different races, though it is impossible to specify precisely what the physical markers of race are that capture all (and only) candidates of a particular group. Genetic heritage is also used as a reference point: if both one's parents are of a specific race then one is also. But this just moves the question back a generation (what determined the race of one's parents?), and also, this merely amplifies the arbitrariness of racial classification since one can always go back far enough to find ancestors who come from parts of the globe not associated with the geography of one's given race. (All human beings may well come from Africa, after all.) Couple this with the fact that a significant percentage of African Americans (for example) have ancestors who were European or American Indian and one sees that so-called 'genetic' classifications of people into races is a social construction that is, in many ways, arbitrary. (For discussion, see Dubois 1995, Haslinger 2000, Collins 1998b, Zack 1999.)[7]

But why is this a question for political philosophy at all, rather than, say, biology or anthropology? It is crucial to political thought because of the way that racial classification figures, for many people, as essential to their own and others' identity. Both self-conceptions and social relations are marked by race, so in so far as such personal and social dynamics are the subject matter of political philosophy, the question of the tenability of race as a concept is a political issue. This relates directly to the question raised in the last chapter about the ways that self-understanding figures in the formulation and justification of principles for a society and whether such formulation and justification can completely abstract from differences in such identities. For if the basic principles of justice make no reference to racial identity, but people living under such principles define themselves essentially with reference to race (or are made to so define themselves because of the racial dynamics of their society), and such self-identifications affect their basic interests, then 'color-blind' principles misrepresent the people to which they are meant to apply.

Racism and 'color-blind' liberalism

As we discussed in Chapter 4, liberalism rests on the view that the individual autonomous person is of ultimate value, and justice is defined as a set of rules which exhibit respect for that autonomy. Justice is protected prior to the promotion of any particular conception of the good for persons or society, and hence toleration for multiple conceptions of the good is fundamental in the liberal state. Moreover, justice applies to 'public' political institutions, those structures whose rules are enforced coercively, such as legal institutions, the economy, and political processes. Cultural activities — those areas of social interaction marked by voluntary participation and spontaneous action — are not directly shaped by the principles of justice. Finally, justice under liberalism concerns fundamentally the *distribution* of basic goods, both the rights and opportunities fundamental to one's moral status as an autonomous person and the economic and material goods necessary to pursue a life plan.

In the critique of liberalism motivated by considerations of race and racism, these components are all placed under critical scrutiny. First, as we noted, the conception of the autonomous person which is the linchpin of liberal principles is articulated without reference to particularities such as race. The autonomy protected by liberalism does not vary according to the race (or gender or sexual orientation) of the person. This implies that the *way* that autonomy is to be respected — what such respect demands in the way of rules of interpersonal dynamics — can be known without knowing the race of the people involved. But some argue that the cause of liberation for oppressed minorities, such as blacks in the USA, can best be served by recognizing the importance of racial identity in the basic interests of African Americans in fighting injustice and pursuing a liberated life plan (Dubois 1995, Cochran 1999, Outlaw 1996; for discussion, see Boxill 1984: 173–204). If the way that autonomy is protected in liberal society fails to give proper emphasis to this need, then there are grounds for critique in this way.

In the last chapter we discussed analogous considerations concerning autonomy and cultural identity. The line of critique considered here rests on the premise that black identity is deeply intertwined with conceptions of value and meaning for people of color.[8] Though this line of critique must posit a connection between autonomy and racial identity that does not imply the valorization of *white* racial pride, at least that it does not imply that races that have enjoyed social superiority can and should formulate their values and define themselves in terms of that superior position. (I assume that such an implication would be problematic on its face.) Moreover, one must also be cautious in claiming a need to protect a racial culture in a way that puts undue pressure on its members to pursue only the 'authentic' lifestyles reflective of their race (Appiah and Gutmann 1996: 93–96). Claims about the value of cultural identity always threaten to denigrate the aspirations of those who inherit that identity but wish to move outside of it in their own self-understandings and life pursuits.

As we noted, liberal theories of justice concern the operation of 'public' institutions and practices, those enforced via the police power of the state. As we also mentioned, however, racism in society occurs at several levels. Some involve the overt violation of basic rights, such as intentionally denying a person a job because of race or, more obviously, racially motivated violence. But a large measure of racial discrimination takes place outside of the explicit parameters of legal rules: subtle and not-so-subtle ways minority citizens are denigrated, avoided, insulted, and disparaged (Cochran 1999, West 1994). More importantly, elements of the public culture reflected in the media, entertainment, public art, modes of dress, popular music, and the like often manifest a marginalization of minority identity (Young 1990a: 53–55). When the standards of beauty and talent that are touted in a society (as reflected in symbolic representations of such standards, from beauty pageants to fashion shows) clearly reflect a race-specific ideal, members of minority races rightly feel excluded and denigrated by their society. And this denigration and marginalization takes place without any laws being broken or overt violation of public rules of justice, as usually understood.

For example, employment decisions are often made on quite intangible and subtle grounds concerning how comfortable the employer feels with the applicant, how confident the latter appears, how distinguished or smooth she is, and the like (depending on the job in question). All of these factors can be (and often are) judged in ways that reflect racist attitudes; yet if the only race-related injustice that is specified in our political principles are those that violate public rules of overt behavior, broad patterns of unequal opportunities and social marginalization will arise in societies that will nevertheless be labeled fully just. It is commonly noted, for example, that African American males have trouble catching a taxicab in New York city because of the racism of cab drivers. This would amount to merely a constant annoyance (which is clearly bad enough), but catching a taxi is sometimes necessary, for example, to get to a job interview. So what is, at best, a mark of cultural derogation and marginalization, is often an indirect block to equality of opportunity in the traditional sense.

Considerations of this sort provide some of the strongest support for affirmative action programs which demand that race be taken into consideration when making hiring decisions, since discriminatory patterns of hiring and promotion continue to be found even after governmental authorities make demands that overt discrimination be ended. Moreover, there is much evidence that a strong determinant of whether one finds a job or advances in one's profession depends on 'who you know' – the informal relationships that lead to recommendations and personal endorsements. And in a highly segregated society (such as the USA and other developed countries), whom one knows is very much affected by these living patterns that are themselves results of recent overt racist behavior (Ezorsky 1991). In so far, then, as such aspects of civil society continue to reflect patterns of racism and exclusion, equality of opportunity will not be achieved despite the existence of formally equal legal rules and principles (Cochran 1999: 103–17).

Finally, liberalism defines justice in essentially distributive terms, where basic rights and opportunities are afforded to all individuals in a way reflective of their equal status. But, as we just pointed out, many elements of social life which are arguably relevant to the justice of a society concern social *relations* – the patterns of people's interaction and relationship to their larger culture that may not be reflected in their access to material goods or basic rights (Young 1990a, Cochran 1999: 53–65). As we have been considering, racism often shows itself in ways not captured in the measure of how much a single person has specific access to (in terms of material goods or opportunities). Rather, it concerns the overall tenor of a social setting, the way that dominant social meanings (such as standards of beauty or character) reflect a narrow cultural view, how aspects of social life for all groups are given support by other members of the community and reflected in public institutions, and countless other ways connected with how people relate to each other rather than how much they (each) have. In these ways, liberal theory seems inadequate to the task of capturing not only what is wrong with racism, but what must be done about it.

These criticisms strike at the heart of liberal theory. This is because they threaten the strict priority liberalism places on the right – enforcing rules of justice for public institutions – over the good – promoting valued patterns of behavior or cultural forms. If racism manifests itself at the level of culture, and can be diminished only if people's attitudes are reformed and voluntary, 'private' behavior is improved, then racism will be eradicated only if the virtues relating to those attitudes and behaviors are promoted. But is there room in liberalism for the promotion of 'healthier' (that is, less prejudiced) attitudes toward others, or will this be in violation of the priority of the right, where rights to hold dissenting attitudes are protected as long as such ideas do not issue in overt rights violations? It appears that such considerations put liberalism in a quandary: if policies are recommended that allow the use of state coercion to alter racist attitudes in order to provide the cultural support for the enjoyment of equality, then the liberal state must take specific, and controversial, stands on the nature of virtue. But this implies taking a stand on the nature of the good, a stand that (in a society containing advocates of white supremacy for example) is not universally shared. Freedom of speech and conscience may be constricted if such attempts to coerce citizens into changing racist attitudes are made into state policy.

A response may be available, however. One could argue that it is justified to advance those conceptions of the good which are necessary for the *full enforcement* of the provisions of liberal principles of justice themselves (cf. Kymlicka, 1995: 83). That is, in protecting the basic right to freedom and equality justice demands, it may be necessary to promote certain cultural forms, ways of life, value commitments, and so on which are necessary for the development of the sense of justice required if such protections are to be effective. Rawls's political liberalism, for example, is structured so that conceptions of the good can be put forward as reasonable assumptions necessary for the full articulation of principles of justice – for example the 'good' of having a sense of justice and being able to form and revise one's own value conception. These are not postulated as universally valid moral values, but merely those objects of commitment necessary for principles of justice to be effective and stable (Rawls 1993: 224–5).

In the case of race relations, those attitudes and values that would be directly detrimental to the cause of justice (protecting people's basic rights to equality and against discrimination for example) can legitimately be discouraged by government policy, as long as such policies do not also directly contravene other basic liberal rights such as freedom of expression and association (though considerations such as promoting justice-related social goods might help in fleshing out the precise meaning and scope of such basic rights). Affirmative action programs, for example, could be seen in this light: promoting the social good of diversity (in education, employment, and the professions) in order to make the protection of basic rights to full equality of opportunity more secure.

We will return to this important issue later. For now, we have before us a complex set of challenges to the standard model of justice provided by consideration (albeit much too brief) of race and racism in modern societies.

Gender, sex, and the challenge of feminism

As with considerations of race, feminism raises issues for political philosophy which not only deserve several book-length treatments (rather than the chapter section it will get here), but also arguably should infuse *all* aspects of political thought. Feminists have plausibly claimed that considerations of gender and gender-related inequalities play a role in the most basic dynamics of social life – in the structure of families, defining identities and opportunities for self-fulfillment, in creating roles and expectations regarding intimate relations, and the like – so that attention to such inequalities is central to the examination of social life and political institutions. What follows, then, is a *very* selective discussion of some of the ways that feminism raises fundamental issues which force a basic alteration and reconstruction (and some would argue wholesale rejection) of mainstream liberal political theories.

There are many kinds of feminisms and the differences among them are as philosophically interesting as are their similarities. In the present discussion, feminism refers generally to a perspective on society, on social relations, and on oneself; it is a perspective that puts the viewpoint and needs of women, and in particular the inequalities and injustices that have involved and do still involve women in society, at center stage. More than a set of shared beliefs or principles, feminism is an *orientation* characterized by focused attention on the ways that women experience the world and have been treated in society, a treatment marked by unfairness, exclusion, and domination in many areas of women's lives. Consequently, this orientation also involves a commitment to alter those conditions (see Offen 1990: especially 15 n. 3 for discussion of the characterization of feminism).

An aspect of social dynamics that is deeply intertwined with the endeavors of the feminist orientation is the predominance of heterosexuality as a norm of social relations and personal identification in modern (if not all) societies. This norm pervades all aspects of social life, from the design of bathrooms to marriage laws to all manner of social roles and expectations. Therefore, analysis of gender-based inequalities must be placed against the backdrop of social norms that pressure women and men to find intimate, romantic connections with the opposite sex. For this reason, problems of gender equality are unique in struggles for social justice (other oppressed groups, whose calls for justice are no less pressing, do not contend with the complicating factor of systematic intimacy between members of the oppressed group and members of the dominant one). This makes the problems of feminism dauntingly complex, as well as fascinating and challenging. (Though, of course, many equate the predominance of a heterosexual norm with male dominance itself – see, for example, Firestone 1971).

Common to all versions of feminism is the acknowledgment of the 'fact' of patriarchy – the ubiquity of gender hierarchies which manifest male power and privilege. Both as an historical fact and as an ongoing aspect of contemporary life, women face comparatively unequal life opportunities, levels of power and prerogative, freedom, and independence, both in public and private life. From inequalities in pay for labor to constant threats of violence, harassment, and discrimination, sexism is a pervasive aspect of all societies in the modern world. While many may disagree on the extent of such phenomena, and there is complex disagreement about their source and precise character, awareness of and sensitivity to the patriarchal aspects of social life function as a working assumption in much contemporary political thought (and certainly in the present discussion).[9]

We will first explicate the themes raised by feminists from within the paradigm of liberal political philosophy, where theorists claim that the injustices faced by women are best captured by the principles justified in liberal theory, even if those principles must be amended to better capture the full nature of those injustices. Next, we will consider arguments to the effect that liberalism must be rejected precisely because of the failure of that approach to take sufficiently into account the multifaceted aspects of patriarchal culture.[10]

Liberal feminism and its limits

Feminism as developed within the scope of liberal theory shares the commitment to freedom and equality basic to the liberal conception of justice and works to bring to light the several ways in which aspects of contemporary patriarchal societies violate them. Several aspects of male dominance in modern cultures blatantly violate basic liberal principles: Women are paid less than men for comparable jobs, enjoy differential opportunities, face greater pressures and expectations concerning marriage, child-rearing, and domestic labor, have less control over their reproductive lives (and hence constricted opportunities regarding life with or without children), encounter harassment and violence in numerous aspects of their private and public lives, and live in cultures where femininity is structured according to the dictates of male heterosexual desires. The essence of liberal feminism, then, is to point out these various factors and the ways in which they violate the basic demands of justice (Kouraney et al. 1992: 261–81, Jaggar 1983: 27–50, 107–206).

Moreover, liberal feminists work to develop *interpretations* of traditional liberal principles of justice in order to better accommodate the needs of women. Conceptions of natural rights, for example, were generally understood to include rights against assault and theft, to acquire property and participate in politics, but rarely were taken to extend to rights over one's reproductive life (one's body in that sense). Similarly, liberal justice demands equality of opportunity, yet opportunities are defined in terms of access to powers and prerogatives of existing social positions (Rawls: 1993: 180–84). But in addition to the countless overt restrictions on women's advancement of their life plans, positions and office *themselves* are defined socially to reflect a male perspective. Legal restrictions on employment positions, for example, may seem to be a thing of the past for women,[11] but the kinds of jobs that women tend to pursue and which are offered to them are systematically lower paid positions with less job security, advancement opportunities, authority, and fringe benefits attached to them (compared to those offered to men). Moreover, the employment positions that tend to be defined by corporate organizational schemes reflect the lifestyles and interests of men (as traditionally regarded), where responsibilities for children are ignored (MacKinnon 1987: 36, 1989: 157–70, Kymlicka 1990: 241–47). And discrimination in the workplace takes on different aspects when one takes seriously the experiences of women in a heterosexist culture, where sexual harassment and offensive work environments are ever present.

Indeed, filling out principles of equality for women and men while taking into consideration aspects of gender *difference* raises the most vexing and complex kinds of problems for feminist theorists and policy makers. For example, job rules that specifically forbid women from doing certain kinds of jobs would clearly be discriminatory; but restrictions on doing certain jobs because of specific dangers to pregnant or possibly pregnant people (hence women) discriminate in a more complex way (Cornell 1998: 71–85). Similarly, parental-leave policies seem clearly called for in order to ensure women an equal opportunity to pursue paid employment while having children, but such policies (when not afforded to men) are based on a recognition of difference – sex-blind policies would have differential and unfair effects in such cases.

Many feminists emphasize that the focal point of women's inequality lies in the structure of marriage and child-rearing arrangements. Women's life prospects are structured according to the roles of heterosexual partnerships, marriage and motherhood, even for those women who do not plan to marry or have children. Child-rearing responsibilities, educational choices, and the very structure of femininity itself is built around the imperative to be attractive to men and be prepared to have and raise children (Bartky 1997, Okin 1989: 134–69). And given that domestic responsibilities (not merely involving child care) disproportionately fall to women (and such responsibilities involve less skill and prepare one less well for positions of paid employment outside the home), women face unequal prospects for the pursuit of a full variety of lifestyles, values, and projects (Weitzman 1985).

So the concept of an opportunity must be fine tuned to reflect sensitivity to gender difference and inequality. However, the liberal egalitarianism we discussed in Chapter 3 does make way for a more nuanced approach to the concept of equal opportunity. For the point of egalitarianism is not simply that people be treated *the same* (without regard to gender), but that they be treated *equally* as defined by an otherwise defensible metric of well-being, for example that they all have access to equal capabilities to achieve valued functionings, or equal resources (broadly defined). In each case, to the extent that women need different resources to achieve equal freedom and success (such as special medical provisions, pregnancy leave, child-care support, special protections against gender-specific dangers, and so on), then liberal feminism can be understood to support such measures.

So some feminists have claimed that liberal (egalitarian) theories of justice can be amended to take into account likely differences in personal responsibilities in society between men and women, for example by building into the procedure for deriving principles of justice (Rawls's original position for instance) a recognition of that likelihood (Okin 1989, Cornell 1998). Others disagree (Young 1990a, Jaggar 1983: 39–50, 185–206). The crux of the matter is whether women's (and men's) place in society can be criticized only if (and because) it manifests unequal enjoyment of autonomy; liberal feminists will view something like autonomy as being denied in situations of gender-related inequalities (Meyers 1989,

Friedman 1993: 62–90 for example), where feminists outside the liberal tradition see autonomy as often irrelevant to the question of injustice, either because autonomy is really a male ideal or because the locus of the injustice in patriarchy lies elsewhere (Scheman 1993, Young 1990a). I will return to this issue below.

In addition to the question of whether the liberal conception of autonomy will be useful in mounting a critique of patriarchal societies, other aspects of the liberal tradition have been targeted by feminists critics as in need of revision (if not wholesale rejection). In particular, the right to privacy has always been seen by liberal theorists as a fundamental aspect of the liberty enjoyed by all citizens in a just society (Mill [1859] 1975). But feminists have raised powerful objections to the way that this right has been traditionally understood, objections that many think push liberal theory to (and some would say beyond) the breaking point in accommodating feminist concerns within its own theoretical limits.

Public and private

As noted earlier, justice concerns the institutions of the basic structure of society. This means that justice concerns those areas of life structured by public, enforceable rules of conduct, specifically those areas governed by law and the coercive arm of the state. But various aspects of life not included in the scope of such rules severely affect and indeed constitute one's pursuit of the good life, and such elements of 'private' life carry over directly to patterns of behavior in the public sphere in a way that makes enforcement of public rules of justice ineffective or deficient (Landes 1998).

Family life can again serve as a focal point for such considerations. Certainly, the traditional view that the private realm protects all aspects of life in the household has been rightly exposed by feminists as ignoring the profound injustice and violence that can take place *within* such households. Domestic violence and spousal abuse was covered up by the traditional respect for the 'privacy' of the home, and marital rape was not even considered a crime in many jurisdictions until recently (MacKinnon 1989: 171–83). The traditional individualism of liberal theory – where the subject of principles of justice was assumed to be an unencumbered atomistic self – is claimed by feminists to be a profoundly sexist conception, since the assumption really is that women and children, whose interests are often tied closely to their relations to other people, and to their family specifically, are simply left out of the equation by that individualist picture (see, for example, Pateman 1988).

But more specifically, even though typical family arrangements are structured by gender hierarchies of authority, power, and privilege, such arrangements are left uncriticized by principles of justice that do not treat family structures as part of the public realm.[12] Feminists argue that such disparities of power, which affect all aspects of women's and men's opportunities inside and outside the home, are unacceptable in a just society, both on their face and because of the effect these arrangements have on the next generation of citizens by functioning as a 'school for (in)justice' (see Okin 1989: 17–24; for an overview of family related inequalities suffered by women, see ibid.: 134–69).

But complications arise when the violations of equal opportunity (concerning such things as domestic labor and child care) are acceded to 'voluntarily' by the women in question. Certainly, most happily married women, even those who bear undue burdens for the unpaid aspects of the household, would never claim that they entered into these situations against their will. So unless injustice can still obtain even if the victim voluntarily accepted her position (and in the case of assault and the violations of basic rights it almost certainly can), the claim that principles of justice should prohibit domestic arrangements that are *per se* unequal is on shakier ground, at least within a liberal framework. For example, how would the rules enforcing equal division of domestic labor be enforced without violating other basic rights? (For discussion see, for example, Okin 1989: 170–86, Babbitt 1996: 39–46, and Cornell 1998: 93–95.)

The liberal emphasis on the protection of autonomy places this question into sharp relief. If marriage contracts are entered into voluntarily (autonomously), they are considered within the 'private' realm and so are protected; in such cases, liberalism would not provide the ammunition for the kind of critique that feminists plausibly mount against systematically unequal domestic arrangements. For this reason, some writers argue that liberalism is insufficient to support resistance to such patterns of oppression (Pateman 1988, Young 1990a, MacKinnon 1989).

But this conclusion depends, again, on what exactly we mean by autonomy and what conditions actually obtain for women (and men) in agreeing to various domestic roles. Taking the second topic first, a strong case can be made that opportunities for women are severely restricted (comparatively) due to the strong social and material pressures on them to marry and have children, take on primary responsibility for those children, curtail or organize their own professional aspirations according to the family's needs, and in other ways take on social roles that include less flexibility for the successful pursuit of a variety of valued life plans. And clearly, poor women, who make up the huge majority of heads of single-parent homes, face severe material pressures to accept whatever employment opportunities will be compatible with putting food on the table for their children (Pearce 1992).

So if autonomy means being governed by forces one chose for oneself (or was not deeply alienated from) against a background of open options, then in so far as women face fewer life options in their choice of family arrangements (compared to men), they are less autonomous and the inequalities involved in such are open to criticism from within liberalism. This means, then, that liberal feminists' critiques of family-related inequalities must be directed at the unequal conditions faced by girls and women in making decisions about what sort of domestic arrangements to enter into, not at the internal domestic arrangements themselves. Put another way, truly gender-neutral principles of justice would not allow differential pressures or opportunities based on sex, and so 'voluntary' choices to enter into marriages which involve unequal responsibilities would not be endorsed (behind, say, a Rawlsian veil of ignorance), but in so far as even unequal roles are chosen autonomously by all affected, liberalism implies state neutrality (that is, inaction) concerning such conditions. (An important qualification must be added: in so far as domestic arrangements, whether voluntary or not, impede the exercise of *ongoing* autonomy, such arrangements can be subject to critique under liberal principles.)

Parallel analyses can be developed toward such things as prostitution, surrogate pregnancy arrangements, and women's participation in pornography: liberal theory focuses attention on decisions about whether to engage in such activities on the part of women, asking whether such decisions are autonomous given the social pressures and limited opportunities available when such decisions are made (Jaggar 1986: 109–111, Satz 1992). Other feminists, however, claim that such a focus is, at best, superficial since it leaves un-analyzed the complex factors that go into the development of women's identity that give rise to such choices (MacKinnon 1993, A. Dworkin 1989, Babbitt 1996).

It has also been argued by some feminists that the tendencies exhibited by women concerning responsibilities in interpersonal relations, child-rearing and child care, and other 'personal' activities is an aspect of (feminine) difference that, in certain forms, is to be celebrated. Traditional overemphasis on the 'public' virtues associated with professional success and material advancement should be criticized rather than insisting that women conform to them. From this perspective, attempts to eradicate gender difference by constructing allegedly neutral principles and insisting that men and women be conditioned to live up to them equally is the source of oppression, not its solution. Let us now turn to this line of argument.

Justice and care

One of the most momentous and controversial contributions to political thought made by feminism in recent decades involves the work of Carol Gilligan, who developed the claim that there exists an approach to morality and social relations that contrasts sharply with that which is based on justice and individual rights of the sort characteristic of mainstream (liberal) theory. The 'care' perspective – a moral orientation that focuses on the value of maintaining relations, acting on interpersonal responsibilities, expressing appropriate emotion and affect, and so on – has been put forward as a moral orientation uniquely connected with the experience and psychology of women, but which has been relegated to secondary status in traditional theories of moral development. Gilligan's work famously suggested that women tend to think more in terms of care and responsibility when considering a moral problem than in terms of impersonal rights and justice, and that moral and political principles which were expressed in the latter terms have essentially silenced women's voices (Gilligan 1982, Gilligan et al. 1988, Brown and Gilligan 1992).

Gilligan questioned the dominant view of psychological development which placed the ability to think in terms of universal, impersonal, principles at the apex of moral thinking, claiming that this reflected the male tendency to value separation, objectivity, and autonomy over connectedness and relationships. Normative principles expressed in terms of justice assume such abilities to detach from personal connections and act on autonomy-based, universal moral principles. Many women, however, tend to approach normative issues in a way which is highly sensitive to obligations toward concrete others, responsible for maintaining or repairing existing relations, and generally responding to particular others with care and connectedness (Noddings 1984, Ruddick 1990).

The basic liberal tenets of protecting autonomy and basic liberties in order to respect the moral equality of all citizens (regardless of particular differences) manifest such an orientation characterized by universal principles and detached judgment. Indeed, the insistence that justice of this sort must be secured prior to advancing the 'good' associated with flourishing relationships, caring connections, particular partnerships, and the like, emphasizes this orientation. So in so far as liberalism places justice first, and justice reflects male thinking and excludes or renders deficient the female-centered care perspective, liberalism faces serious objections from this corner.

But claims of a 'different voice' are crucially ambiguous. Such claims can be understood to assert a significant and general difference between males and females (in Western societies for example) concerning how they think morally; or the claim of difference can be taken as simply a criticism of the dominant approach to morality (justice) for underemphasizing a style of thinking some or many women engage in (as do some men), along with the presentation of an alternative vision which better reflects the perspective, social position, and experience of women. The latter view need not rest on any empirical claims about significant sex differences in moral thinking. Rather, the claim is that modes of moral thinking that are *associated* with female social roles, and which express the experience of many or most women, must be considered as a valid alternative to the orientation (justice) that reflects the experience and social roles of males. The difference between these two interpretations is important since research following Gilligan's original findings in fact raised questions about the empirical basis for her implied claim of significant sex differences in moral orientation (or at best yielded inconclusive results – see Larrabee 1991, Christman 1995: 19–24, Friedman 1997: 666f., especially n. 6; for discussion, see Stocker 1987, Sommers 1987, and Sher 1987).[13]

Regardless of the claim that women and men tend to think differently (to a statistically significant degree), the challenge to liberalism remains clear. If the value priorities and general orientation manifested in liberal principles unduly reflect the perspective of males, and the life experiences and social patterns associated with (and lived by) women are de-emphasized, liberal political thought can rightly be accused of bias. The question, then, is whether liberal principles can place value on, protect, and help foment flourishing caring relationships in ways which adequately value the social roles associated with the feminine.

The challenge is that the terms used to formulate political principles manifest the perspective of generalized, impersonal values, thereby leaving no conceptual room for the specification of the value of particular relationships and localized needs (Benhabib 1987). The same might be said of the use of the language of individualized rights in such principles (see, for example, Friedman 1993, W. Brown 1995, and P. Williams 1991). But in so far as the principles in question are *political* – that is, applicable to broad patterns of behavior in society (even if some such behavior occurs in the traditionally 'private' realm) – such generality is necessary.[14] The question is whether political principles expressed in terms of justice actually denigrates or devalues, or at least does not sufficiently encourage, the particular and emotionally grounded relations by which many people (especially women) frame their lives.

There are at least four ways that government policy can relate to the promotion of caring relations: first, such relations (and the virtues necessary to carry them out well) are promoted *directly*; second, such relations are promoted *indirectly* (by such things as tax breaks for family expenses, policies designed to allow people more time to participate fully in close relationships, and so on); third, government policy attempts complete *neutrality* concerning such relations; and fourth, state policy actively *discourages* fulfilling caring relations among citizens. Now no one recommends this last option, but critics of traditional liberal theory often claim that its policies are guilty of this, that the atomistic, hyper-mobile, and unencumbered citizens that liberal policies tend to produce have a tougher time building close relationships and living up to responsibilities arising from them. We discussed this charge in the last chapter, and concluded that nothing about liberal theory itself carried these implications, and the blame lay on patterns of capitalist development that some versions of liberalism (egalitarian liberalism for example) may themselves provide grounds for resisting.

But what of the other possibilities? As we mentioned, strict neutrality concerning the promotion of the good for citizens can be weakened to allow the promotion of those patterns of behavior and character development that are necessary for the effectiveness of principles of justice. So in so far as flourishing personal relations and stable families are necessary for an effective sense of justice, state policies can promote them (though see below for an important qualification).

Now, one way that such stability is established concerns raising the next generation of citizens. Children must be raised in caring environments for the next generation of citizens to come on to the scene, presumably with these same kinds of virtues intact (Rawls 1971:405–09, Okin 1989: 17–24). Traditionally, this pattern of development would simply be *assumed* in that families were considered natural and part of the private realm of the household, so that state action concerning families was not unjust, it was simply unnecessary – nature took care of that itself. Feminists have rightly pointed out the difficulty of this traditional picture (Pateman 1988, Okin 1989). First, relegating the responsibilities of family life to the private realm essentially makes invisible the world of many women, implying that women will simply assume their natural roles and do the dirty work of taking care of the home and raising the children. Such silence about domestic life in traditional political theories reveal that these theorists were simply not considering the lives of woman at all (Elshtain 1981, Benhabib 1987, Landes 1998). But also, actual family life is typically patriarchal and authoritarian, so that assuming that family life is 'natural' implies that one accepts a hierarchical authority structure as natural. And this, clearly, is an unacceptable idea (though we must remember that the rejection of such hierarchies is at best a recent development and is still not universally accepted).

But that leaves the question of *how* the state should promote those patterns of relationships which help form the characters necessary for cooperative citizens. The answer must be a highly qualified and guarded one. For if one accepts the feminist claim that promoting care and responsibility (to particular others) pays more adequate heed to the perspective and orientation of the feminine world, one must nevertheless constantly remind oneself of the *varieties* of interpretations of caring relations. For example, realizing that families are crucial in fostering such caring relations (in particular concerning children) might induce one to support government policies that make family life easier. But which families? Heterosexual families? The so-called 'nuclear' family where the two parents are married and raise their biological offspring? There is a multitude of types of caring relations and any reference to a particular type in the justification of state policy always runs the risk of valorizing merely one particular conception to the detriment of others (cf. Kymlicka 1991). The argument for the priority of right, whatever version of it we want to hold on to in the end, is based on respect for pluralism of conceptions of the good, so feminist claims for the recognition and promotion of moral values associated with women should be accepted, but only in a form which remains consistent with this respect.

Departures from liberalism: gender, culture, and identity formation

Liberal rules of the political order extend to those actions that overtly violate the basic rights of citizens, those associated with freedom and equality defined neutrally across genders, races, classes, and so on. But as we saw with race-based critiques of that view, feminists point out that aspects of cultural life that do not involve overt coercion or explicit rights violations can contribute greatly to the continuation of power hierarchies and oppressive social patterns (Young 1990a: 61–63). This relates to the question discussed earlier concerning whether principles of justice must include provisions for correction of predictably unjust social conditions found in modern communities, especially if those unjust conditions create and foster a pattern of inequality that those principles are designed to condemn. Aspects of modern culture in many ways reflect an overwhelmingly (heterosexual) male perspective. The aesthetic and symbolic face of modern (Western) culture pervasively reflects the priorities of (straight) males concerning the availability and sexual attractiveness of women, the status associated with wealth for men but beauty and sexuality for women, and so on. The ubiquity of prostitution and pornography, for example, which is overwhelmingly geared toward the desires of heterosexual males, shows how cultural patterns mirror the perspective and priorities of males and denigrate or ignore the perspective of women. As long as such patterns do not involve the explicit violation of autonomy-based rights, liberal principles of justice will not apply to them and will declare even the most (culturally) patriarchal and sexist society perfectly just.[15]

But the assumption in modern societies is that cultural life is *voluntary* in a way that shields it from the force of principles of justice; so if social and aesthetic tastes tend to reflect the desires of one class of citizens over another, the correct response is to exert social pressure rather than legal coercion in order to effect changes in such tastes (such as boycotts, protests, and public argument) (Mill [1859] 1995: 32–33). This position, however, may well underestimate the degree to which public laws tend to underwrite and support social patterns (rather than leaving them to the independent control of the citizenry). For example, laws banning pornography which is 'obscene' based on its overall offensiveness, but not for its degrading depictions of women, inscribes male-biased perceptions and attitudes (A. Dworkin 1989). The prosecution of laws against prostitution which are aimed solely at the (female) prostitute rather than the (male) clients reflect and perpetuate sexist views about the men's rights to the sexual availability of women. This points to the way that cultural life is shaped directly and indirectly by the substance of legal restrictions on public behavior and hence predictably mold behavior in ways that directly foster the continuation of oppressive social forms.[16]

Principles of justice which prize freedom and equality concentrate on the ability of people to pursue their own (authentic) value conceptions. Inequalities in people's ability to act on such conceptions manifest injustice on this view. What this approach leaves unevaluated, however, are patterns of personal (and child) development that *bring about* those value conceptions. If social factors operate so as to predictably mold people's characters in a way that supports and reiterates power hierarchies, then liberal principles will not be sufficient to respond (negatively) to that pattern. Principles of justice that condemn slavery, for example, are impotent to respond if large segments of the population are socialized strongly to be 'voluntary' slaves. Feminists claim that in similar ways, patriarchal society operates so as to aid in the construction of gender identities that do virtually that (MacKinnon 1989, Bartky 1997, Ferguson 1997). Femininity, they argue, is a social construct that arises from the forces of patriarchy and results in special pressures to conform to those patriarchal structures in the process of character development for women.

Consider the relation between being feminine and being physically attractive to men. Huge industries – fashion, make-up, hair and beauty products, and various entertainment and media industries connected with these – rotate around women's needs to be slim, pretty, and sexy. Femininity (as well as masculinity) is molded by a heterosexist imperative: to be fulfilled and successful one must be able to attract the opposite sex not only for potential marriage partners, but also as a public display of one's own success and well-being.[17] Whether such patterns result from psychological dynamics in childhood development (Chodorow 1978), material conditions arising from the division of labor under capitalism (Ferguson 1997), or more generally a manifestation of male power hierarchies (MacKinnon 1989), the relationship between patriarchal society and self-development and identity is easy to pinpoint.

If it can be clearly shown that patterns of child development systematically foster gender identities that include, say, passivity, obedience, and attractiveness in girls, but independence, self-confidence, and industriousness in boys, should a state committed to realizing just social conditions remain neutral and silent about such patterns? Should, for example, public education be geared to counteract such patterns of development? On the other hand, can a program of counteracting such sexist gender roles maintain respect for those members of the society – religious conservatives for example – who self-consciously support gender-specific personal values and social roles? The question arises whether the commitment to social equality extends to using public policy to affect those cultural and personal patterns that predictably contribute to unequal opportunities and status.

However, the claim that social pressures mold the personalities and gender identities of citizens in ways that reflect patriarchal social patterns is in tension with assumptions of agency and autonomy on the part of women (and men). Mounting a critique of the construction of femininity first presupposes a specific value conception about character development (passivity and obedience are inferior to independence and power), defensible though these conceptions might be. Second, such critiques run counter to the attribution of self-definition and agency that most women themselves feel, and most feminist theorists want to promote. If we assume that gender identity is fully constructed by social forces, then we must conclude that women themselves play no role in responding to those forces and forging new identities for themselves.

In these ways, feminism that engages in analysis and critique of the *formation* of identities departs decidedly from liberalism. Psychoanalytic feminism, for example, utilizes the theoretical and therapeutic insights of psychological analyses, in particular those in a Freudian or neo-Freudian strain, to attempt to understand the development and ongoing dynamics of gender identities and hence patriarchy (Flax 1993, Benjamin 1988, Chodorow 1978, Meyers 1994, and the essays in Rhode 1990). The role of unconscious mechanisms, both in the process of personality development and in adult mental lives, is linked with the construction of gender, the play of power dynamics between and within subjects, and the nature of family relations which mirror and support patriarchal social patterns.

We will touch again on such material in the next chapter (though, even there, only briefly), but let us note three points here: First, theoretical critiques of the *formation* of values, identities, and self-concepts from a political point of view run directly counter to the liberal contention that the autonomous subject is both the ground and the ideal of political principles, and any critique that does not take as a starting point the ability of agents to freely reflect on their own values and the institutions of their society is problematic from that perspective. Second, any particular theoretical analysis of mental life and development is only as powerful as the social-psychological theory that frames its claims (for a discussion of feminist misgiving about psychoanalytic approaches, see Meyers 1994: 86–91). Third, such critiques of the formation of personality themselves rest on normative principles and hence require philosophical justification and support. In complex modern societies where there is disagreement about whether such roles are in fact ones of subordination, such justifications cannot be simply assumed.

Further departures: The feminist critique of objectivity and reason

Political philosophy emerging from the European Enlightenment is based on the idea that human reason, detached from all bodily and emotional aspects of character, can function to uncover fundamental truths about the conceptual, empirical, and moral worlds. Such reasoning must be conducted in a way that makes irrelevant the particularities of the body, historical context, character, class, and so on, of the thinking person. And just as philosophical *theory* should be conducted according to the dictates of detached reason, public deliberation about the meaning and justification of social principles should also reflect the ideals of objectivity, detachment, and neutral reason.

Feminists, and other critics of the Enlightenment tradition (including some race theorists), have raised issues about this general presumption, issues that pinpoint the several ways that this model of human thinking not only excludes or downgrades the experience of women (and other subordinated groups), but also gives a false picture of the objectivity and detachment involved in reasoned reflection. These critiques follow several paths and we can discuss only a few (while leaving the main discussion of them to the next chapter). The idea that detached reason is the source of philosophical truth can be questioned by saying that this 'detachment' – the abstraction from one's own particular circumstances in making judgments – is always incomplete and so surreptitiously biased, that it reflects merely one (male) mode of thinking and deliberating, and that it is a false ideal in any case since much of what is relevant to particular judgments concerns those very circumstances ignored in such thinking (Young 1990a: 111–16, Phelan 1996).

The ideal of reasoned reflection under scrutiny here amounts to the idea that moral principles are discovered only through cognitive reflection that abstracts from all particular contingencies of the reflector's person and of the particular object of reflection. The priority of right insisted upon by liberalism can be seen to rest on this ideal in that rules of justice can be determined (it has been thought) by detached reflection based on practical reason, while conceptions of the good are particular, laden with emotional elements, and concern particular attachments and circumstances (and hence cannot be specified 'objectively' for all).

Critiques of this ideal of reflection have taken place along several lines, some emphasizing the impossibility of the *thinker's* detachment and objectivity (and the relevance of his or her biography to judgment), others pointing to the relevance of the concrete particulars of the *object of thought*, especially if such an 'object' is a person or kind of person (see the essays in Anthony and Witt 1993). More specifically, defenders of so-called 'standpoint theory' have claimed that those in positions of relative powerlessness have unique insights into the experience and dynamics of power differences, implying that the assumption of a detached, objective evaluation of such dynamics will be incomplete at best, and biased toward the perspective of the powerful at worst (Jaggar 1983: 370–85, Harstock 1997, Mills 1997: 109–11). In so far as moral judgments involve interpretations and evaluations of particular experiences, those with unique perspectives on those experiences introduce factors that cannot simply be reduced to a neutral (in particular a gender-neutral) standpoint. Consider the harms involved in the crimes of rape and sexual harassment: is there an objective, neutral, standpoint which can appraise such harms? Is there a neutral perspective from which to judge whether advances are too forceful or expressions of voluntary participation fully genuine? Feminists have argued strongly that attempts to utilize such an allegedly neutral viewpoint surreptitiously import a male perspective (as in the 'reasonable man' standard in the law) (MacKinnon 1989: 171–83). Given radical differences (especially gender differences) in personal experiences and general interaction with others, the idea of an objective viewpoint from which principles defining such phenomena can be determined seems obviously a dangerous ideal.

A difficulty here, however, is that *all* judgments generalize across types of people, whether it be women and men or people of different races, classes, sexual orientations, and so on. Feminists themselves have wrestled with the tensions of decrying traditional, supposedly all-embracing categories used in political judgments ('rational agents as such' for example) while at the same time having to make reference to groups and subgroups themselves in order to specify the very excluded groups being talked about (Young 1997a: 12–37, Haslinger 2000, Spellman 1997). To say that the standard reference to all human beings in traditional philosophy glosses over differences between, say, men and women, runs immediately up against the claim that *these* categories – women and men – are subject to the very same critique.

But liberal theories can certainly be challenged to the extent that the articulation of their central principles is always in *danger* of glossing over relevant differences among groups whose interests are being represented (cf. Babbitt 1996: 207–12). Feminists have rightly claimed that until quite recently, virtually all allegedly neutral theories promulgated and defended by (mostly) men in a male-dominated culture in fact failed to adequately represent the experiences and interests of women (and other marginalized groups). Only when women themselves, and those who listen sensitively to the different voices among genders and between them, speak from their particular points of view can we have any confidence that the various values and interests at stake have been fully expressed; and even then such judgments must be seen as fallible and subject to revision when new or previously silenced voices enter the discussion. In this way we again see the centrality of democracy to fully worked out principles of justice (cf. Young 2000, Fraser 1997: 11–41, Benhabib 1996b).

So feminists have raised several challenges to the liberal model, some of which may be accommodated within that model subject to modifications of it, while others may force more radical revisions.[18] But as we noted at several points, these challenges highlight the important role that the conception of autonomy plays in liberal principles, a conception that must be understood in a more nuanced fashion than traditionally done. Moreover, liberal theory is not poised to render evaluations of the manners in which identities are formed and values adopted, except in so far as those processes make autonomy (however it is defined) impossible. But liberalism prizes freedom and equality of (adult) persons, and passes no direct judgment about the forces that go into the construction of that identity. As we will see in the next chapter, many will argue that this is the ultimate limitation of liberal theory in all its forms and provides the strongest reason for its rejection.

Identity, injustice, and democracy

One final word should be added about the implications of both race-based and feminist lines of critique for principles of justice. Such principles must be formulated in terms of formal categories: rights, freedoms, and equality with reference to abstract conditions that provide an index of position (such as wealth, status, or happiness). As we discussed in Chapter 3, equality of condition can be measured in a number of ways, with reference to resources, capabilities, welfare (happiness), or opportunities. Critics of liberalism point out, however, that this formal characterization of justice will not provide a set of concepts that are fine tuned enough to adequately capture the conditions of injustice that are actually found in modern societies. Experiences of racism, sexism, and other forms of oppressive relations are not reducible, they argue, to the abstract categories of unequal rights, freedoms, income and wealth, or other such measures of just conditions (Young 1990a).

Injustice, these critics argue, has an irreducibly experiential element, unique characteristics that only victims of such treatment can adequately express. Yet theoretical accounts of social justice must refer to such experiences in general terms, for example in terms of rights and freedoms (to vote, to avoid assault and abuse, and so on). Conceptions of inequality, then, must be formulated according to such abstractions, ones which refer to broad categories of human beings. But each such categorization necessarily blurs over differences among the members of those groups – class differences within races and genders, differences in sexual orientation, physical ability, age, and the like – that represent significant contrasts in the way that social life and relations are experienced.

One answer to such a quandary has been mentioned at various times in this work (and indeed is a major theme), namely that democratic institutions play a basic role in defining justice, institutions that allow members of such groups to *speak for themselves*. Democracy involves mechanisms of collective, public expression of one's experiences in social conditions, expressions that may well not be translatable readily into formulas for measuring comparative condition (Young 1990a: 183–91, 2000). Democratic institutions provide formulas for decisions on how to weigh relative injustice which cannot be completely set out theoretically in advance, but must result from actual deliberative interaction among those affected by the policies in question.

Of course, this move does not solve the problem completely. For democracy itself must be structured in a way that preserves fairness. Procedures concerning who gets to speak, how votes are counted, and what gets on the agenda are all reflective of previous decisions about justice. Some democratic theorists have responded that *all* normative provisions, even those in place which define the democracy itself, should be open to debate and collective reconsideration, at least eventually (see, for example, J. Cohen 1996, Benhabib 1996b). But democratic procedures are structured in a certain way, not because people collectively decided (or would decide) to have them so structured, but because it would be *unjust* not to do so. Such requirements as full and equal participation of all citizens, protection of the independence and autonomy of participants, enjoyment of equal political power, and so on, all reflect a prior commitment to principles of freedom and equality definitive of just institutions.

So the dialectic we have just traced is ongoing but informative: theoretical categorization of just social relations will always be incomplete due to the experiential elements that can only be weighed and evaluated through first-person accounts;[19] democratic procedures allow for this, at least indirectly, and hence will function as a constitutive element in just institutions; but democracy itself presupposes a conception of justice based on the fundamental values of freedom (autonomy) and equality, while the specific interpretations of these values might always be open to debate. In this picture, constitutional provisions guaranteeing certain individual rights and freedoms – as well as setting out the institutional framework for governments – are understood as necessary, not to fully define just social relations, but to put in place the normative structure of a functioning democracy which, as a whole and over time, will do so.

Chapter summary

Two of the most powerful and politically energized critiques of mainstream political philosophy were considered here, and both brought forth problems for liberal theory to which it might be hard pressed to respond. For both race-based and gender-based critiques, the question was raised whether any ideal political theory such as liberalism should acknowledge and help analyze the existing injustices and oppressive practices found in the society to which they apply. Idealizations, it was charged, tend to ignore, and hence leave intact, practices that are known to be endemic to modern societies, but which are not noted in the abstract principles themselves (such as inequalities of wealth and opportunity that stem from *past* discrimination).

In the case of critical race theory, the question of the meaning of 'race' was considered, where it was concluded that such a concept is a social construction but, none the less, one that deeply shaped many people's self-understanding and interaction with others. Racism was analyzed as were the numerous ways that racist attitudes can manifest themselves, often in ways that fall between the cracks of public, legal rules. We also considered the ways that racial identity might ground claims for specifically cultural protections of the sort that were mentioned in Chapter 5 (though we also noted some dissension among race theorists themselves about this position). More tellingly for liberalism, however, is the manner in which racism manifests itself in a variety of settings not specified by public, legal rules of behavior, such as cultural patterns, informal relations among people, and various behaviors that crucially affect the lives of victims of such prejudice. Liberalism's limited focus on only state actions grounded criticisms of the ability of standard liberal views to adequately respond to such racism in all its varieties. The relevance of these lines of critique to the liberal insistence on the priority of right was discussed. It was mentioned that there is room in liberal frameworks to justify state promotion of those cultural forms that turn out to be necessary for the effective enforcement of rules of justice, though the potential conflict between such promotion and the protection of other basic liberal rights, such as the right to free speech, was noted.

Next, feminist political thought was discussed, where we gave a general characterization of feminism as well as outlining the aspects of 'patriarchy' (male dominance and gender inequality) found in modern societies. We considered the approach to these phenomena by liberal feminism, though the claim was made that principles of liberal justice, such as the guarantee of full equality of opportunity, must be reinterpreted in order to respond more adequately to women's experiences and interests. Specifically, unequal opportunities based on differential expectations and material position regarding family life (pregnancy, child care, domestic labor) were discussed, and it was argued that full justice for women would not be secured as long as such traditional gender roles and pressures remained in place. We also mentioned, however, the quandary that this creates for feminist analysis regarding whether current gender differences should be acknowledged (and even celebrated) or ignored by social policy aimed at securing justice. Liberal feminism amounts to the position that in so far as gender-specific policies are necessary to ensure real equality (not just superficial sameness of treatment), the recognition of gender difference is justified.

This led, however, to an examination of the protections afforded to the 'private' sphere. The traditional separation of private and public, feminists argue, has led to state policies which simply ignore the abuse and oppression of women inside of such spheres as the household or the marriage bedroom. Liberal feminists must rethink the line between private activity and areas of life subject to social control, though the way in which that line is drawn for liberals will always refer to the meaningful exercise of individual autonomy in such spheres.

But the liberal emphasis on securing justice prior to promoting the good was seen to draw direct critical attention from those feminists who claim that promotion of 'care' and flourishing relationships better reflects the moral thinking of some, or most, women. These views, influenced by the work of Carol Gilligan and others, rest on an assumption that an ethic of care is not only distinct from justice, but also reflects a moral orientation closely associated with women's experiences. We acknowledged the ways that traditional liberal theory suppressed the development of caring relations for all citizens by assuming such activity belonged in the 'natural,' 'private' realm of family relations. But also a cautionary note was sounded about the justification of social policies that try to promote, directly or indirectly, caring relations among citizens (such as healthy family connections and the care of children), as such policies could well ignore the profound differences among the members of the society over how such relations should be understood and organized.

More pronounced departures from liberalism were next outlined in raising questions about the processes of personality (that is, gender) development and the ways that feminists have critically analyzed those processes as found in patriarchal societies. Since liberal principles assume as their subject a fully formed, autonomous individual, questions about character development and value formation do not appear on the normative agenda of liberal views. And questions were raised about the methodological and normative presuppositions behind critiques of gender development which assume the acceptability of certain models of both psychological development (especially psychoanalytic models) and normative categories (such as 'subordinated' social roles), though further discussion of such strategies was left for the next chapter.

A final note was voiced concerning the ramifications for liberal political theory of both the race-based and gender-based approaches.

Specifically, the importance of questioning all general categories of social classes which form the subject matter of political critiques (such as race, gender, class, and the interests allegedly associated with each) was emphasized, and the experiential element in any specification of the interests aligned with such categories was noted. This led us, once again, to stress the constitutive role that robust and complex mechanisms of democracy must play in the theory and practice of just institutions.

Case to consider

Imagine a society much like one's own, but where the medical and technological capability to completely alter the physical manifestations of one's race or biological sex was available (and inexpensive). That is, with an operation no more complicated than, say, an appendectomy, one could alter all of the physical marks associated with race (whatever those marks turn out to be) or one's biological sex (akin to having an effective sex-change operation). Several questions can be raised about such a scenario. Would this be a more ideal society, given that any advantages or disadvantages stemming from race or sex could be eradicated by choice? Would we then treat people not as of a given race or sex, but as autonomous individuals who have chosen that race or sex? Would the entire *idea* of racial and sexual categorization cease to be comprehensible in such a society? Would people tend to change their race or sex under such conditions? Why or why not? (It may be necessary to take the case of 'race-change' and 'sex-change' separately and fill in the different details that would be relevant in even imagining each of the scenarios.)

If one thinks that such a thought experiment is completely unrealistic (apart from the obvious fact that it is under-described), this itself is philosophically instructive. After all, sex-change operations happen now; and plastic surgery is available to alter skin tone and other conventional markers of race. But if one thinks that, nevertheless, such operations would not succeed in altering one's 'true' race or sex (or gender), what does that say about the true nature of racial and gender identity?

Finally, what would both liberal theorists and their critics say about such a scenario? Would liberals necessarily be in favor of such developments, since they further enable people to exercise autonomous choice about those elements of their being that (for whatever reason) society continues to view as significant? And would critics of liberalism reply that for that very reason, *because* liberalism clearly implies that such technologies would be ideal (and, clearly, they are not), liberalism ought to be abandoned in the struggle against race- and sex-based injustice?

Notes on further reading

For discussions of the limitation of ideal theory (in relation to ongoing injustices), see Geuss 1981 and Hampton 1997: xiii–xv; specifically in relation to considerations of gender and race, see Okin 1989, and Mills 1997: 120–23, 1999: 17ff. The controversy concerning the definition of race is discussed in Appiah 1992, 1996, Outlaw 1996, 1999, and the essays in Zack 1997, in Babbitt and Campbell 1999, especially Part II, and in Blackburn 2000. A sustained critique of the idea of race as a scientific concept can be found in Blackburn 2000.

Discussions of liberalism motivated by considerations of race can be found in Boxill 1984, West 1994, Mills 1997, Cochran 1999. Among the many important discussions of race and political philosophy generally, see, for example, the essays in Harris 1983, Bell et al., 1996, and Babbitt and Campbell 1999.

Feminism also, of course, contains a vast literature. An excellent overview of dominant themes in recent feminism can be found in Meyers 1997, but see also the essays in Kittay and Meyers 1987, Kourany et al. 1992, and Kourany 1998. Jagger 1983 remains a valuable resource (though cf. also Jagger 1994). Liberal feminism, in particular, is critically discussed in Jaggar 1983: 27–50, 173–206, 355–57; it is defended in Okin 1989 and (with many qualifications) Cornell 1998. Feminism and autonomy is specifically examined in Meyers 1989, Friedman 1993: 62–90, and Christman 1995; and it is critically appraised in Young 1990a: 96–121 and Scheman 1993. The feminist critique of the public-private distinction is discussed in Elshtain 1981, Pateman 1988, Benhabib 1987, Kymlicka 1990: 247–62, and the essays in Landes 1998.

The justice-care distinction has also elicited much discussion. Gilligan's views can be found in Gilligan 1982, 1988, Gilligan et al. and Brown and Gilligan 1992. See also the essays in Kittay and Meyers 1987. For specific treatment, see Noddings 1984, Ruddick 1990, Christman 1995: 19–24, and Friedman 1997. For a bibliography on work on the issue (up until 1991), see Larrabee 1991.

The construction of gender in patriarchal society is examined in Chodorow 1978 (though this is criticized in Young 1997b), Bartky 1990 and 1997, and Ferguson 1997. Psychoanalytic approaches to feminist issues can be found in Benjamin 1988, Flax 1993, and Meyers 1994. The feminist rejection of Enlightenment standards of impartial reason is discussed in, among other places, the essays in Anthony and Witt 1993. Feminist theorization of democracy is usefully developed in Benhabib 1996b, Fraser 1997: 11–41, and Young 1990a and 2000.

CHAPTER 7

Radical critique
Marxism and post-modernism

- The legacy of Marx and Marxism
- Post-modern departures
- Epilogue: The hope of liberalism
- Chapter summary
- Case to consider
- Notes on further reading

The approaches to political philosophy discussed in this chapter represent a more 'radical' departure from not only liberalism specifically, but from the broad tradition of Enlightenment philosophy in general. There is some overlap between them (there are post-modern Marxists for example) and there are many strands of the critiques we examined in the last chapter that could easily fall under one or both of these headings. And certainly the labels 'Marxist' and 'post-modern' are disputed in their meaning and range of application. But in both cases, new and unique challenges to mainstream political philosophy are raised, ones that do more than offer a competing set of normative principles but also question both the methods and the proper subject matter of political philosophy.

In their paradigmatic forms, Marxism and (what usually falls under the label of) post-modernism are actually quite different families of thought. We discuss them here together if only because they each ask that mainstream political philosophy be altered fundamentally if not rejected altogether. Given their differences, however, I will consider the two in turn, with only passing reference to the ways that they overlap. I will then close the chapter with a brief discussion of liberalism in light of the various critical departures from it we will have examined. This will allow us to take stock of the most powerful lines of attack and to consider directions that defenders of liberalism might take in response.

The legacy of Marx and Marxism

Outside of academia, it may seem strange to consider Marxism as a major competitor in discussions of political systems, since outside of a few countries (albeit very large ones in some cases!), democratic capitalism reigns supreme as the only acceptable framework of government and economic organization (for discussion, see G. Cohen 1995: 245–65). But this judgment is based on several fundamental misconceptions: first, Marxism comes in various forms, and few political philosophers calling themselves Marxists would point to China, North Korea, or Cuba as their model for Marxist political systems; second, Marxism is not by nature or by implication (according to its defenders) anti-democratic. Indeed, left-wing critics of capitalist societies plausibly claim that the vast inequalities in wealth and power that capitalism fosters is precisely antithetical to democracy (is your impact on the outcome of government policies really equal to a billionaire's?). Moreover, most varieties of Marxism being defended these days include a vital role for economic *markets* in the production and distribution of goods (for discussion of the complexity of distinguishing capitalism from socialism, see Christman 1994: Chapter 2). And third, Marxism represents more than a blueprint for throwing off capitalism and adopting socialism (though that is certainly a crucial part of it), it is also a *method* for conducting social theory itself, one which carries with it a certain critical stance toward capitalism, but is not reducible to that stance nor to the recommendation of any particular form of socialism. It is an approach to social theory which calls into question the fundamental normative and methodological assumptions of traditional political philosophy (and it is this aspect of Marxism that we will stress here – for discussion of what is essential about Marxism see, for example, Lukács 1971: 1, Althusser [1969] 1996, Elster 1985 and Roemer 1988).

Marx was a tenacious and powerful thinker who left a broad intellectual and political legacy. Here, we will selectively examine three major contributions to political thought emanating from his work. These are historical materialism, the theory of ideology, and his critical interpretation of capitalism.

Historical materialism

Historical materialism is a complex view of the structure of societies and of the changes that occur in them, but its basic components are fairly straightforward. At any given time, a society should be seen in terms of its economic organization which will explain other aspects of its structure – its legal and political system in particular, though some would argue also its culture, social mores, and dominant morality. Specifically, a society should be seen as structured by three interrelated elements: its productive forces – the material resources available at any give time, including natural resources, labor, and technology; the relations of production – the patterns of control that people have over those resources, reflected in the legal system (granting property rights over the productive forces); and the 'superstructure' – the other aspects of the political, cultural, moral, and religious elements of a society. The productive forces, moreover, tend to *develop* over time, due to new discoveries of natural resources and technology as well as a natural human propensity to be increasingly productive in the face of scarcity. So the best way to understand the mechanisms driving the history of societies is in terms of the level of development of its material resources (rather than, say, its political system, dominant morality, or the actions of its government leaders). Understanding historical change in this way will also explain why major shifts in the political and economic organization of societies have taken place, as well as how future 'revolutions' from the dominant capitalism of the present age (to socialism and communism) are in fact inevitable.[1]

Historical materialism, then, implies that *at a time*, the structure of a society is best explained by the level of productive forces available within it. *Over time*, changes in the productive forces are the fundamental factor in explanations of changes in both the relations of production and the superstructure. That is, changes at the 'social' level are explained with fundamental reference to changes at the economic level for a society, and this includes shifts in moral principles, political structures such as forms of government, dominant religion, and so on.[2] Finally, the expanding level of the productive forces, which generally are supported and stabilized by the legal and political institutions of a state, will eventually grow to a point where they will put pressure on the existing relations of production, making the latter a kind of 'fetter' on the continued development of productive forces. At these times, a revolution of some kind eventually occurs, where those types of productive relations (and the rest of the superstructural elements in the society) will be thrown off and a new system of productive relations – a new economic system – will be ushered in.

Let us consider these theses separately. The first claims that societies primarily function to serve the (development of) the economic forces at its disposal; its laws, government, and social forms will be those that tend to stabilize and foster the productive capacities of the society. Feudalism, for example, best served the kinds of material and modes of production (agriculture and small-scale craft technologies) that were available in the Middle Ages. Capitalism, where private ownership of the productive forces predominates, best serves the kinds of resources (natural resources, technology, and labor) available in modern societies. So to understand why a society recognizes private property as a basic right (and protects various other individual liberal rights), one should not look to the intellectual, moral, or political reasons for that system, or the arguments and activities of the leaders of those societies. One must look at the basic economic imperative operating in them – to use available resources, technologies, and human labor for the general satisfaction of needs. Arguments for the 'rights of man,' basic justice, and other moral claims are all window dressing for the real forces at work in the society, the use and development of economic goods.

For the most part, this stabilizing and fostering effect that the relations of production have on the productive forces remains robust, and those forces grow and develop in normal ways. However, at certain times in history, the productive potential of a society (or region) will outpace its laws and governmental forms, just as the discovery of the 'new world,' the establishment of trade routes to Africa and Asia, and the increase in the population of potential laborers, put pressure on the old feudal forms in Europe and eventually caused their 'overthrow' and the onset of capitalism.[3] At such times, the relations of production, as well as the cultural and political aspects of a society, will act as a fetter on the development of the society's economic potential. This conflict will not last and a new form of social and economic organization will be developed, one which better serves this potential. And just as capitalism (private property) was developed in order to better serve the productive potential of the European states after the Middle Ages, socialism (and ultimately communism) will be necessary to fully utilize the labor and technological potential that, eventually, capitalism will frustrate (because of its tendency to exploit and alienate workers and to overuse resources).[4]

One element in this story that should be noted is that it includes a view of societies in which differences in *class* are fundamental. As Marx and Engels wrote: 'The history of all hitherto existing society is that of class struggle' (Marx and Engels [1848] 1998: 34). A class, for Marx, is a social group defined by its members' relation to the means of production. One's relation to the means of production concerns the degree of control (ownership) that one has over productive forces, including the productive force of labor. In capitalism, there are basically two classes – those who own the means of production (as well as their own labor power), called the bourgeoisie, and those who own no external means of production but own *only* their labor power, called the proletariat. The direct conflict of interest between members of these two classes under capitalism can be seen by considering that the bourgeoisie (the 'capitalists') want to buy labor and produce goods as cheaply as possible, while the proletariat has precisely the opposite desire. They compete and bargain and, depending on their relative options (what access they have to assets outside of those being bargained over), they will come to an agreement. This will, almost always, involve the capitalist hiring the services of the worker for a wage.

Also, a fundamental element in Marx's approach to human nature and the structure of human motivation is *labor*, the basic human drive to work and produce (Marx *Economic and Philosophic Manuscripts*, McLellan 1977: 80–81). For Marx, one's mode of labor is a crucial component in one's self-realization – what one makes of oneself – and the relation one has to the resources necessary to undertake this activity will structure and determine one's ability to be self-realizing. Having to sell one's labor in order to live means that one must accept the terms and conditions of that laboring that one faces (the kind of work done, the length of the working day, the social positions defined by various jobs). And for the proletariat, no direct control over those conditions are afforded to them, so control over the real physical determinants of self-realization are not in their hands. Therefore, real freedom (and equality), which Marxists define in terms of these actual abilities to labor in self-fulfilling ways, will be blocked under unequal economic and material conditions.

But is power over the means of production the most fundamental force driving society's structure and historical transformations? Marx was adamant about denying the view that *ideas* had any independent force in changing society; this was the grounds for his break with Hegel and other previous philosophical traditions (Marx *Critique of Hegel's 'Philosophy of Right,'* McLellan 1977: 26–35). This also shows that historical materialism rests importantly on his theory of ideology, that elements of society thought to be independent of economics, and indeed able to exercise a kind of force to reshape it (by way of social criticism), are actually themselves shaped by the nature of those economic forces. It is to this view, then, that we now turn.

Ideology

Generally, ideology is a set of beliefs (generally held in a population) that may be thought to be valid because of their own power and truth, but are really held because they tend to serve the interest of the ruling class. That is, the relations of production in a society explain the dominant ideas there, not vice versa. The belief in the power of ideology manifests Marxism's unique approach to social theory because it fundamentally redirects our gaze in appraising and interpreting social forms, from the justifications of those forms to the material dynamics that give rise to those justifications. Ideology forces us to look beyond ideas to economics (Geuss 1981: ch. 1, Elster 1985: ch. 8).

More precisely, ideology refers to a set of beliefs consciously held (though some might claim they can be unconscious) by members of a society, beliefs which are *about* some aspect of society but which are also *caused* by the material structure of that society. In particular, the interests of the ruling class, and the positions of all citizens in relation to that class, explain the dominance of various philosophical, religious, moral, and cultural ideas concerning social forms. A simple example of ideology is the generally held view under capitalism that capitalists both deserve their position in the economic structure of society and generally act in a way that benefits all its members. Nothing serves the interests of the capitalist class more than the general belief that the riches it controls are ones it morally deserves and that the decisions it makes to further enrich itself actually benefit those from whom those riches are taken. (At least this is the formulation that a Marxist would give of the matter.)

As Marx himself puts it:

> Morality, religion, metaphysics and all the rest of ideology as well as the forms of consciousness corresponding to these, thus no longer retain the semblance of independence. They have no history, no development; but men, developing their material production and their material intercourse, alter along with this their actual world, also their thinking and the products of their thinking.
> (Marx *The German Ideology*, McLellan 1977: 164)[5]

But the fact that moral judgments are examples of ideology for Marx indicates the precariousness of using Marx's views to mount a normative critique of capitalism itself, saying, for example, that it is unjust and therefore ought to be altered. Claims about the nature of ideology face the obvious objection that, in some of their forms, they are either self-refuting or empty. That is, if all pronouncements about society are really to be explained by the economic structure of that society, then so is the claim about ideology itself.

Moreover, to say that a belief system has social causes is not, by itself, to say it is false. For some views that are really the result of capitalist control of the economy may nevertheless be reasonable claims, in the same way that my paranoid beliefs that my government is spying on me, say, which are based purely on irrational fear, might turn out to be true (R. Miller 1991: 73, Geuss 1981: 88–95). So either the fact that a belief has material causes discredits that belief (discrediting the claim of ideology itself) or it does not (since the belief might still be true); if the latter holds, though, describing a dominant belief as 'ideological' does nothing to subvert its validity.

There are stronger and weaker forms of claims about the ideological nature of beliefs. One version, associated with the critical theory of the early Frankfurt School, in particular of Theodor Adorno, Max Horkheimer, and Walter Benjamin, assumes that the very epistemic *standards* by which we judge beliefs and normative claims – our own as well as those dominant in a society – are relative to the historical/economic context in which they occur, and hence subject to ideological pressure (Horkheimer and Adorno [1944] 1998, Geuss 1981: 63). The purpose of critical theory, then, is to reveal the social forces underlying the belief system and hopefully liberate the holder of that belief from the constraining effects of those forces (that is, inducing revolutionary action). Such criticism can only be addressed to those who populate the historical context and who are guided by the epistemic standards underlying such judgments, for any cross-contextual criticism that goes beyond this will lack a foundation.

Other writers in the Marxist tradition, however, view such a position as overly relativistic, since it implies that there is no standpoint from which to judge the very claim that standards of knowledge reflect the class interests of the economic powers in the society (see Habermas 1995: 106–30, Geuss 1981). They adopt, in turn, a weaker version of the ideology thesis, one which assumes that, at least for extremely broad socio-historical contexts (such as 'modernity'), fixed epistemic and normative standards can be identified that can ground judgments, but social forces nevertheless plague such judgments by promoting only those that serve the ruling class (Habermas 1975, 1996b).

Now even this thesis admits of stronger and weaker degrees. The stronger claims that all judgments are determined by the economic structure functioning in the interest of the ruling elite, while a weaker version has it that there is a strong *tendency* for beliefs to reflect the forces underlying the economic structure. That tendency is manifested in a kind of 'filtering' effect that economic systems have on normative ideas, allowing ideas that are friendly to their continued operation to flourish and strongly pressuring critical ones out of existence (Elster 1985: 470). The latter formulation escapes the charge of self-refutation since it implies that criticisms of dominant social forms (such as the ideology thesis itself) are examples of those beliefs that have evaded the pressures of economic forces and therefore can sustain a moral critique of existing society in a way that, potentially, functions independent of the internal forces of that society.[6]

Moreover, the question of the material pressures that give rise to belief systems is, as we said, independent of the plausibility or power of those ideas. Even if we were convinced that the socio-economic structure of capitalism gave rise to certain political principles (or at least exerted a kind of filtering effect on them), we must still inquire about whether, independent of those pressures, we should accept those principles. Libertarian liberalism, for example, strongly supports the interests of rich capitalists and so is ripe for accusations of simply serving ideological purposes. Whether or not that is so, libertarianism must be considered on its own philosophical merits. Pointing out the service such a view provides to the ruling classes becomes irrelevant.

Finally, just as we questioned whether economic forces are the only source of historical and social change in our discussion of historical materialism, we can here inquire whether ideas can ever exert pressure *back* on the relations of production that make up the base of the economic system. For instance, one of the most prominent examples of ideological thinking for Marx is racism, since it so systematically serves the interests of capitalists by dividing workers and retarding the process of worker unification and resistance (for discussion see R. Miller 1991: 78–79). But social and philosophical opposition to racism might function as an autonomous social movement, attacking the ideas and attitudes of racism as well as their political and legal manifestations, so that the question of racial justice arises independent of attacks on capitalist power relations. Correspondingly, many race theorists and feminists claim that Marxism focuses too narrowly on economic domination and leaves out of account the independent force of racial and sexual inequalities found in modern societies (see, for example, Jaggar 1983: 69–78, 229–43, and Boxill 1984: 52–72).

But two lessons arise from this discussion of ideology that are worth underscoring, and both can be gleaned from even the weakest version of the claim – that moral and political (and generally philosophical) judgments about society are always in danger of emanating from a social nexus that serves the interest of the elite in a way that tends to undercut their truth. The first is that the specific economic and social contexts out of which ideas are generated and (more importantly) take hold are worthy of particular study and critical suspicion. Especially given the broad control that capitalists can directly exert on both governments (through such things as capital flight, interest rate manipulation, financial pressure on politics, and the like: see Gilbert 1991: 176–80, R. Miller 1991: 68–69) and culture (through control of the mass media: see McCallister 1996), there is much prima facie evidence that ideas reflect the interests of the powerful in capitalist societies. There is much reason for political philosophy to broaden its methodological parameters (in some instances at least) to include critical interpretation of such sociological, historical, and psychological processes.

The second concerns liberalism. In so far as beliefs are formed as a result of social pressures that are designed to serve certain interests, then social theory which abstracts completely from such processes of value and character formation is problematically incomplete. As we saw in our discussions of feminism, liberal principles that take as their subjects fully formed autonomous adults, and do not provide the conceptual means for analyzing the values such autonomous adults have come to guide their lives by, will be mute about patterns of injustice and domination caused by the *manner* in which those values are developed. As we have seen repeatedly, the conception of the autonomous person underlying those principles will be the chief focus of this type of critical discussion.[7]

Capitalism, alienation, and exploitation

The third avenue of analysis that Marxism provides concerns the critical interpretation of capitalism as an historically located socio-economic system. The two elements of this critique that most commentators have centered on (though only one of which will be discussed in detail here) are that intrinsic to the structure of capitalism is the alienation and exploitation of the worker, respectively. Both of these, Marx thought, were *structural* aspects of capitalism, in that wage labor, a division of labor organized by the capitalist, and profits reverting to the owners of the means of production (all of which are alienating and exploitative) are all defining elements of capitalist relations of production, so alienation and exploitation inheres in capitalism.

The worker is alienated in several ways, for Marx: from his *labor* (or hers – though Marx refers only to men), since those he works for control the conditions under which that labor will be exercised; from *fellow workers* (since capitalist competition pits workers against each other); and from his *'species being*,' since he is separated from a defining element of his (human) nature (Marx *Economic and Philosophic Manuscripts*, McLellan 1977: 77–87). This means that, given that workers must use their labor power to produce things others will control (and under conditions the workers do not design or control), they are estranged from those aspects of themselves that, Marx thought, define their basic humanity, namely to labor in ways that freely express their own self-realization.

Marx's claims about the alienation of the worker occur almost exclusively in his earlier writings, and many current commentators avoid heavy reliance on this line of critique. But even assuming that alienation is endemic to capitalist systems, this charge amounts to a normative critique of the conditions of labor under capitalism (which may be the reason Marx himself ceased to emphasize it). And while the claim certainly has intuitive pull (wouldn't it be better to work under conditions where you control both the work environment and the product of your labor?), it amounts to a kind of 'perfectionist' argument of the sort we surveyed in Chapter 4. That is, to claim that alienated labor should be reduced or eradicated is to take a critical stand on modes of life and labor that people themselves may well be willing to accept (if, for example, the wages were high enough, the conditions flexible enough to leave free time for other activities, and the like). The view that only when one exerts one's labor under certain self-controlling conditions does one express one's true 'species being' is to rely on a specific (and contentious) view of human nature from which we might reasonably dissent (for discussion, see Kymlicka 1990: 186–92).

Exploitation, however, is a slightly different matter. Exploitation loosely means taking advantage of someone or someone's situation and, in so doing, extracting more from the interaction than the other person receives from it. Marx's views on exploitation are rather complex and for the most part rely on his particular view of value and labor. Marx famously developed a version of what was called the 'labor theory of value,' an economic model of the value of commodities that arose from the eighteenth-century theories of Adam Smith and David Ricardo. Roughly, this view is that all value (of an object in an economy) arises from, and is directly proportional to, the socially necessary labor used in its production. This view is notoriously difficult to articulate coherently and fully defend, as Marx himself partially realized (see *Capital*, vol. 3, McLellan 1977: 488–507, for his struggles to work out its details). Indeed, most contemporary Marxists have abandoned any reliance on the labor theory of value in defending the exploitative nature of capitalism (see, for example, Roemer 1982, and cf. Elster 1985: 127–65).

However, the charge concerning exploitation can be generally summarized as follows:[8] capitalism relies on growth and growth requires the generation of profit by the capitalist. Profit amounts to the income which is left over after all costs of production, including labor costs, interest on debts, material used in production, and so on are paid and the produced object is sold on the market. If labor is the chief source of all value (things like machines are merely 'embedded labor'), and the process of production produces a thing whose value is greater than the costs the capitalist lays out in that process (by definition, otherwise there would be no profit), then the worker contributes more value to the process than he or she is paid. This happens specifically because the wage rate is fixed by competition among workers (and given the presence of a 'reserve army of the unemployed,' wages always gravitate to mere subsistence, Marx argued). Therefore, this process operates only by the capitalist taking advantage of the worker due to her constrained position and extracting more value from her than is returned. Hence exploitation (Marx *Capital,* vol. 1, McLellan 1977: 455–70).

Now this version of the critique assumes the labor theory of value – that the worker's contribution is the ultimate source of value for the commodity, so selling the commodity for more than the worker is paid (marginally) exploits the worker. But as we said, this view that the source of economic value emanating from (only) labor has been almost universally abandoned, so the argument must be put in terms of the comparative income and relative bargaining positions of the workers and the capitalist. On that version, we must assume that the 'value' added to any factor in production is simply the price paid for it in the local competitive market. Therefore, the exploitation that occurs is a function of the differential incomes that workers and capitalists each bring to the bargain and leave with after the workday. On those (overly simplistic) terms, we can still mount a fairly powerful intuitive case that there is exploitation occurring, since (assuming that the capitalist and worker put in equal amount of effort during production) the fact that capitalists tend to earn *many times* more than the average worker in successful firms seems to show that the relatively constrained bargaining positions of the workers explain the differential in incomes. Therefore, exploitation – defined as taking advantage of a person's constrained circumstances and emerging from an interaction with her with more than she takes away – seems inherent in capitalism whenever profits are generated.[9]

This, then, shows that the heart of exploitation is the unequal distribution of productive resources in capitalist society, where exchanges take the form of 'free' transfers but produce highly unequal results (Kymlicka 1990: 176–77, Roemer 1985). From this angle, then, it appears that Marxism is hard to distinguish from egalitarian liberalism.

But this is to miss an important element in the Marxist critique of capitalist exploitation that, while not ruled out of consideration in liberal egalitarianism, is certainly not stressed by it. Inequalities under capitalism characterize not merely the relative positions of the (individual) citizens living there, but also their *relations*. Capitalists' relative superior position give them not only greater income, but greater social power than the workers. Furthermore, this power is used *over* the worker, in the form of designing production and employment to meet their needs (increasing production, growth, and profit) rather than the needs of the workers. Owners of capital, through managers at various levels, have authority over workers (they can fire them, demand overtime, that they relocate across the country, and so on); but they also exert indirect power, making decisions about how production will be organized, goods will be manufactured, advertising will be shaped, and the like. And since workers are also consumers, workers' lives both at work and elsewhere are 'controlled' by the capitalist (see Elster 1985: 199 and 211–16).[10]

Exploitation, then, involves the power relations that go along with unequal access to the means of production that allow one class of people to benefit disproportionately from the position they occupy in the relations of production, at the expense of another class. The Marxist remedy for this is the *social* ownership of productive goods, where democratically constituted mechanisms of collective control over the economy replace private property and markets (except where use of markets, say to determine factor prices, is favored by the people). Now, there are many lines of criticism of this 'solution' to the alleged problem of exploitation in capitalism. The most famous such line is that socializing the means of production will be intolerably inefficient, a point which sparked a protracted debate about the productive efficiency of socialism (for discussion, see Christman 1994: ch. 6).

More importantly, however, the social control of the economy through democratic institutions will not guarantee an absence of exploitation and inequality, for majorities in such a society can act collectively to secure a greater share of resources in a way that allows for the exploitation of the minority. In so far as trade and market mechanisms are allowed in some fashion under a post-capitalist regime, even if all citizens begin with equal resources and equal control over productive processes (or the opportunity through representatives to exercise such control), inequalities of wealth are possible over time through the different choices people make as well as the different attitudes toward risk and consumption they adopt (Kymlicka, 1990: 171–83, Roemer 1988, Arneson 1981).

There are two kinds of response one might make to this problem. One is that we can assume that people's desires for domination and unequal power will be relinquished following the overthrow of capitalism and the fundamental social reorganization that socialism will bring about. This prediction can certainly be traced to Marx's writings where he blames all competitive impulses on the ideology of capitalism (for example in *The German Ideology*, McLellan 1977: 159–91), but the view that all desires for comparative advantage will vanish with the overthrow of capitalism is an aspect of Marx's thought that seems to many to be the most strikingly utopian (Elster 1985: 82–92).

The second response is to urge that a constitutional structure be put in place that limits inequalities allowable via democratic action, where principles (of justice?) constrain the full operation of democratic institutions to prevent such damaging effects. But the argument for such principles amounts to the claim that such inequalities are *unjust*, a claim that is in some tension with Marx's theory of ideology and his many expressions of disdain for justice-based critiques of economic structures. The question then arises, does Marx provide the materials for a critique of the *injustice* of inequality, such that unjustified inequalities would be condemned both under capitalism and under whatever socialist regime would replace it? This turns out to be a complex methodological and interpretive question, since as was noted earlier, Marx did not view the proper role of social theory to be that of providing a normative critique of social institutions abstracted from an analysis of their operation (for overview of the literature, see Geras 1989). But in so far as Marxism can be understood to provide the grounds for a view about justice, then Marxism and liberal egalitarianism would then become very close cousins, if not variations on the same theory. A brief discussion of this issue, then, is in order.

Marxism and justice

The basic problem of deriving judgments of injustice from an orthodox Marxist framework concerns Marx's views on ideology. For Marx, judgments of political principle, such as claims of injustice, operate in the realm of ideas and so are part of the superstructure. Therefore, they are in place because (and only because) they tend to serve, or at least do not seriously threaten, the development of the productive forces in society. (Though as we noted above, this does not close off questions of their truth.) In capitalism, justice is defined by the law of free contract, where 'free' individuals trade goods voluntarily, according to standards set by the bargaining position of each. There can be no 'injustice' in such a transaction since such a term is defined by the procedure of making these very types of trades, and therefore there exists no outside standard with which to judge them. Justice, then, is simply a 'bourgeois virtue' and, as such, must be superceded by an overthrow of capitalist relations of production, where a new era of communism can be ushered in which is 'beyond' justice.

There is much debate about whether a society can be imagined which in fact has no need of rules of social interaction of the sort that justice provides (Kymlicka 1990: 161–69, Buchanan 1982: ch. 4).[11] But that leaves the question of what we can say about life before reaching the communist utopia, whether Marxists can claim that capitalism is itself unjust (because, for example, of the exploitation of workers it inevitably involves) and so thereby provides reasons for moving *toward* such a utopia. Marx himself, in several places, seemed clearly to reject the language of justice and rights to critically appraise exploitation (or life under capitalism in general), and yet, at the same time, he *does* systematically condemn such exploitation (for references, see Geras 1989: 214–17). Can one, then, be a 'justice Marxist' – condemning capitalism as unjust and thereby promoting an alternative social conception based on superior principles – and still pay heed to the materialist conception of history and the theory of ideology that it supports?

Marxists must agree that conceptions of justice are strongly shaped by the socio-economic structures of the age. That view seems to suggest that therefore capitalism is not unjust by the standard of its own age. However, justice-Marxists can claim that the particular ideas 'dominant' in the modern age that seem to provide ideological support for capitalism (for example that whatever is freely contracted into is just and so wage labor and income inequalities are justified) are indeed mere emanations of the economic forces of capitalism and serve the class interests of the elite. But these are merely *interpretations* of more abstract principles available in that age, namely the principles of Enlightenment liberalism, whose general contours are not so easily reducible to the need to serve class interests. Indeed, alternative and more philosophically defensible interpretations of those abstract principles could be put forward and defended, and applied to capitalism to show its injustice. Also, such a philosophical view can be used to design alternative social systems that would amount to a moral improvement over capitalism, one which would better live up to the humanitarian and egalitarian strains in this tradition.

However, one element of orthodox Marxism should remain in such an account. That is, no philosophical critique of existing economies can plausibly by mounted without a detailed understanding of the material forces and power dynamics in that society. This is part of Marx's repeated condemnation of 'reformist' social movements (see, for example, *The Critique of the Gotha Program*, McLellan 1977: 564–70), namely that the voicing of philosophical arguments against a social form without practical analysis of how the power structure of that social form can be upended and reconstituted is futile. This makes use of the remnant of historical materialism operating in the weak version of ideology described above — that economic forces will have a strong tendency to filter out threatening voices, so unless this power is resisted, such voices will be nothing but empty words. The lesson here is that theory without praxis may well be empty; but theory along with an interdisciplinary analysis of the social forces operating in the arena being critiqued (providing the basis for a kind of praxis) need not be relativistic and hence self-refuting. Rather, it must merely be realistic (see Geras 1989: 227–30 for a similar argument).

But this supposes that some version of liberal egalitarianism (or indeed some alternative theory of justice that could apply realistically to modern conditions) can be fully defended. I do not assume that this has been done. Nevertheless, we have extracted from the Marxist tradition several ideas that urge both a methodological and a substantive shift in the focus of social and political theory. These are that societies must be understood primarily in terms of the material forces at work in their economic systems (historical materialism); that politics, culture, and indeed philosophical critiques are all under pressure from those material conditions to be cast in terms that serve the class interests of the economic elite (the theory of ideology); but critiques of the inequalities inherent in capitalism (and potentially socialism) may nevertheless proceed by utilizing the conceptual tools of egalitarian liberalism, as long as they do so in a way that includes explanatory analysis of the mechanisms of economic and social forces at work in such societies.

However, there are many who think that relying on the traditions of Enlightenment thought in this way is doubly misguided, since that tradition itself rests on foundations that can be very much thrown into doubt, a subject to which we now must turn.

Post-modern departures

The term 'post-modern' means different things in different contexts, sometimes describing a period in history (more or less contemporary times), an aesthetic style (a reaction against 'modernism') or a pattern of social organization (see Harvey 1989, and Butler 1995a: 36–40). Most often, however, it refers to a range of philosophical views that share a suspicion of those grand foundationalist theories that arose from the Enlightenment and which assume that reasoned reflection is able to discover universal truths about the world. As described by Jean-François Lyotard (one of the few writers in this tradition to fully embrace the term 'post-modernism'), it is generally characterized by suspicion of the 'metanarratives,' including such things as Marxism, Hegelianism, and Kantianism, which attempt to yield universal truths about the human condition discovered by the use of objective reason (Lyotard 1997: 37). Post-modernism not only rejects epistemological and moral foundations, it also abandons the idea that rational reflection, whether utilized philosophically or in scientific contexts, can yield reliable and stable truths. As will soon be apparent, this will pick up on the discussion near the close of the last chapter concerning feminist rejections of the standards of impartial reason.

Lines of post-modern thought have arisen with a specifically political cast, where critiques of the normative models of reasoned reflection and the autonomous person have generated views with a decidedly social focus. For this reason, the project of liberal political philosophy is a principle target of post-modernist critique. In our discussion here of these lines of critique, the versions of post-modern thought discussed by feminists will be featured, if only to focus on a single set of themes, but post-modern challenges to liberal philosophy motivated by considerations of race, culture, sexuality, and combinations of these could also have been considered. (For a general overview, see White 1991.)

There are two separable strands in this post-modern critique that can be usefully teased apart (cf. Young 1990b: 303–05). In one, the idea that there are overarching, if not universal, normative propositions that apply to persons irrespective of their particularities, such as their gender, race, class, or the dynamics of ongoing political struggles, is rejected. This critical view rests on a particular theory of language, one which departs from the 'structuralist' accounts of meaning and reference to be described below (hence 'post-structuralism' is often used interchangeably with 'post-modernism'). The second set of themes concerns the rejection of the idea of persons as unified, stable, and self-transparent rational agents, able to freely and rationally grasp universal principles by which to autonomously guide action. Theorists who develop this theme, some of whom are informed by psychoanalysis, emphasize that a close examination of the mechanisms of personal reflection reveals in the subject a disjointed and unstable motley of motives, identifications, ways of thinking, and modes of behavior. As we have noted, the traditional liberal conception of the autonomous person is one of a rational agent able to subject all aspects of herself to reflection and to alter herself in light of principles and values she sees as valid (universally valid, according to some conceptions of autonomy).

This model of the person is thoroughly dismantled by the post-modern views being considered here: rationality is either an illusion or provides only a narrow, oppressive, hierarchical standard of thought; the self is opaque to reflection rather than transparent, comprised of unconscious and conflicting elements which are constructed from the dynamics of surrounding (social) power relations as well as individual past experiences; and wholesale abilities of self-transformation are illusory (see, for example, Foucault 1995: 135–56, 1984: 341–51, 1990a). Let us look at these strains of post-modern thought in more detail, taking the second of them first.

The fragmented self

A helpful starting point for explicating post-modern thought is to consider the Cartesian approach to subjectivity and the person and its connection to standards of knowledge. For Descartes, the essence of a person is her reflective capacity and access to clear and distinct, that is, *a priori* ideas. The mental, internal life of pure thought is the Archimedean point of both self-identity and knowledge. Aspects of the 'external' world – the body, physical objects, and all contingencies of time and space – are set at a distance from, and considered only as represented through, this mental faculty. The person, then, is the dualistic combination of mental and physical properties, whose essence lies on the mental side of the divide. All contingencies of bodily comportment, interpersonal dynamics, social structure, one's place in history, and the power dynamics that bear on all of these, can be grouped outside of the workings of the core self, and hence only indirectly relevant to the person as knower. Knowledge results, then, from deductive inference and inductive generalization, untempered in its operation by these contingencies.

The post-modern rejection of this picture of the person takes it apart piece by piece. The assumption of the essential rationality of the thinking subject, for example, is undercut by general suspicion of the powers of reason and self-reflection, informed in some instances by psychoanalytic models of unconscious (and non-rational) drives and relations. The separation of the mental aspects of self from the physical, with the attendant assumption of the centrality of the mental and the relative unimportance of the physical, is rejected by theorists of 'the body' who insist on the fundamentally physical, embodied nature of experience and reflection.[12]

We will return to this theme shortly, where it will be developed further; in order to do so, however, we must first examine the post-modern conception of language and meaning.

Rejecting the language of universal principles

Connected with this rejection of the Cartesian model of the self and its powers of reason is a fundamental shift in the understanding of language. In the traditional view, made famous by the linguistic philosophy of Gottleib Frege and Bertrand Russell, meaning could be understood as a function of atomistic linguistic elements whose logical relations – syntax – form sentences which express truth-functional propositional content. Meaning, on this view, is determined by the internal logical structure of those linguistic elements and the relation between those elements and the world (via reference) (for discussion, see Hacking 1975 and the essays in Rorty 1967). For the linguists and philosophers in the 'structuralist' (and eventually 'post-structuralist') camp, meaning should not, indeed cannot, be seen one sentence at a time like this, in isolation from the interplay of the entirety of the linguistic structure of which it is a part. Such sentences and their constitutive elements (words) gain semantic significance by virtue of their differential operation relative to other elements in the system. These systems of signifiers operate in tandem with social and political forces that structure the uses of language, communication, and thought.

For Frege and Russell, the logical structure of language can be determined by the analysis of sentences, and hence explicated independently of historical forces and social relations; second, semantics is related to syntax in that truth and meaning are, as far as possible, a function of the internal logic of sentences and the causal relation of language to the world.[13] Both these tenets are rejected by (post-) structuralist theories: meaning cannot be determined independently of the dynamic operation of entire sign systems (hence linguistics and anthropology, not to mention social theory and politics, are all of a piece); and meaning is not a precise and determined relation of word to world, but rather is a product of 'difference,' the contrast between particular signs functioning in a larger system.

This last point is crucial in the post-structuralist approach. Meaning is not a matter of causal connection between sentences and some non-linguistic reality, nor is it a function of the internal coherence of sign systems. Rather, it is a function of difference – the gaps and contrasts between signs that explain the appropriateness of one over the other in a given context. This appropriateness rests not on the characteristics of the sign in question – 'red' – but on the contrast or difference between that sign and another – 'blue' (that is, not red). This play of difference determines meaning, and is located in a larger structural matrix that forms the language – the *langue* – operative in a given cultural site. This means that reference is a relation between one sign and another according to the dominant patterns of use in that site (and not, of course, between the sign and the world). (For discussion, see Jameson 1972: 101–216.)

For structuralists of this sort, meaning resides in the binary opposition of signifiers whose contrast denotes sense: inside/outside, light/dark, nature/culture, man/woman, and so on. The *post*-structuralist turn in this theory of language takes this view of meaning and brings to greater prominence the implications of seeing meaning as difference and semantics as the indefinite play of signifiers. These writers emphasize both the open-endedness of this 'play' as well as the larger implication of these contrasts. Such binary pairs imply a hierarchy buried in the fact that meaning affixes to a dominant element of the pair while its 'other' is defined relative to it, and hence derivatively. This dominance is reflected in a priority of focus as well as a relegation of the subsidiary term to secondary status, if not to outright insignificance (see White 1991: 15, and Eagleton 1983: 133ff.).

Julia Kristeva echoes this point when she emphasizes the fluidity and multiplicity of linguistic expression. Rather than seeing language as cemented in rule-bound orders of meaning, Kristeva emphasizes the 'process' of linguistic meaning and communication: meaning is produced through the play between literal and figurative, representational and musical aspects of speech. Non-discursive elements, such as metaphor, modes of bodily expression, figurative turns of phrase, suggestive associations, and varieties of connotation all add to the conveyance of ideas among language users. The rules fixing the meaning of such elements are open-ended, subject to negotiation and change, and, most importantly, are a function of the complexities of social dynamics inherent in the interchange of *actual* communication and the institutional and social settings defining that interchange (Kristeva 1980, 1987; for discussion, see Young 1990a: 141–48, and Meyers 1994: 100–01).

Once language is seen in this manner, the interplay between social forces and semiotic meaning takes center stage.[14] In so far as the thinking subject is understood as the operation of meaning-bearing elements (rather than the pure, unfiltered reflector of Descartes), the self is understood as a construction emerging out of the socially mediated play of signification just described. In more specific terms, key categories in the reflective understanding of the self – sanity, reason, guilt, responsibility, desire, sexuality – operate inside this historically unfolding dynamic of social relations. And where there are social relations, there is *power* at work in the shape and direction of that relation. So the self is constructed out of the power dynamics of present and past social structures, in particular institutional structures whose conceptual legitimation arises from, and in turn reshapes, that dynamic of power and meaning (what Foucault calls 'power/knowledge') (Foucault 1965, 1995).

The implications for the formulation of general normative principles, then, is clear: since meanings are neither stable nor independent of socially embedded use, moral and political principles cannot be expressed in politically neutral language that operates separately from the social milieu from which those principles get their meaning. Liberal principles, for example, attempt to express such normative propositions in neutral language applicable to all rational agents regardless of particularities of their identity (as discussed in the last chapter). However, post-modern critics of this view emphasize the instability of the conceptual categories used to specify the subjects in question, categories which always serve to suppress the difference among those coming under them as well as the contested nature of the boundaries of those categories (who counts as 'rational' for example). As we saw, on this view of language, all concepts are contested and serve to surreptitiously conceal a particularized agenda manifesting the existing power structures dominant in the society out of which these categories and principles emerge. A telling case of this comes from the writings of a prototypical liberal humanist, J. S. Mill, whose views on freedom and individuality (and the utilitarianism upon which they were based) bore all the pretensions of universality one could expect from modernist theorizing. 'Over himself, over his own body and mind, the individual is sovereign,' he writes, implying a broad application of this and other normative claims. But tucked away a few lines later is the, to him obvious, qualification, that '. . . we may leave out of consideration those backward states of society in which the race itself may be considered as in its nonage . . . Despotism is a legitimate mode of government when dealing with barbarians' (Mill [1859] 1975: 13–14). And Mill's position in the colonial administration in India, in the East India House, adds a chilling aspect to this qualification (W. Thomas 1985: 1–3).

This view, however, takes us back to the post-modern rejection of a unified self, as it bears on the conception of the person that such linguistic practices under review here underwrites. The new social movements that arose in Europe and the US in the 1960s, for example, demanded a re-evaluation of this humanist conception of justice because it had failed to give specific weight to the full variety of unique needs, perspectives, and experiences of participants in those movements, producing what came to be called 'identity politics' (White 1991: 10f., Young 1990a: ch. 6). The emphasis on general rights derived from the

RADICAL CRITIQUE: MARXISM AND POST-MODERNISM

conception of the autonomous person neutrally described allowed no special mention of the unique manner in which minorities, women, and gays and lesbians confronted narrow opportunities and constraining social structures. Moreover, the assumed bearer of those rights, while purporting to neutrally include all persons as such, merely replicated the conceptions of the good and of justice held by those in power – heterosexual white men (in the manner we discussed in the last chapter). Motivated by arguments such as this, claims have been made that only specific and particularized conceptions of the subject of justice can adequately represent the needs of diverse populations (Phelan 1996). The argument is that the idea that self-conceptions, motivations, and the definition of needs vary essentially across various groups, and that such variations matter crucially to the articulation of principles of justice.

Here, however, lies one of the crucial instabilities of the post-modern critique of liberal principles. On the one hand, post-modernists claim that all purportedly universal principles utilize categories which range over entities whose internal differences are politically important, but ignored by those principles. But on the other, they also urge that no category term can be taken as stable or meaningful independent of the fluid contingencies of the power dynamics of a society. However, the claim that *sub*-categories of persons within the general concepts of liberal principles ('women', 'racial minorities', 'homosexuals', and so on) pick out politically important differences among groups implies that *those* concepts – gender, race, sexuality – are stable enough to express identity and unique needs. This last claim runs counter to the deep suspicion leveled at all generalized categorizations by post-modern theorists.

For this reason, critics of liberal humanism work very hard to pick out specific categories of difference without essentializing the identities of the constituents of those groups. Though she is not herself a post-modern thinker *per se*, Iris Young brings out clearly the post-modern rejection of those liberal paradigms of justice that utilize what she calls 'totalizing' theories of universal morality (ones stated in general and allegedly neutral terms which assume an unproblematic identity among all of the subjects to which they apply). She is similarly critical of the concept of a unified, independent autonomous agent as the subject of political principles (Young 1990a: ch. 4). Young argues, alternatively, that individuals are constituted by the groups of which they are members: 'Groups . . . constitute individuals. A person's particular senses of history, affinity, and separateness, even in the person's mode of reasoning, evaluating, and expressing feeling, are constituted partly by her or his group affinities' (ibid.: 45).[15] But in specifying 'affinity' as a mark of group membership, Young includes a partially subjective element in her account of identity. Though the affinity in question is shaped by ongoing social processes (rather than fixed attributes) and admits of shifting and blurry boundaries, it is a condition of identity that it involves affective bonding, sharing common assumptions, and active networking among members (ibid.: 172), activities that take place as a result of voluntary choices on the part of group members.[16] But the presence of a voluntaristic element of this sort in models of identity will dilute severely the contrast between such models and the liberal humanism they are meant to replace. Liberal conceptions of autonomy can all accept the historical nature of group membership and identity, but they insist that the ability to rationally appraise and, if it is wished, to revise those connections is fundamental in the normative positions concerning rights, recognition, and respect underwritten by the model of the autonomous person. Only if a fundamentally unchosen element remains in the model of identity will views of this sort provide true alternatives to liberal conceptions of the self.

This points to the internal tension in post-modern conceptions of political action – feminist accounts for example – that, on the one hand, reject conceptions of stable self-conceptions but, on the other, advocate forms of political resistance that themselves presuppose sincere self-expression, basic interests rooted in a fixed identity, and authentic political engagement. For example, Foucault claims that the interplay of social forces, as embodied in the disciplinary practices of dominant institutions of society, not only limit and constrain the development of a self but *constitute* that self (Foucault 1990a, 1995; cf., however, Foucault 1988: 2–5). In a similar vein (though influenced more by psychoanalysis), Judith Butler argues that categories of identity, such as 'female,' are unstable and malleable as well as produced through the power dynamics of reigning social forces (Butler 1990: 1–35, 1997). Just as all conceptual categories are unstable and socially constructed, those concepts that organize one's self-conception such as gender, race, and so on do not refer to settled and fixed characteristics or ways of being. Rather, she argues, gender is 'performed' in a non-intentional and non-cognitive sense, in that it is enacted by the styles of life adopted and constructed by the dominant meanings one's culture provides (and which, of course, reflect patterns of power in that culture) (Butler 1990, 1995b).

But if there is nothing authentic in the identities from which agents are moved to resist regimes of power that are taken to exemplify domination, then it is unclear what the ground could possibly be, short of individually motivated passions, for organized political action to resist that domination (Benhabib 1995). Only if the 'performance' of one's identity is somehow rooted in either a self-conception or a set of basic interests that can be specified prior to the activity that they motivate and justify can the social interaction resting upon them find a grounding. And the view that positing identity can be used purely 'strategically,' as a trope by which to motivate action but based on conceptualizations that are, theoretically, no longer seen as grounded (Butler 1995b: 128–29; Rorty 1989: 73–95) simply skirts the crucial issue: for the idea of a strategic undertaking assumes a settled and defensible idea of the *goal* of that undertaking as well as a perspective from which such goals can be justified, both of which are fundamentally in question from a post-modern point of view.

We have said nothing to challenge the view of language (as fundamentally fluid and unstable) and the conception of self-constitution that motivates the post-modern critique, and certainly those claims deserve their own specific scrutiny. But even if the linguistic concepts utilized in normative principles are always in danger of masking exclusionary categorizations (as we saw with Mill), and even if selves (and their interests) can be thought of as socially constructed out of the dynamics of power, we still need a way of conceptualizing principles of political critique that rest on some settled concepts and fixed identities. Saying that all concepts are open to critical reappraisal is certainly compatible with making normative claims that utilize such concepts. But what are also necessary are normative guidelines which direct social action that involve *deliberation* about those very contested meanings, normative guidelines that find full expression in a view of collective choice and deliberation, a theory (once again) of democracy.[17] *Liberal conceptions of democracy may well be fully disposed to provide a framework in which such basic interests (albeit resting, perhaps, on fluid identities) can be expressed in a way protective of fundamental rights and basic justice.*

Epilogue: The hope of liberalism

It won't be necessary to rehearse, in detail, the various critical claims made about liberal political philosophy in the past several chapters, but it will be helpful to bring out certain major themes. Concerning its basic value commitments, liberalism faces challenges from two diametrically opposed viewpoints: at one end of the spectrum are perfectionists and, in a different way, communitarians and conservatives, all of whom claim that liberalism's commitment to some form of neutrality runs counter to specific value commitments that certain citizens will hold as objectively valid (and which, perfectionists claim, *are* objectively valid).

The priority of the right over the good inherent in liberalism is in conflict with those political philosophies which advocate the promotion of substantive goods for citizens, whether those are understood as objectively valid for human beings as such or simply grounded in the communal practices which provide the structure of the values citizens themselves pursue. The principle of legitimacy we discussed in Chapters 2 and 4, where political principles are considered acceptable only if embraced as legitimate by the citizenry, is threatened when the values which motivate citizens' own commitment to public principles run counter to or diverge from the allegedly neutral values underlying public principles of justice.

Chiming in from the other direction are those thinkers, such as postmodernists and some feminists and race theorists, who claim that liberalism is not pluralistic *enough*. For their claim is that values are more fragmented and plural than liberalism assumes, in that the supposedly neutral categories of persons assumed in liberal principles of justice (which do not mention particularities of gender, race, and so on) fail to respect the heterogeneity of self-conceptions and commitments found in modern populations. Feminists and race theorists claim, for example, that basic interests tied to gender and race are glossed over in those principles of liberal justice which make no mention of such categories, serving to ignore those aspects of entrenched injustice found in current societies and thereby supporting the power hierarchies of the status quo. Moreover, liberal attention to formal justice, as focused on the public institutions of the basic structure of society, fail to attend to the varieties of injustice manifested in informal, personal, and cultural aspects of society.

Post-modern theorists take these issues further by claiming that the very *language* of liberalism (or any other reason-based, allegedly universal normative social theory) belies the instability and exclusionary tendencies of any reliance on conceptual categories and are based on models of unified personhood and stable identity that can no longer be sustained. Values and interests which principles of justice serve to protect are not only more plural and varied than liberalism assumes, they are more conceptually blurry, fluid, and revisable than the language of Enlightenment philosophy as a whole admits.

Orthogonal to these concerns is the challenge of Marxism, as well as aspects of feminism and critical race theory, questioning the theoretical methods of liberal political philosophy, methods which assume a sharp distinction between idealized normative principles and real world descriptive analysis. Marxists, and others, argue that full theoretical treatment of social conditions must include interpretive analysis of historical processes and current material conditions in order to fully articulate the nature of injustice (or oppression, exploitation, domination, and so on). Indeed, they claim, liberal theory already does this by assuming (without articulating them) various background facts concerning such things as the psychological make up of citizens and the rules governing the organization and operation of social institutions (in particular economic mechanisms). Whether or not one agrees with the normative presuppositions of Marxism, this call for a more thoroughgoing interdisciplinarity (including use of material from the social sciences) is a powerful one.

These challenges, and several related ones mentioned in these pages, call in many cases for a response from, if not a full reconstruction of, liberal theory. In the case of the perfectionist challenge, this highlights the liberal commitment to an irreducible pluralism of values, a plurality which blocks us from locating any specific set of fixed objective values that can be posited as valid for all in the society. More deeply, this exposes the liberal commitment to a certain version of value constructivism, according to which values can be understood to apply validly to individuals only if they, in some sense, can come to embrace them from a reasonable point of view which reflects their unique history and place in the world. Value *realism*, which understands values as definable apart from the reasoned embrace of those values by those whose values they are, must be rejected by liberal views discussed here. That rejection can only come, of course, from more detailed philosophical arguments than those surveyed in this book, but it is not a prospect that appears hopeless on its face.

A similar response might be made to the challenges raised by communitarian critics and those motivated by considerations of the social construction of the self. The liberal conception of the person (and autonomy) must be spelled out in a way that is consistent with the idea that we are not fully self-made, our self-concepts, values, motivations, and identities are constructed in virtue of our embeddedness in historically and culturally situated social structures. No conception of the autonomous person will be acceptable if it denies this. However, we did put forward, in quite schematic terms, a conception of autonomy which requires only that the person have those cognitive and emotional capacities to reflect on aspects of herself that form her character and values, and be able to reject such aspects (or conditions that form them) when she is deeply alienated from them. This does not imply that she be able to separate herself from all contingent conditions of her identity or her social situation to be autonomous, nor does it demand that she see herself as independent of the social context that forms her personality.

Rather, it merely requires that she be able to consider her situation and embrace it (in some minimal sense) in light of considerations of its history and social context. Nothing in the communitarian challenge to liberalism (if the arguments behind that challenge are all accepted as plausible) rules this out. (In a moment we will consider a post-modern challenge to this idea of self-reflection that will not so easily be avoided.)

Those criticisms that demand that principles of justice be sensitive to differences in interests relating to gender, race, and other aspects of identity (and historical victimization) must also be addressed. But as we noted, only in so far as such differences can themselves be specified in ways that do not assume their own problematic (essentialist) conceptions of identity will such a response be called for. In so far as group interests vary in ways not acknowledged by the general categories of justice (protecting basic rights understood in particular ways, for example), then such categories fail to apply neutrally to all citizens and are subject to challenge.

Similarly, those aspects of injustice that are found outside of official public contexts, relating to social relations, informal dynamics of behavior, language and cultural expression, are subject to political evaluation and critique. However, as we noted, such patterns of behavior, in many cases, may reflect sincerely held value commitments that a pluralistic society must attempt neutrality toward (religious doctrines that assume hierarchies of power and status for example), as long as such practices do not deny their adherents basic autonomy and dignity (they allow freedom of exit, for example, and are not imposed on others without consent). But in many cases, there may well simply be deep conflict between respect for pluralism and the need to eradicate conditions that cause (or are the result of) injustice. This is a balancing act that liberal theories need to attend to more directly.

The versions of liberal theory being assumed here can all be seen as rejecting a kind of moral foundationalism which its founders (such as Locke and Kant) embraced. Rather, as we found in Rawls's version of this view, liberalism can be seen as an historically situated approach to the fact of pluralism, one which grew out of the Enlightenment and came to fruition in the constitutional democracies of the modern age. These political frameworks all assume that citizens share at least an abstract commitment to respect for autonomy and the equal status of persons, without which social relations devolve into mere power struggles among fundamentally opposed groups (power struggles that no independent theory of justice can hope to adjudicate). In this way, the framing principles of respect for autonomy and equality of moral status are inherited as a cultural legacy but embraced from a variety of points of view, each of which grounds those values in different moral conceptions and value frameworks. This is the essence of 'political' liberalism discussed in Chapter 4. The fundamental issue left facing that view, as we discussed, was whether it is possible to demand that citizens bracket away from public discussion the details of those moral conceptions that are not shared by other citizens. This is a contention to which liberalism must also find a way to respond.

This shows an aspect of current political thought not fully emphasized here, and that is the wide *variety* of liberal theories. While attending to this variety in various places (Chapter 4 for example), I have not stressed the numerous differences among adherents to this general picture which would show up in a more detailed treatment of this area. One can only mention in passing, then, that what I have been calling 'liberalism' here is actually quite a disparate and contentious set of complex philosophical positions.

For many of these challenges, we discussed the need to include the call for instituting democratic procedures among the basic principles of justice, not merely as an added mechanism to aggregate preferences in an already just society, but as a constitutive element of just institutions. The operation of robust methods to facilitate social discourse, collective deliberation, and public expression and discussion is essential for principles of justice to be fully articulated and operational. Only if actual voices, represented in forums for public interaction, are invited to articulate the specific interests, value perspectives, identities, and particular experiences that make up an increasingly differentiated social world, will the norms regulating social interaction be fully worked out. Prior to hearing those voices, all such normative principles run the risk of over-simplification, exclusion, and bias that have historically marked virtually all attempts at constructing 'neutral' principles in advance of social engagement. Justice and democracy, then, are interlaced and mutually dependent.

The 'hope' of liberalism, then, is merely the hope of justice: in order to peacefully and respectfully acknowledge our place an increasingly pluralistic but interconnected world, we must hope that accepting as legitimate principles of justice that do not rest on specific moral conceptions, but do guarantee certain rights and protections will lead us to the collective and individual pursuit of life plans that are themselves meaningful. The hope is both that justice be formulated in a way that pays full respect to the varieties of value and identity found in the modern world, but also at the same time allows each person or group to pursue their moral, religious, and philosophical convictions in a way fully reflective of their sense of the ultimate validity of those convictions.

Liberalism, then, attempts a precarious reconciliation between the twin forces of the modern condition: strong moral commitment and increasing plurality of voices.

Chapter summary

This chapter included surveys of two radical departures from the Enlightenment humanism that underwrites liberal theory. I summarized the dominant themes of the Marxist critique at the close of that section and so won't repeat them here. Though we should note that in examining the Marxist claim that economic relations under capitalism are inherently alienating and exploitative, we came to the view that this critique is actually closely allied with liberal egalitarian views of the injustice of capitalism, in that both advance the argument that it is the economic inequalities between workers and capitalists that explain the exploitation (and hence the injustice) of capitalist social forms. But this charge of 'injustice' gave rise to our discussion of whether Marxists could consistently engage in charges of injustice, given the view of ideology earlier defended. We concluded they could, but only if they adopted the weakest of the versions of the ideology thesis we examined.

We then turned to the post-modern critique of modernist (liberal) political thought, where we considered the two foci of post-modern thought in turn. First, we looked at the rejection of the assumption of a unified, rational, self-aware person that models of, for example, liberal autonomy rest upon. And we considered the various ways that post-modern thinkers reject that model as illusory. Next we considered the post-structuralist view of language that motivates post-modern rejections of the use of generalized normative principles in political theory. But we noted a tension between these two lines of thought in that, in so far as language is too unstable and variable to allow us to express normative judgements, and 'selves' are really only fragmented and fluid collections of motives and ideas, then there is no ground for the kind of liberatory political action that many post-modern writers (feminists for example) very much urge us to engage in. In particular, we looked at this tension in certain attempts, on the one hand, to undercut liberal assumptions of a neutral subject whose interests political principles must protect, and, on the other, to advance the cause of certain subgroups (women, racial minorities, and so on) whose interests are left out of those general principles. In so far as all language is too unstable to admit of meaningful categories, the struggles of the politics of identity lacks the same grounding that is allegedly absent in liberalism. We noted that theories of democracy, though ones which followed generally along liberal lines (guaranteeing basic equality and autonomy to participants), were needed to work out these tensions in the post-modern critiques.

We ended with reflections on the entire project of the book, and remarked that liberal political theory faces numerous challenges arising from the various discussions in Part II of this survey. We noted, however, that despite the fundamental question raised about liberal political theory, there may well be hope for that approach – in one of its many varieties – after all.

Case to consider

The final issue we will reflect upon is very broad, and invites discussion along many of the lines developed in this book, though I propose particular focus on the themes of this chapter. Increasingly, governments of both developed and developing countries around the world are turning to globalized capitalism to strengthen both their own economies and, they claim, promote the growth of other countries. This is meant to take place by opening markets, dropping tariffs and trade barriers, and generally facilitating the flow of capital and products across borders. This move is fueled by growing communication among disparate societies as well as technological advances easing information and product transfer across long distances. The theory behind these moves is that expanding capitalist free markets will allow a rising tide of economic growth to 'raise all boats' and aid the flow of wealth and goods to those areas most in need of such resources. In addition to libertarian arguments for the sanctity of capitalist property rights (of the sort we considered in Chapter 3), there are consequentialist arguments that expanding free markets across borders will benefit all concerned.

Of course, critics of these trends vociferously object that these rationales are merely cover stories for the real motive driving these moves – the increased concentration of economic power into the hands of the corporate elite. Any predictions of overall benefit (and consequentialist justifications of globalization based on them) are examples of mere subterfuge masking the true motivations at work – the collusion of world governments with corporate capital interests.

Consider these critiques, in particular as they might utilize Marxist methods to undercut philosophical justifications of global economic policies. In addition, though, consider whether the language of capitalist free markets (and presumably the liberal democratic political structures that are associated with them) can be applied globally in a way that is sufficiently sensitive to the fundamental differences among groups in far corners of the globe, separated by language, tradition, culture, and values. In other words, can a single normative language, such as the language of liberal democracy, be applied universally to disparate cultures without ignoring the fundamental differences among people in the world. Consider the work of post-modernist thinkers on this topic, who would surely balk at the idea that universal principles can be articulated in a common conceptual language and applied, without exclusion or violence, across the globe.

Notes on further reading

For ease of reference I have referred all Marx quotations to McLellan 1977 (a reader containing parts of the major works; but see also Tucker 1978), though I have also included the titles of the specific work by Marx or Marx and Engels so they can be found in other sources as well. The reader is encouraged to seek out the full original work for detailed study of the ideas mentioned.

For general discussion of Marx's ideas, some helpful starting points are Althusser [1969] 1996, Lukács 1971, G. Cohen 1978 and 1988b, Wolff 1984, Elster 1985, Roemer 1988, Gilbert 1990 Part II, Kymlicka 1990: 160–98, Wright et al. 1992, and the essays in Callinicos 1989, and Carver 1991. Marx is also critically appraised in Arnold 1990. Some recent theorists very much inspired by Marxism are Laclau and Mouffe 1985, and W. Brown 1995. Historical materialism is specifically discussed in G. Cohen 1978, though it is considered in all of the works just mentioned as well. For material on the concept of ideology, see Horkheimer and Adorno [1944] 1998, Habermas 1975, Geuss 1981, Elster 1985: ch. 8, and Eagleton 1991. And the concept of Marxian exploitation is specifically examined in Roemer 1982, 1985 and 1988, and Elster 1985: 166–234. The question of whether Marx's framework can support a critique of the injustice of a society is dealt with in Buchanan 1982, and Kymlicka 1990: 161–69. The question is thoroughly discussed (with exhaustive references to date) in Geras 1989 as well.

Post-modernism is a multifaceted phenomenon and few, if any, single sources will examine all of its features (or not take controversial stands on its meaning). Examples of worthwhile attempts, however, are Jameson 1972: 101–216 (especially on post-structuralist views of language), Harvey 1989, White 1991 (especially for its connection with political philosophy), and Lyotard 1997. If one wishes to read the original progenitors of these views, one can start with Derrida 1982: 1–28 and 109–36, and 1994, and Foucault 1984, 1990a and 1990b, and

Rorty 1989. Feminist post-modernism is developed in Kristeva 1980 and 1987, Grosz 1994, Butler 1997; and discussed in Meyers 1994, and Young 1990a: ch. 4, as well as in the essays in Nicholson 1990 and 1995 (especially the latter where discussion of some of the questions about the tensions of post-modernism I raised above are discussed), and Oliver 2000.

The topic of liberalism, its many varieties and its tenability, has been touched on throughout this work. In addition to works already mentioned, one can find useful discussions in Kateb 1992, Gray 1989 and 1993, Taylor 1991, Larmore 1996, Habermas 1996b, and Rawls 1999a.

Notes

1 Introduction

1 Indeed, some theorists have claimed that the defining focus of mainstream political philosophy consists in questions of distributive justice. (See Young, 1990: 15–24).
2 Prior to Rawls's work, ethics and political philosophy in the analytic tradition was very abstract, focusing, for example, on the structure of moral language, rather than the plausibility of particular positions concerning substantive political issues.

2 The problem of political authority

1 It is important to reflect upon the precise meaning of the terms 'liberty' and 'freedom' in this context, and there exists a vast philosophical literature on that question (Berlin 1969, McCallum 1967, Feinberg 1973: 4–19, Christman 1994: ch. 4). One alleged and much commented upon distinction is between a 'negative' sense of freedom – the absence of restraints on action – from a 'positive' sense – the capacity to effectively act upon one's own authentic desires (along with variations on each of these). Another useful distinction is between those concepts of freedom that assume it refers only to morally permissible acts, where being free means, by definition, being able to act within moral strictures, and those views that see freedom as simply the ability to act on one's desires *period*, whether or not they issue in morally permissible acts (see G. Cohen 1988a, Christman 1994: 68–70). Finally, other writers have attempted to declare any such debate about the 'proper' understanding of freedom as essentially misguided since different uses of that idea will presuppose substantive normative conclusions buried in the definitions of the word 'freedom,' so reference to it cannot be made to *support* such normative conclusions; this, they say, makes the concept 'essentially contestable' (see Connolly 1983: chs 1 and 5–6).
2 This is the received view of Hobbes. Some, such as Jean Hampton, have suggested that Hobbes is not, strictly speaking, a psychological egoist, at least not in the *Leviathan*, since he mentions various capacities for fellow feeling in the motivational structure of humans (see Hampton 1986:

20–24). But Hampton also concedes that 'for purposes of his political argument, he might as well be a psychological egoist . . . because other-interested desires play no role whatsoever in his justification or explanation of the formation of the state' (ibid.: 22).

3 This description of these decision-theoretic problems is pitched at a general level and leaves many details unspecified. For more precise discussions of these issues, see Hampton 1986: ch. 2, Hardin 1982, Elster 1986: 1–33, Elster and Hylland 1986.

4 This is implicitly to defend the 'passions' account of the inevitable conflict in the state of nature, described by Gauthier (Gauthier 1986: 114–16), and criticized by Hampton (Hampton 1986: ch. 2); this interpretation claims that, for Hobbes, life in the state of nature would not be as horrible as he describes if all acted rationally; only their passions muck things up. Generally, though, the question of whether cooperation would ensue spontaneously, even when all are acting from rational self-interest alone, depends on the payoffs and costs of (unilateral and mutual) cooperation and non-cooperation.

5 This is what Hampton calls Hobbes's 'radical individualism.' See Hampton 1986: 6–11.

6 The argument in this section follows Hampton (Hampton 1997: ch. 3, 1986: ch. 9).

7 Moreover, the *moral* legitimacy of regimes based on this kind of convention can be established on utilitarian grounds, based on the prediction that in so far as citizens endorse (and at least minimally participate in) the government in question, that government generally can be said to maximize the well-being of those citizens (otherwise, the government could be replaced with an alternative or the society break apart into competing coalitions). (See the Introduction above for discussion of utilitarianism). For discussion of this line of argument, see Hampton 1997: 99–100.

8 This argument is made by Thomas Christiano (Christiano 1994).

9 This means, then, that when Locke refers to 'liberty' or 'freedom' he understands these terms in what we could call a 'moralized' manner, where being free means (by implicit definition) being unimpeded in acting *within the strictures of the moral law*, which for Locke meant not violating the natural rights of others. In fact, he says just this: 'But though this [state of perfect freedom] be a *State of Liberty*, it is *not a state of Licence*' (Locke [1690] 1963: 311). The liberty we would naturally enjoy in the state of nature ('of perfect freedom') is a liberty to live within the natural law (given to us by reason) and not, *à la* Hobbes, being unimpeded by external forces from doing whatever we happen to desire.

10 These criticisms parallel what Simmons calls the 'standard critique' of Locke's theory of political obligation (Simmons 1993: ch. 7).

11 What Rawls calls the 'basic structure' are those institutions, such as the government, the legal system, the economy, and the like, which fundamentally

shape a person's life plan and order of values. (See Rawls 1971: 6–10, 1993).
12 As with Rawls's theory generally, these principles are subtly altered as he refines his views, a point to be discussed in Chapter 4. This formulation is taken from Rawls 1982: 165.

3 Distributive justice

1 It should be noted that while it may seem that the state only 'intervenes' in cases where capitalist markets are somehow regulated or interfered with, governments *always* actively 'intervene' in the economic life of citizens, because it defines the property rights citizens hold over their goods, even in so-called 'free market' capitalist economies. For discussion of this point, see Christman 1994: ch. 2.
2 Some libertarians' insistence that property rights encompass *all* rights is misleading: only if one defines 'rights' as having an enforceable claim over something and then defines 'property' so broadly as to include one's body, the space in which one moves, and so on, are all rights then property rights; but there is a quite straightforward use of the term 'property' which is more restrictive than this, and of course this more restrictive range of rights is what is controversial about the libertarian position. (See Narveson 1988: 66–67.)
3 We should stress that the package of property rights that the libertarian identifies as 'ownership' is merely one type of package among many others. Ownership is a complex relation and need not include (and in fact never does in actual societies) the full rights to possess and use property however one wants (free of zoning restrictions, pollution controls, and so on), as well as rights to keep whatever gains one might acquire from transactions with others (without any taxation at all). For discussion of the complexity of ownership, see Christman 1994: chs 1 and 2; for a similar point, see Nielsen 1985: 267f.).
4 This is despite Narveson's careful attempts (Narveson 1988: 13–40) to define 'liberty' in a sense that does not presuppose established (and controversial) rights and norms. A key step in this analysis is where Narveson claims that active interference with a person's action counts as a limitation on liberty, but merely refusing to help does not. Some of his reasons for this position are conceptual (saying inaction amounts to an interference implies that we are all interfering with someone all of the time – 1988: 38). But the '[m]ost fundamental reason of all,' he writes, is that 'to insist that there is no difference between B's actually preventing A from doing x and B's merely not doing what might have enabled A to do x is to trample *B's* freedom into the dust . . . [that is] . . . we are saying . . . that B's liberty doesn't count or doesn't matter. The libertarian wants to say that it *does* matter' (1988: 39, italics in the original). (For further discussion, see also Narveson 1984.) So the

NOTES

libertarian says we all have a right to liberty but liberty is defined by what *matters* (at least to the libertarian). This is a normative conception, then, of liberty.

5   While not strictly utilitarian, see Friedman 1962 for a well known defense which can be considered as broadly consequentialist. In addition, there have been 'social Darwinist' defenses of the free market, such as those popular early in the twentieth century. See Spencer 1972.

6   I am admitting this for the sake of argument, but there are several reasons to question it, especially when considering the perhaps irreversible effect such development has had on the environment. Also, as I will discuss in a moment, the 'first appropriators' of resources in most places hardly left the surrounding people alone when they, often murderously, acquired their goods.

7   At least one libertarian writer has claimed (albeit tentatively) that there are no duties to care for one's children directly, except to prevent the possible future harm to society that one's neglect may cause when the child grows up to be a delinquent! (Narveson 2000: 319.)

8   Presumably! Clearly there are countless examples of wasted taxes and unfair redistributive schemes. The point being made here is that the unqualified bar to *any* such redistribution based on the right to liberty is implausible. For discussions of the distinctions among kinds of property rights relevant to this issue, see, for example, Radin 1993 and Christman 1994: ch. 7. Many have made the claim that libertarians fail to justify the specifically capitalist rights they claim to: see, for example, Nielson 1985: 267, Christman 1994. For discussion, see Narveson 1988: 62–68.

9   See Narveson 1988: Part II, 1995, and 2000: 320–24. This line of argument is based on views developed in more detail in Gauthier 1986. For an earlier version of this strategy, see Buchanan and Tullock 1965.

10 This is tremendously simplified, of course: it leaves open the question of what ends of ours we are aiming to satisfy: the ones we have now or the ones we can predict we will adopt in the future? Should we balance the satisfaction of one set over the satisfaction of another, and if so, what metric of comparison should we use? As we will see, particular answers to those questions assume aspects of human psychology that are highly variable and hence cannot be simply assumed as true of all people without importing a normative position about how one thinks they ought to be.

11 One attempt to show the various benefits of libertarian policies can be found in Narveson 1988: Part III.

12 For the original discussion of this principle, see Rawls 1971. Rawls subsequently revised this principle in significant ways: see Rawls 1999a ('The Basic Liberties and Their Priority') and 1993: 331–40. For an argument that the equal opportunity principle may be otiose, see Arneson 1999a.

13 In the original formulation of the theory, Rawls claimed that the primary goods are things that will be valued no matter what else it is that a person

values – as universal means to the widest variety of ends (Rawls 1971: 54–55). In later versions of the theory this was altered, and primary goods were defined as those things that will be thought valuable for persons conceived in a particular way, namely as agents with highest order interests to form, revise, and pursue their own conceptions of the good within publicly accepted principles of justice. This conception of the person is not meant to apply to *everyone*, but rather is to be utilized as an artificial conception around which we real people can gain a consensus. The meaning and importance of this shift will be discussed in the next chapter. In the text I combine these two formulations. (See Rawls 1982, 1993: 178–87.)

14 As we will see, well-being is sometimes understood to mean simply 'welfare.' But I will reserve the latter term for conceptions of a person's good that see it as a function of desire-satisfaction, pleasure or happiness (utility). I will use 'well-being' as a catch-all term for whatever it is that turns out to be the aspect of persons' lives that must be equalized according to the principles we discuss.

15 These comments can be found in G. Cohen 1989. Dworkin has responded to these criticisms; see R. Dworkin 2000: ch. 7.

16 See Arneson (1989). It should be noted that in later work, Arneson suggests that although the term 'welfare' is used in the equality of opportunity for welfare scheme, it can (and he argues should) be thought of much more broadly to include whatever subjective goods and objective values comprise a good life for a person (Arneson 2000a).

17 Sen admits that any list of this sort is bound to be contentious and indeterminate, and he acknowledges the need for sensitivity to the wide variety of life forms in various cultures, ones which will each demand different schedules of basic capabilities. One writer who is much less shy about attempting to craft a universally applicable conception of basic capabilities (based forthrightly on a theory of human nature) is Martha Nussbaum (see Nussbaum 1993).

18 In the case of Rawls this is explicit, since inequalities (in the enjoyment of primary goods) are *allowed* as long as they serve to benefit the worst off group; this is because the more fundamental equality of moral status is protected by the mechanism of the original position and the veil of ignorance, from which the Difference Principle is derived (Rawls 1971: 86–93, 118–23).

19 Some anti-egalitarians might also claim that at the upper reaches of prosperity there is really nothing to distinguish the lot of the rich compared to the very rich, since at that level well-being cannot be meaningfully compared (cf. Raz 1986: 217–44). But if that is so – if conditions at that level are arguably the same – then this provides no counterexample to egalitarianism, but merely an instance where its demands have been met, that despite minor income disparities, such people are equal on any plausible measure.

4 Toleration, pluralism, and the foundations of liberalism

1 One aside: in literature dealing with this issue, the object of neutrality is often described as the person's 'conception of the good' or some such equivalent locution. But we should note the undue narrowness of that phrase. For what is involved in the pursuit of value and meaning in a person's life may well involve a host of factors, such as her self-conception, her embrace of emotional ties, her religious commitments, her embeddedness in cultural, racial or other networks, and the like. Such factors may well not be properly described as the person's 'conception' of the good, since the latter phrase connotes a cognitive (and hence fully voluntary and detached) judgment about what is good or bad, and in this way fails to capture the affective and non-cognitive elements in value commitment.

2 It should be noted that liberalism would not prohibit the use of state power to advance the good of citizens if this was carried out in a way respectful of autonomy. At this point, liberalism and perfectionism converge (though via different routes: the perfectionist claims that the violations of autonomy are simply ineffective, while the liberal says that they are impermissible).

3 In particular, the variant of liberalism we have described as libertarianism (discussed in the last chapter) has rested quite often on considerations of utility, especially by theorists influenced by the thinking and methods of economics (Buchanan and Tullock 1965).

4 This ideal may appear to conflict with the liberal approach to value defined above (constructivisim), which claimed that values are valid for a person only if she could autonomously embrace them. These views are consistent, however, if one considers the external source of value being described here as merely *part* of what validates a value for a person, her autonomously embracing it being also necessary for that validity.

5 In work subsequent to *Political Liberalism*, Rawls has stressed that justice as fairness is merely one of a family of views that could be the subject of an overlapping consensus of this sort (see Rawls 1999b: 140–41). I am grateful to Lori Watson for conversations that have helped me clarify these points.

6 In this way, Habermas is influenced by the tradition of American Pragmatism, in particular the work of George Herbert Mead (see Habermas 1990: 65, 88–89).

7 In his earlier work, Habermas developed a theory of 'the ideal speech situation,' which was meant to model the justification of norms independent of actual face-to-face discourse (1990: 43–115). As his views have developed, however, it has become clear that he thinks that those norms that guide public political doctrine gain their validity only as a result of actual discourse in public space (see Warnke 1989–90).

5 Conservatism, communitarianism, and the social conception of the self

1 In the last thirty years or so, especially in the US and Britain, a 'neo-conservative' movement has become prominent that, while stressing policies of the sort listed, has also insisted upon 'minimal government' and the protection of free markets, thereby including elements of libertarian liberalism into their platform. Whether this has created a new (and unstable) hybrid position or is a further development of conservative philosophy generally considered will be a question we will leave open here.
2 This may be part of the reason that, historically, conservatism has not been studied as a distinct philosophical view (for discussion of this charge, see Kekes 1998: 2).
3 The following exposition of conservatism is largely based on Kekes (1998); but it should be noted that he claims specifically that conservatism is anti-perfectionist in the sense he uses the term, in that it reflects skepticism about rationally establishing fixed value systems in advance and it is pessimistic about the possibilities of human perfection (ibid.: 41–45). That is consistent, however, with being perfectionist in our sense, since all we mean by the term is that governments should promote the good lives of its citizens overall and in doing so forsake the priority of the right definitive of liberalism.
4 For liberals, typically, penal systems are justified only in so far as they continue to show respect for the basic dignity and moral worth of the criminal, since on such a view wrong actions do not indicate a loss of autonomy (unless, of course, the wrongdoer has lost the basic capacities definitive of autonomy, through mental illness and the like). As an implication, liberals tend to push for more 'humane' prison practices. Conservatives, on the other hand, hold as a basic value the protection of established social order against the threat of 'evil' forces, and hence tend to favor harsher penal policies. For discussion, see Kekes 1998: 68–90.
5 The conservatism we are discussing here is a sort which is relativistic *vis-à-vis* particular communities (and hence will have much in common with aspects of communitarianism to be discussed below). An alternative version of conservatism can be labeled 'absolutist' in that its claim that governments should promote valuable lives for its citizens is based on conceptions of value that are universal and known by reasoned reflection. In recent decades a version of this view has been defended under the label of the 'new natural law' theories; see, for example, Finnis 1980, Grisez and Shaw 1988, and Weinreb 1987. Some aspects of Alasdair MacIntyre's views are also in line with this approach (MacIntyre 1984). For criticism, see Hittinger 1987.
6 Communitarians tend to be influenced in these views by Aristotle (MacIntyre 1984), Hegel (Taylor 1979), and in some cases Heidegger (Bell 1993). The exposition in the text blurs over distinctions among these very different traditions (though it owes much to the presentation of the communitarian view in Bell).

7 Communitarian claims about personhood were initially taken to mean that liberals implausibly assume that persons can stand back from *all* their values at once, and liberals were quick to reply that they meant no such thing, only that any *particular* commitment can be subject to reflective scrutiny (Kymlicka 1989). So communitarians must reject even this model of personhood, that an individual can stand back from any specific commitment or value and reflectively appraise it while holding other factors (provisionally) intact.
8 Communitarians can meaningfully reply here that such value judgments would have no *basis* unless the person's perspective was oriented by prior constitutive commitments. But the liberal rejoinder would be that as long as these reflections take place in a piecemeal manner, holding prior commitments (which provide the basis for the judgments) fixed, there remains a basis for judgment.
9 And it should also be noted that the sociological basis of these claims arises from a specifically American (US) context. Though the tensions analyzed in the text are not peculiar to US policy or history and are claimed to inhere in liberal cultures wherever they develop.
10 A deep division in communitarian thinking reveals itself here, namely whether the ultimate ground of the validity of shared norms lies in the fact of their being shared or in some external source of objective value. Michael Sandel argues that pursuit of a common good by members of a community must proceed on the assumption that such a good is grounded 'externally' and not merely a reflection of what is 'done around here' (see Sandel 1982: ix–xvi). Daniel Bell and Michael Walzer can be interpreted to claim that no moral horizons beyond the local value orientation of one's community is available to ground 'objective' values (Bell 1993: 76, Walzer 1983, 1987).
11 As we noted in the last chapter, there are also 'perfectionist' liberals who think that there are certain objective values whose grounds are independent of human choices about them.
12 Kymlicka's argument relies crucially on a distinction between those cultures that have been incorporated (involuntarily) into a larger nation and those whose members have (voluntarily) immigrated into a host nation. For critical discussion of that distinction, see Kukathas 1997.

6 Race, gender, and the politics of identity

1 It could be alleged that this critique apparently confuses questions of 'values' (what is wrong with racism or sexism) with questions of 'fact' (whether a particular society is racist or sexist), as was discussed in Chapter 1 above. But as Charles Mills argues (Mills 1997: 120–23, 1999: 17), political philosophy should be understood to include both evaluations of social patterns and institutions as well as descriptions and analyses of those patterns; indeed, the latter is crucial for a full understanding of the former, if

NOTES

these two enterprises can be separated at all. Moreover, this is one of the areas where the *distinction* between the purely descriptive and the purely normative is open to question. And regarding the kinds of phenomena alluded to here – slavery, overt discrimination, violence, and so on – labeling these things 'unjust,' 'oppressive,' and the like should hardly be controversial.

2 The Voting Rights Act in the USA, for example, which was necessary to ensure full and equal rights to vote for African Americans, was only passed in 1964; if that is a benchmark of this acceptance of full equality regarding race (and it is a highly imperfect one at best), this indicates how very recent such general acceptance actually is.

3 Boxill considers the claim that the reason that reference to race should not be made in principles of justice is that no such reference should be made to factors for which the person is not *responsible*; he argues, however, that this guideline cannot plausibly be generalized: see Boxill 1984: 15–18. Also, the discussion in the text connects directly to the complex question of the justification of affirmative action, a topic we leave to the side here (except for a brief comment below); for discussion, see Boxill 1984: 147–72, Goldman 1979, Ezorsky 1991, and Cochran 1999: 141–44.

4 Due to considerations of brevity and by way of exemplification, I focus here (for the most part) on racism in the context of life in the United States, though the problems raised here can apply (with variations) to other areas. I also focus primarily on the dynamics of racism as they involve 'whites' and 'blacks' in America, acknowledging that the experiences and struggles against oppression by Native Americans, Latinos, Asian Americans, and the other groups there also deserve direct attention (and raise unique problems). But some of the issues raised here can be applied to those groups as well as those areas of the world where the legacy of colonialism, cultural expansion, imperialism, and the like have created patterns of discrimination and prejudice based on race, ethnicity or geographical origin. I should say also that I use the terms 'white' and 'black' (noncapitalized) while knowing that doing so is controversial. The use of any such terminology papers over complex controversies about race, identity, and the language of ongoing political struggles. In a fuller examination of these subjects, such controversies would indeed be taken up directly.

Finally, I use the term 'critical race theory' to refer broadly to critical political philosophy centering on issues of race. I am aware that this term is also used to refer to a specific body of work in legal theory concerning race and politics. For discussion of this latter area, see Delgado and Stefancic 2001.

5 There is much literature on the nature of racism and clearly the full picture is more complex than this (see, for example, West 1994, and the essays in Zack 1997, in Babbitt and Campbell 1999: especially Part II, and in Blackburn 2000). David Haekwon Kim, for instance, argues that racism must be seen as involving *contempt* for the other, and indeed is a fundamentally emotional, rather than cognitive phenomenon (Kim 1999).

NOTES

6 These are mere examples, of course, and are all controversial, both concerning the terminology used to describe them as well as the groupings picked out by them. ('Asian' is a geographical category after all.) They are also, as noted before, examples taken specifically from the US context.
7 Of course, the categorization of people into 'races' often rests on the view that there are *other* characteristics of people that corresponded significantly to these physical markers. Moral, psychological, social, and cultural tendencies of various sorts are identified as true of particular races; it was for this very reason that racist ideas about the inferiority of certain groups relative to others developed (Appiah and Gutmann 1996, Outlaw 1999).
8 This connection between black identity and values can be made through the examination of culture, as we saw earlier, though this is a claim that some race scholars themselves have questioned, whether, for example, there is an identifiable and unique black culture in a place like the United States (Appiah and Gutmann 1996: 83–99).
9 There are parallel controversies concerning the ultimate sources of gender *difference* as well as the ultimate explanation of patriarchy itself (see, for example, Chodorow 1978, Ferguson 1997, MacKinnon 1989: 37–80, and the essays in Rhode 1990).
10 Other analyses of feminism have divided the field into different theoretical perspectives (liberal feminism, socialist feminism, radical feminism, etc. – see Jaggar 1983, Kourany et al., 1992). My approach is oriented around issues and principles rather than theoretical frameworks, though the background question concerns the degree to which feminist claims force us to move beyond the liberal theoretical picture.
11 Though barriers remain, of course: various positions in the US military, for example, are closed to women independent of their overall qualifications for them.
12 It should be noted that the very legal definition of marriage (in most jurisdictions) as involving one male and one female already makes lifelong intimacy between members of the *same* sex devoid of legal standing. The question of whether heterosexism, as such, involves identifiable injustice is also relevant here.
13 There has been much discussion of this controversy, with some claiming that the different orientations are simply situation specific – care dominating in certain settings and justice in others, perhaps corresponding with typical male and female roles. Gilligan herself can be read at times as taking this view (Gilligan 1987: 19–33). Moreover, even if women and men do in fact differ in their moral thinking in this way, the *sources* of these differences are open to question, perhaps reflecting sexist gender roles themselves (see, for example, Chodorow 1978, and the essays in Rhode 1990).
14 See Young 1990a: 96–121, who accepts that principles must take on a certain level of generality (ibid.: 105). Also, I leave open here the question of whether the language of rights is similarly defensible.

15 Some feminists, of course, argue that pornography of various sorts actually does involve the violation of basic rights. See MacKinnon 1993, and A. Dworkin 1989.
16 It should also be stressed that some feminist writers claim that many facets of the overtly sexual aspects of Western culture, including the availability of pornography, should be embraced by women and turned into forms more reflective of their own sexual lives (rather than condemned outright). See, for example, Bright 1999. This raises the issue of pluralism once again, where condemnation of elements of culture often carries with it presuppositions about value orientations that are very much in question.
17 Often unmentioned in these discussions, however, is the obvious implication that *male* character development is equally constructed in accordance with the dynamics of this power structure, in particular the heterosexist imperative that prizes male power and structures sexual desire in a manner that objectifies the female 'other'.
18 I have raised those challenges which I think have the most surface plausibility, but of course calling for alterations in a political theory because it does not properly account for certain unjust conditions assumes those conditions are in fact unjust. Indeed, certain writers on feminism argue strenuously that traditional theories need not be altered to accommodate these critiques; rather it is these critiques that need to be rethought. See, for example, Sommers 1995, Fox-Genovese 1991).
19 This is, of course, an exaggeration, in that requiring first-person accounts of injustice for any large society is unwieldy. Patterns of *representation* will be necessary. And representational schemes themselves manifest abstract categorization of citizens and their interests, raising yet again the question we are discussing.

7 Radical critique: Marxism and post-modernism

1 Marx's statement of his theory of history is best found in his *Preface to the Critique of Political Economy* of 1859 (McLellan 1977: 388–92) and the *Communist Manifesto* (Marx and Engels [1848] 1998). For discussion, see G. Cohen 1978, and Wright et al. 1992.
2 There is debate among Marxist scholars about whether historical materialism should be understood as claiming that changes in the productive forces *determine* changes in the superstructure or whether changes in productive forces are the effects, which nevertheless explain, changes in the superstructure. The latter formulation utilizes a functional explanation – where the effects of some cause explains that cause because of the way that cause 'functions' to produce that effect (through filtering or feedback mechanisms for example). For discussion, see Elster 1985, Wright et al. 1992: 13–46, and G. Cohen 1978 and 1989.
3 This description of the shift from feudalism to capitalism indicates that such 'revolutions' need not be violent on Marx's view (though plenty of

NOTES

wars occurred during the period), nor need it be specifically intended as such. For Marx's description of the rise of capitalism, see Marx and Engels [1848] 1998: 36–40.

4 This illustrates the dynamic in which changes from one economic epoch to another take place, epochs which include: ancient slave owning society, feudalism, capitalism, socialism, and communism. Each epoch operates under different sets of fundamental economic organizing principles, especially concerning who controls the basic means of producing goods in the society.

5 Another illustration of ideology is what Marx calls 'commodity fetishism,' where the objective nature of a valued object is seen in terms of its market value instead of the human labor that went into its production (Marx, *Capital,* vol. 1, McLellan 1977: 435–43). The use-value of an object is replaced by its exchange value, so that what an object represents is nothing more than whatever other objects (or capital) it can be exchanged for, instead of any inherent usefulness or value it may have for its possessor. In capitalist economies, especially those with massive corporate control of advertising via mass media, culture is 'commodified' in that all forms of leisure, entertainment, personal activity, and consumption are shaped by those in control of economic resources into a form that is easily bought and sold, and it is valued for this reason. The prevailing idea in capitalist societies of 'consumer sovereignty' then is merely ideological, on this view (see Horkheimer and Adorno [1944] 1998: 120–67; for discussion of corporate control of media in the USA, see McCallister 1996).

6 However, deflationary claims about the true social sources of ideas themselves must be presented and defended with evidence. Often, ideological critique proceeds without providing what Elster calls 'microfoundations,' explanations of how the dissemination of beliefs actually works, and its precise relation with the advance of ruling-class interests (see Elster 1985: ch. 8). For analysis of ways that economic systems relate to beliefs and motivations (though within the rubric of empirical social psychology and rational choice theory, respectively), see Lane 1991, and Elster 1983b.

7 Some theorists specifically define autonomy in relation to the historical processes of development of the person's values and character: see Christman 1991, and Mele 1995).

8 The discussion of these ideas glosses over the myriad disagreements about the correct interpretation of them. For more detailed discussion, see Wolff 1984, G. Cohen 1980, Arnold 1990, and Elster 1985.

9 For example, the typical CEO in the United States makes 160 times the average worker's salary (for discussion of this point, see Christman 1994: 115–17). That means that unless there is exploitation going on, the capitalist is contributing to the overall value of the items produced 160 times more than the worker. Now, perhaps CEOs have highly valuable skills in choosing markets, organizing production, management, and so on

(though none of these are strictly necessary for the capitalist to perform — she can hire people to do them), but to say that these contributions amount to this much more than our hard-working laborers strains credulity (and seems implausible on its face when we realize that these ratios of owner income to worker income are highly *variable* around the world).

10 Another departure from the liberal egalitarian model of injustice that Marxists will make is that the relation of exploitation and inequality is not best seen at the level of the individual, but rather at the level of *class*. Capitalists *as a group* benefit from capitalists' productive relations and workers *as a group* suffer from them. Even though particular workers may be able to earn income which gives them options other than to work in unpleasant circumstances, and some workers can 'move up' and enter the capitalist class, it is not the case that *most* workers have these options. For discussion of this idea of 'collective unfreedom,' see G. Cohen 1988a. For a similar point about seeing exploitation as essentially a property of economic systems as a whole, see Elster 1985: 176.

11 The question involves, among other things, the issue of whether rules of justice are meaningful only when the 'circumstances of justice' – moderate scarcity and limited egoism – are in place, so that in a future communist utopia (where scarcity is eradicated) justice is not needed or even meaningful. But (as Kymlicka argues in 1990: 166–67) rules of social coordination will always be needed even under conditions of abundance.

12 See, especially, Butler 1993, and Grosz 1994. Note, however, that this is not merely the position described as 'physicalism' in the philosophy of mind (namely that persons are nothing but physical organisms and all mental properties must be expressed in physical language). It is a broader claim that thought itself is an embodiment of not only physical processes, but social dynamics and institutional interplays of power (which may not be expressed in naturalistic or physicalist terms at all).

13 This way of putting things privileges only one strand of this modernist approach to language, one that rests on a correspondence between propositions and the world; such a view is controversial and contrasts with more 'coherentist' approaches to meaning and truth that have been developed within the modernist rubric. What I am calling here the 'traditional' account of meaning, from which the post-modern view departs, is much more heterogeneous than I have described. I simplify here to clarify the contrasts with post-modernism. See Hacking 1975 for a fuller overview.

14 Some post-modern writers also utilize the work of 'speech-act' theory, which emphasizes the role of performative actions in the fixing of meaning for a language. And since such performance involves real actors in actual social settings, the ambiguities of intention and understanding, and the power relations that infuse those settings, all become crucially relevant to meaning. See, for example, Lyotard 1997: 9–11.

15 It should be noted that Young specifically claims that she utilizes the methods of critical theory rather than post-modernism (Young 2000: 10–11). However, her critique of the liberal paradigm expresses clearly the themes of post-modern writers of interest to us here (so the claims in the text are not intended as a direct criticism of Young's work specifically, but merely a critical discussion of those larger themes). Also, in utilizing the notion of 'affinity' she notes the work of Donna Haraway, a thinker who is usually identified as post-modern: see Haraway 1997.

16 For example, on Young's view, cultural revolutions initiated by social groups take place precisely because 'these movements have self-consciously constructed the culture that they claim defines the distinctiveness of their groups.' (Young 1990a: 172)

17 Some writers such as Iris Young fully accept this implication, and indeed have written extensively on the topic of democracy as a fundamental component of justice (Young 1990a, 2000), and for this reason she is not well described as a 'post-modern' thinker. For similar views, see also Benahib 1996b, Connolly 1991, and Fraser 1997. It is also unclear just how much Butler opposes the postulation of foundational normative categories, as long as they are never to be taken as unrevisable (Butler 1995b: 130–33).

Bibliography

Ackerman, Bruce (1980) *Social Justice and the Liberal State.* New Haven, CT: Yale University Press.
Althusser, Louis ([1969]1996) *For Marx.* London: Verso.
Anderson, Elizabeth S. (1999) 'What is the Point of Equality?' *Ethics* 109, 2: 287–337.
Anthony, Louise, and Charlotte Witt, eds (1993) *A Mind of One's Own: Feminist Essays on Reason and Objectivity.* Boulder, CO: Westview Press.
Appiah, K. Anthony (1992) *In My Father's House: Africa in the Philosophy of Culture.* New York: Praeger.
——, and Amy Gutmann (1996) *Color Conscious: The Political Morality of Race.* Princeton, NJ: Princeton University Press.
Aristotle (1958) *The Politics.* Trans. Ernest Barker. Oxford: Oxford University Press.
Arneson, Richard (1981) 'What is Wrong with Exploitation?' *Ethics* 91, 2: 202–27.
—— (1985) 'Freedom and Desire' *Canadian Journal of Philosophy* 15, 3: 425–48.
—— (1989) 'Equality and Equal Opportunity for Welfare' *Philosophical Studies* 56: 77–93.
—— ed. (1992) *Liberalism.* 2 Vols. Northampton: Edward Elgar Publishing.
—— (1997) 'Egalitarianism and the Undeserving Poor' *Journal of Political Philosophy* 5, 4: 327–50.
—— (1999a) 'Against Rawlsian Equality of Opportunity' *Philosophical Studies* 93: 77–112.
—— (1999b) 'Egalitarianism and Responsibility' *Journal of Ethics* 3: 225–47.
—— (2000a) 'Luck Egalitarianism and Prioritarianism' *Ethics* 110: 339–49.
—— (2000b) 'Perfectionism and Politics' *Ethics* 111, 1: 37–63.
Arnold, N. Scott (1987) 'Why Profits are Deserved' *Ethics* 97, 2: 387–402.
—— (1990) *Marx's Radical Critique of Capitalist Society.* Oxford: Oxford University Press.
Arthur, John (1987) 'Resource Acquisition and Harm' *Canadian Journal of Philosophy* 17, 2 (June): 337–47.
Avineri, Shlomo, and Avner de-Shalit, eds (1992) *Communitarianism and Individualism.* New York: Oxford University Press.
Avnon, Dan, and Avner de-Shalit (1999) *Liberalism and its Practice.* New York: Routledge.
Babbitt, Susan (1996) *Impossible Dreams: Rationality, Integrity, and Moral Imagination.* Boulder, CO: Westview Press.
——, and Sue Campbell, eds (1999) *Racism and Philosophy.* Ithaca, NY: Cornell University Press.
Barry, Brian (1973) *The Liberal Theory of Justice.* Oxford: Oxford University Press.
—— (1980) 'Justice as Reciprocity,' in Kamenka, ed. (1980): 50–78.
—— (1989) *Theories of Justice.* Berkeley, CA: University of California Press.
Bartky, Sandrah (1990) *Femininity and Domination: Studies in the Phenomenology of Oppression.* New York: Routledge.
—— (1997) 'Foucault, Femininity, and the Modernization of Patriarchal Power,' in Meyers, ed. (1997): 92–111.

BIBLIOGRAPHY

Beiner, Ronald (1997) *Philosophy in a Time of Lost Spirit: Essays on Contemporary Theory.* Toronto: University of Toronto Press.
Bell, Bernard W., Emily R. Grozholz and James B. Stewart, eds (1996) *W. E. B. Dubois on Race and Culture.* New York: Routledge.
Bell, Daniel (1993) *Communitarianism and its Critics.* Oxford: Clarendon.
Bellah, Robert N., et al. eds (1985) *Habits of the Heart: Individualism and Commitment in American Life.* Berkeley, CA: University of California Press.
Benhabib, Seyla (1987) 'The Generalized and the Concrete Other: The Kohlberg-Giligan Controversy and Feminist Theory,' in *Feminism as Critique.* Ed. S. Benhabib and D. Cornell. Minneapolis, MN: University of Minnesota Press.
—— (1992) *Situating the Self: Gender, Community and Postmodernism in Contemporary Ethics.* New York: Routledge.
—— ed. (1995) *Feminist Contentions: A Philosophical Exchange.* London and New York: Routledge.
—— ed. (1996a) *Democracy and Difference.* Princeton, NJ: Princeton University Press.
—— (1996b) 'Toward a Deliberative Model of Democratic Legitimacy,' in Benhabib, ed. (1996a): 67–94.
Benjamin, Jessica (1988) *The Bonds of Love: Psychoanalysis, Feminism, and the Problem of Domination.* New York: Pantheon.
Benn, Stanley (1988) *A Theory of Freedom.* Cambridge: Cambridge University Press.
Beran, Harry (1987) *The Consent Theory of Political Obligation.* New York: Croom Helm.
Berlin, Isaiah (1969) 'Two Concepts of Liberty,' in *Four Essays on Liberty.* London: Oxford University Press, 118–72.
Berofsky, Bernard (1995) *Liberation from Self.* New York: Cambridge University Press.
Blackburn, David (2000) 'Why Race is Not a Biological Concept,' in Lang, ed. (2000): 3–26.
Bowie, Norman, ed. (1988) *Equal Opportunity.* Boulder, CO: Westview Press.
Boxill, Bernard (1984) *Blacks and Social Justice.* Totowa, NJ: Rowman and Allanheld.
Brenkert, George (1983) *Marx's Ethics of Freedom.* London: Routledge.
Bright, Susie (1999) *Full Exposure: Opening Up to Sexual Creativity and Erotic Expression.* San Francisco, CA: Harper Books.
Brook, Andrew (1994) *Kant and the Mind.* New York: Cambridge University Press.
Brown, Lynn Mikel, and Carol Gilligan (1992) *Meeting at the Crossroads: Women's Psychology and Girls' Development.* Cambridge, MA: Harvard University Press.
Brown, Wendy (1995) *States of Injury: Power and Freedom in Late Modernity.* Princeton, NJ: Princeton University Press.
Buchanan, Allan (1982) *Marx and Justice: The Radical Critique of Liberalism.* London: Methuen.
—— (1985) *Ethics, Efficiency and the Market.* Totowa, NJ: Rowman and Allanheld.
—— (1989) 'Assessing the Communitarian Critique of Liberalism' *Ethics* 99: 852–82.
Buchanan, James, and Gordon Tullock (1965) *The Calculus of Consent.* Ann Arbor, MI: University of Michigan Press.
Burke, Edmund (1968) *Reflections on the Revolution in France.* Ed. Connor Cruise O'Brien. Harmondsworth: Penguin.
Bushnell, Dana, ed. (1995) *Nagging Questions.* Savage, MD: Rowman and Littlefield.
Butler, Judith (1990) *Gender Trouble: Feminism and the Subversion of Identity.* New York: Routledge.
—— (1993) *Bodies That Matter.* New York: Routledge.
—— (1995a) 'Contingent Foundations,' in Nicholson, ed. (1995): 35–58.
—— (1995b) 'For a Careful Reading,' in Nicholson, ed. (1995): 127–44.
—— (1997) *The Psychic Life of Power.* Stanford, CA: Stanford University Press.
Callinicos, Alex, ed. (1989) *Marxist Theory.* Oxford: Oxford University Press.
Carver, Terrell, ed. (1991) *The Cambridge Companion to Marx.* Cambridge: Cambridge University Press.

BIBLIOGRAPHY

Chodorow, Nancy (1978) *The Reproduction of Mothering: Psychoanalysis and the Sociology of Gender*. Berkeley, CA: University of California Press.
Christiano, Thomas (1994) 'The Incoherence of Hobbesian Justifications of the State' *American Philosophical Quarterly* 31: 23–38.
—— (1996) *The Rule of the Many: Fundamental Issues in Democratic Theory*. Boulder, CO: Westview Press.
Christman, John (1986) 'Can Ownership be Justified by Natural Rights?' *Philosophy and Public Affairs* 15, 2: 156–77.
—— ed. (1989) *The Inner Citadel: Essays on Individual Autonomy*. New York: Oxford University Press.
—— (1991) 'Autonomy and Personal History' *Canadian Journal of Philosophy* 21, 1 (March): 1–24.
—— (1994) *The Myth of Property: Towards an Egalitarian Theory of Ownership*. New York: Oxford University Press.
—— (1995) 'Feminism and Autonomy,' in Bushnell, ed. (1995): 17–39.
—— (1998) 'Autonomy, Independence, and Poverty-Related Welfare Policies' *Public Affairs Quarterly* 12, 4: 383–406.
—— (2001) 'Liberalism, Autonomy, and Self-Transformation' *Social Theory and Practice* 27, 2: 185–206.
Cochran, David (1999) *The Color of Freedom*. Albany, NY: SUNY Press.
Cohen, G. A. (1978) *Karl Marx's Theory of History: A Defence*. Princeton, NJ: Princeton University Press.
—— (1980) 'The Labor Theory of Value and the Concept of Exploitation,' in M. Cohen et al. (1980): 135–57.
—— (1986a) 'Self-Ownership, World-Ownership, and Equality,' in *Justice and Equality Here and Now*. Ed. F. Lucash. Ithaca, NY: Cornell University Press.
—— (1986b) 'Self-Ownership, World-Ownership, and Equality: Part 2' *Social Philosophy and Policy* 3, 2: 77–96.
—— (1988a) 'The Structure of Proletarian Unfreedom,' in G. A. Cohen, ed. (1988b), 255–85.
—— (1988b) *History, Labor, and Freedom: Themes from Marx*. Oxford: Oxford University Press.
—— (1989) 'The Currency of Egalitarian Justice' *Ethics* 99: 96–104.
—— (1995) *Self-Ownership, Freedom and Equality*. Cambridge: Cambridge University Press.
—— (1998) 'Once More Into the Breach of Self-Ownership: Reply to Narveson and Brenkert' *The Journal of Ethics* 2: 57–96.
Cohen, Joshua (1986) 'Autonomy and Democracy: Reflections on Rousseau' *Philosophy and Public Affairs* 15: 275–97.
—— (1996) 'Procedure and Substance in Deliberative Democracy,' in Benhabib, ed. (1996a): 95–119.
Cohen, Marshall, Thomas Nagel and Thomas Scanlon, eds (1980) *Marx, Justice, and History*. Princeton, NJ: Princeton University Press.
Collins, Patricia Hill (1998a) *Fighting Words: African-American Women and the Search for Justice*. Minneapolis, MN: University of Minnesota Press.
—— (1998b) 'It's All In the Family: Intersections of Gender, Race, and Nation' *Hypatia* 13, 3 (Summer): 62–82.
Connolly, William (1983) *The Terms of Political Discourse*. Princeton, NJ: Princeton University Press.
—— (1991) *Identity/Difference: Democratic Negotiations of Political Paradox*. Ithaca, NY: Cornell University Press.
Cornell, Drucilla (1998) *At the Heart of Freedom: Feminism, Sex, and Equality*. Princeton, NJ: Princeton University Press.
Crittenden, Jack (1992) *Beyond Individualism: Reconstituting the Liberal Self*. New York: Oxford University Press.

BIBLIOGRAPHY

Cummins, Robert, and Thomas Christiano, eds (1999) *Modern Moral and Political Philosophy*. Mountain View, CA: Mayfield Publishing Co.
Daniels, Norman (1975) 'Equal Liberty and Unequal Worth of Liberty,' in Daniels, ed. (1975): 253–81.
—— ed. (1975) *Reading Rawls: Critical Studies on Rawls's 'A Theory of Justice'*. New York: Basic Books.
Davion, Victoria, and Clark Wolf, eds (2000) *The Idea of Political Liberalism: Essays on Rawls*. Landham, MD: Rowman and Littlefield.
Delaney, C. F., ed. (1994) *The Liberalism-Communitarianism Debate*. Lanham, MD: Rowman and Littlefield.
Delgado, Richard, and Jean Stefancic (2001) *Critical Race Theory: An Introduction*. New York: New York University Press.
Derrida, Jacques (1982) *Margins of Philosophy*. Trans. Alan Bass. Chicago, IL: University of Chicago Press.
—— (1994) *Specters of Marx: The State of the Debt, the Work of Mourning, and the New International*. Trans. Peggy Kamuf. New York: Routledge.
Dryzek, John (2000) *Deliberative Democracy and Beyond: Liberals, Critics, Contestations*. New York: Oxford University Press.
Dubois, W. E. B. (1995) *The Souls of Black Folk*. New York: Penguin.
Dunn, John (1969) *The Political Thought of John Locke*. Cambridge: Cambridge University Press.
Dworkin, Andrea (1989) *Pornography: Men Possessing Women*. New York: Plume.
Dworkin, Gerald (1988) *The Theory and Practice of Autonomy*. New York: Cambridge University Press.
Dworkin, Ronald (1977) *Taking Rights Seriously*. London: Duckworth.
—— (1978) 'Liberalism' in *Public and Private Morality*. Ed. S. Hampshire. Cambridge: Cambridge University Press.
—— (1981). 'What is Equality? Part I: Equality of Welfare; Part II: Equality of Resources' *Philosophy and Public Affairs* 10, 3–4: 185–246, 283–345.
—— (1985) *A Matter of Principle*. Cambridge, MA: Harvard University Press.
—— (1986) *Law's Empire*. Cambridge, MA: Harvard University Press.
—— (1987) 'What is Equality? Part III: The Place of Liberty' *Iowa Law Review* 73, 1: 1–54.
—— (1988) 'What is Equality? Part IV: Political Equality' *University of San Francisco Law Review* 22, 1: 1–30.
—— (1989). 'Liberal Community' *California Law Review* 77, 3: 479–504.
—— (1990) 'Foundations of Liberal Equality,' in *Tanner Lectures On Human Value*. Vol. XI. Ed. Grethe B. Peterson. Salt Lake City, UT: University of Utah Press, 1–119.
—— (2000) *Sovereign Virtue: The Theory and Practice of Equality*. Cambridge, MA: Harvard University Press.
Eagleton, Terry (1983) *Literary Theory: An Introduction*. Minneapolis, MN: University of Minnesota Press.
—— (1991) *Ideology: An Introduction*. London: Verso.
Elshtain, Jean Bethke (1981) *Public Man, Private Women: Women in Social and Political Thought*. Princeton, NJ: Princeton University Press.
Elster, Jon (1983a) *Explaining Technical Change*. Cambridge: Cambridge University Press.
—— (1983b) *Sour Grapes*. Cambridge: Cambridge University Press.
—— (1985) *Making Sense of Marx*. Cambridge: Cambridge University Press.
—— ed. (1986) *Rational Choice*. New York: New York University Press.
——, and A. Hylland, eds (1986) *Foundations of Social Choice Theory*. Cambridge: Cambridge University Press.
Etzioni, Amitai, ed. (1998) *The Essential Communitarian Reader*. Lanham, MD, and Oxford: Rowman and Littlefield.

BIBLIOGRAPHY

Eze, Emmanuel Chukwudi, ed. (1997) *Race and the Enlightenment: A Reader*. Cambridge, MA: Blackwell.
Ezorsky, Gertrude (1991) *Racism and Justice*. Ithaca, NY: Cornell University Press.
Feinberg, Joel (1970) *Doing and Deserving*. Princeton, NJ: Princeton University Press.
—— (1973) *Social Philosophy*. Englewood Cliffs, NJ: Prentice Hall, Inc.
—— (1980) *Rights, Justice and the Bounds of Liberty*. Princeton, NJ: Princeton University Press.
Ferguson, Ann (1997) 'On Conceiving Motherhood and Sexuality: A Feminist Materialist Approach,' in Meyers, ed. (1997): 38–63.
Finnis, John (1980) *Natural Law and Natural Rights*. New York: Oxford University Press.
Firestone, Shulamith (1971) *The Dialectics of Sex: The Case for Feminist Revolution*. New York: Bantam.
Fischer, John Martin, ed. (1986) *Moral Responsibility*. Ithaca, NY: Cornell University Press.
Flathman, Richard (1989) *Toward A Liberalism*. Ithaca, New York: Cornell University Press.
Flax, Jane (1993) *Disputed Subjects: Essays on Psychoanalysis, Politics, and Philosophy*. New York: Routledge.
Fox-Genovese, Elizabeth (1991) *Feminism Without Illusions: A Critique of Individualism*. Chapell Hill, NC: University of North Carolina Press.
Foucault, Michel (1965) *Madness and Civilization: A History of Insanity in the Age of Reason*. Trans. Richard Howard. New York: Vintage Books.
—— (1984) *The Foucault Reader*. Ed. Paul Rabinow. New York: Pantheon Books.
—— (1988) *The Final Foucault*. Ed. J. Bernauer and D. Rasmussen. Cambridge, MA: MIT Press.
—— (1990a) *The History of Sexuality: An Introduction*. Trans. Robert Hurley. New York: Vintage.
—— (1990b) *The Use of Pleasure*. Trans. Robert Hurley. New York: Vintage.
—— (1995) *Discipline and Punish: The Birth of the Prison*. Trans. Alan Sheridan. New York: Vintage Books.
Frankfurt, Harry (1987) 'Equality as a Moral Ideal' *Ethics* 98, 21–43.
—— (2000) 'The Moral Irrelevance of Equality' *Public Affairs Quarterly* 14, 2: 87–103.
Fraser, Nancy (1997) *Justice Interruptus*. New York: Routledge.
French, Peter A., Theodore E. Uehling Jr, and Howard K. Wettstein (1988) *Ethical Theory: Character and Virtue*. Notre Dame, IN: University of Notre Dame Press.
Frey, R. G., and Christopher W. Morris, eds (1993) *Value, Welfare, and Morality*. New York: Cambridge University Press.
Friedman, Marilyn (1993) *What are Friends For? Feminist Perspectives on Personal Relationships and Moral Theory*. Ithaca, NY: Cornell University Press.
—— (1997) 'Beyond Caring: The De-Moralization of Gender,' in Meyers, ed. (1997): 664–79.
Friedman, Milton (1962) *Capitalism and Freedom*. Chicago, IL: University of Chicago Press.
Galston, William (1980) *Justice and the Human Good*. Chicago, IL: University of Chicago Press.
—— (1991) *Liberal Purposes: Goods, Virtues, and Diversity in the Liberal State*. Cambridge: Cambridge University Press.
Gaus, Gerald F. (1996) *Justificatory Liberalism*. New York: Oxford University Press.
—— (1999) *Social Philosophy*. Armonk, NY: M. E. Sharpe.
Gauthier, David (1986) *Morals by Agreement*. Oxford: Oxford University Press.
Geras, Norman (1989) 'The Controversy about Marx and Justice,' in Callinicos, ed. (1989): 211–67.
Geuss, Raymond (1981) *The Idea of a Critical Theory: Habermas and the Frankfurt School*. New York: Cambridge University Press.

BIBLIOGRAPHY

Gilbert, Alan (1990) *Democratic Individuality*. Cambridge: Cambridge University Press.
—— (1991) 'Political Philosophy: Marx and Radical Democracy,' in Carver, ed. (1991): 168–95.
Gilligan, Carol (1982) *In a Different Voice: Psychological Theory and Women's Development*. Cambridge, MA: Harvard University Press.
—— (1987) 'Moral Orientation and Moral Development,' in Kittay and Meyers, eds (1987): 19–36.
——, Jane Ward, Jill Taylor and Betty Bardige, eds (1988) *Mapping the Moral Domain: A Contribution of Women's Thinking to Psychological Theory and Education*. Cambridge, MA: Harvard University Press.
Goldman, Alan (1979) *Justice and Reverse Discrimination*. Princeton, NJ: Princeton University Press.
Gough, J. W. (1957) *The Social Contract: A Critical Study of its Development*. Oxford: Clarendon Press.
Gould, Carol (1988) *Rethinking Democracy*. Cambridge: Cambridge University Press.
Grant, Ruth (1987) *John Locke's Liberalism*. Chicago, IL: University of Chicago Press.
Gray, John (1986) *Liberalism*. Minneapolis: University of Minnesota Press.
—— (1989) *Liberalisms: Essays in Political Philosophy*. New York: Routledge.
—— (1993) *Post-Liberalism: Studies in Political Thought*. New York: Routledge.
Green, Leslie (1988) *The Authority of the State*. New York: Oxford University Press.
Greenawalt, Kent (1988) *Religious Convictions and Political Choice*. New York: Oxford University Press.
—— (1995) *Private Consciences and Public Reason*. New York: Oxford University Press.
Griffin, James (1986) *Well-Being: Its Meaning, Measurement, and Moral Importance*. Oxford: Oxford University Press.
Grimshaw, Jean (1986) *Philosophy and Feminist Thinking*. Minneapolis, MN: University of Minnesota Press.
Grisez, Germaine, and Russell Shaw (1988) *Beyond the New Morality: The Responsibilities of Freedom*. Third edn. Notre Dame, IN: University of Notre Dame Press.
Grosz, Elizabeth (1994) *Volatile Bodies: Toward a Corporeal Feminism*. Bloomington, IN: University of Indiana Press.
Gutmann, Amy (1985) 'Communitarian Critics of Liberalism' *Philosophy and Public Affairs* 14, 3: 308–22.
Guyer, Paul (1988) *Kant and the Claims of Knowledge*. New York: Cambridge University Press.
Habermas, Jürgen (1975) *Legitimation Crisis*. Trans. Thomas McCarthy. Boston, MA: Beacon Press.
—— (1985) 'Questions and Counterquestions' in *Habermas and Modernity*. Ed. R. Bernstein. Cambridge, MA: MIT Press.
—— (1990) *Moral Consciousness and Communicative Action*. Trans. Christian Lenhardt and Shierry Weber Nicholsen. Cambridge, MA: MIT Press.
—— (1995) *The Philosophical Discourse of Modernity*. Trans. Frederick Lawrence. Cambridge, MA: MIT Press.
—— (1996a) 'Three Normative Models of Democracy,' in Benhabib, ed. (1996): 21–30.
—— (1996b) *Between Facts and Norms*. Trans. William Rehg. Cambridge, MA: MIT Press.
—— (1998) *The Inclusion of the Other: Stories in Political Theory*. Ed. Ciaran Cronin and Pablo De Greiff. Cambridge, MA: MIT Press.
Hacking, Ian (1975) *Why Does Language Matter to Philosophy?* New York: Cambridge University Press.
Hampton, Jean (1986) *Hobbes and the Social Contract Tradition*. New York: Cambridge University Press.
—— (1997) *Political Philosophy*. Boulder, CO: Westview Press.

BIBLIOGRAPHY

Haraway, Donna (1997) 'A Manifesto for Cyborgs: Science, Technology, and Socialist Feminism in the 1980s,' in Meyers, ed. (1997): 501–31.
Hardin, Russell (1982) *Collective Action*. Baltimore, MD: Johns Hopkins University Press.
——(1988) *Morality Within the Limits of Reason*. Chicago, IL: University of Chicago Press.
Harris, Leonard, ed. (1983) *Philosophy Born of Struggle: Anthology of Afro-American Philosophy from 1917*. Dubuque, IN: Kendall Hunt Publishing Co.
Harsanyi, John (1982) 'Morality and the Theory of Rational Behavior,' in Sen and Williams, eds (1982): 39–62.
Harstock, Nancy (1997) 'The Feminist Standpoint: Developing the Ground for a Specifically Feminist Historical Materialism,' in Meyers, ed. (1997): 461–83.
Hart, H. L. A. (1979) 'Are There Any Natural Rights,' in Lyons, ed. (1979): 14–25.
Harvey, David (1989) *The Condition of Postmodernity*. Cambridge, MA: Basil Blackwell.
Haslinger, Sally (2000) 'Gender and Race: (What) Are They? (What) Do We Want Them to Be?' *NOUS* 34, 1: 31–55.
Hayek, F. A. (1960) *The Constitution of Liberty*. London: Routledge & Kegan Paul.
Held, David (1987) *Models of Democracy*. Stanford, CA: Stanford University Press.
Hill, Thomas (1992) *Dignity and Practical Reason in Kant's Moral Theory*. Ithaca, NY: Cornell University Press.
Hittinger, Russell (1987) *A Critique of the New Natural Law Theory*. Notre Dame, IN: University of Notre Dame Press.
Hobbes, Thomas ([1651] 1986) *Leviathan*. Harmondsworth: Penguin Books.
Holmes, Stephen (1989) 'The Permanent Structure of Antiliberal Thought,' in *Liberalism and the Moral Life*. Ed. N. Rosenblum. Cambridge, MA: Harvard University Press.
Horkheimer, Max, and Theodor Adorno ([1944] 1998) *Dialectic of Enlightenment*. New York: Continuum Publishing.
Hume, David ([1739] 1978) *A Treatise of Human Nature*. Ed. L. A. Selby-Bigge. Oxford: Oxford University Press.
——(1985) *Essays Moral, Political, and Literary*. Ed. Eugene F. Miller. Indianapolis, IN: Liberty Press.
Hurka, Thomas (1993) *Perfectionism*. New York: Oxford University Press.
Jaggar, Alison (1983) *Feminist Politics and Human Nature*. Totowa, NJ: Rowman and Allanheld.
——(1986) 'Prostitution,' in Pearsall, ed. (1986): 108–22.
——(1994) *Living with Contradictions: Controversies in Feminist Social Ethics*. Boulder, CO: Westview Press.
Jameson, Frederick (1972) *The Prison House of Language*. Princeton, NJ: Princeton University Press.
Johnston, David (1994) *The Idea of a Liberal Theory: A Critique and Reconstruction*. Princeton, NJ: Princeton University Press.
—— ed. (2000) *Equality*. Indianapolis, IN: Hackett.
Kamenka, Eugene, ed. (1980) *Ideas and Ideologies: Justice*. New York: St. Martin's Press.
Kant, Immanuel ([1785] 1983) *Grounding for the Metaphysics of Morals*, in *I. Kant Ethical Philosophy*. Trans. James W. Ellington. Indianapolis, IN: Hackett.
——([1797] 1999) *Metaphysical Elements of Justice*. Ed. John Ladd. Indianapolis, IN: Hackett.
Kateb, George (1992) *The Inner Ocean: Individualism and Democratic Culture*. Ithaca, NY: Cornell University Press.
Kavka, Gregory S. (1986) *Hobbesian Moral and Political Theory*. Princeton, NJ: Princeton University Press.
Kekes, John (1997) *Against Liberalism*. Ithaca, NY: Cornell University Press.
——(1998) *A Case for Conservatism*. Ithaca, NY: Cornell University Press.

BIBLIOGRAPHY

Kelly, Michael, ed. (1990) *Hermeneutics and Critical Theory in Ethics and Politics.* Cambridge, MA: MIT Press.

Kernohan, Andrew (1998) *Liberalism, Equality, and Cultural Oppression.* New York: Cambridge University Press.

Kim, David Haekwon (1999) 'Contempt and Ordinary Inequality,' in Babbit and Campbell, eds (1999): 108–23.

Kirk, Russell, ed. (1982) *The Portable Conservative Reader.* New York: Viking Penguin.

Kittay, Eva Feder (1999) *Love's Labor: Essays on Women, Equality, and Dependency.* London: Routledge.

——, and Diana T. Meyers, eds (1987) *Women and Moral Theory.* Savage, MD: Rowman and Littlefield.

Kneller, Jane, and Sidney Axxin, eds (1998) *Autonomy and Community: Readings in Contemporary Kantian Social Philosophy.* Albany, NY: State University of New York Press.

Kourany, Janet, ed. (1998) *Philosophy in a Feminist Voice.* Princeton, NJ: Princeton University Press.

——, James Sterba and Rosemary Tong, eds (1992) *Feminist Philosophies.* Englewood Cliffs, NJ: Prentice Hall.

Korsgaard, Christine M. (1996) *The Sources of Normativity.* New York: Cambridge University Press.

—— (1997) 'Taking the Law into Our Own Hands: Kant on the Right to Revolution' in Reath et al., eds (1997): 297–328.

Kraus, Jody (1993) *The Limits of Hobbesean Contractarianism.* New York: Cambridge University Press.

Kristeva, Julia (1980) *Desire in Language.* New York: Columbia University Press.

—— (1986) *The Kristeva Reader.* Ed. Toril Moi. New York: Columbia University Press.

—— (1987) *Tales of Love.* Trans. Leon S. Roudiez. New York: Columbia University Press.

Kukathas, Chandran (1997) 'Multiculturalism as Fairness: Will Kymlicka's Multicultural Citizenship' *Journal of Political Philosophy* 5: 406–27.

——, and Philip Pettit (1990) *Rawls: A Theory of Justice and its Critics.* Cambridge: Polity Press and Basil Blackwell.

Kupfer, Joseph H. (1990) *Autonomy and Social Interaction.* Albany, NY: State University of New York Press.

Kymlicka, Will (1989) *Liberalism, Community and Culture.* Oxford: Clarendon.

—— (1990) *Contemporary Political Philosophy: An Introduction.* Oxford: Clarendon.

—— (1991) 'Rethinking the Family' *Philosophy and Public Affairs* 20, 1 (Winter): 77–97.

—— ed. (1992) *Justice in Political Philosophy.* 2 Vols. Brookfield, VT: Edward Elgar.

—— (1995) *Multicultural Citizenship: A Liberal Theory of Minority Rights.* Oxford: Clarendon.

—— (1998) 'Introduction: An Emerging Consensus' *Ethical Theory and Moral Practice* 1: 143–57.

Laclau, Ernesto, and Chantal Mouffe (1985) *Hegemony and Socialist Strategy: Towards a Radical Democratic Politics.* New York: Verso.

LaFollette, Hugh, ed. (2000) *Blackwell Guide to Ethical Theory.* Oxford: Blackwell.

Landes, Joan, ed. (1998) *Feminism, the Public and the Private.* New York: Oxford University Press.

Lane, Robert (1991) *The Market Experience.* Cambridge: Cambridge University Press.

Lang, Berel, ed. (2000) *Race and Racism in Theory and Practice.* Langham, MD: Rowman and Littlefield.

Larmore, Charles (1987) *Patterns of Moral Complexity.* Cambridge: Cambridge University Press.

—— (1996) *The Morals of Modernity.* New York: Cambridge University Press.

Larrabee, Mary Jeanne (1991) 'The Care Ethics Debate: A Selected Bibliography,' *APA Newsletter on Feminism* 90, 2: 103–9.

BIBLIOGRAPHY

Levine, Andrew (1976) *The End of Autonomy: A Kantian Reading of Rousseau's Social Contract*. Amherst, MA: University of Massachusetts Press.
—— (1988) *Arguing for Socialism*. London: Verso Press.
—— (1993) *The General Will: Rousseau, Marx, Communism*. New York: Cambridge University Press.
Lilla, Mark, ed. (1994) *New French Thought: Political Philosophy*. Princeton, NJ: Princeton University Press.
Locke, John ([1689] 1955) *A Letter Concerning Toleration*. Indianapolis, IN: Bobbs-Merrill, Co.
—— ([1689] 1996) *An Essay Concerning Human Understanding*. Ed. Kenneth Winkler. Indianapolis, IN: Hacket Publishing Co.
—— ([1690] 1963) *Two Treatises of Government*. Ed. Peter Laslett. New York: Cambridge University Press.
Lomasky, Loren (1987) *Persons, Rights, and the Moral Community*. Oxford: Oxford University Press.
Lukács, Georg (1971) *History and Class Consciousness*. Cambridge: Cambridge University Press.
Lukes, Stephen (1985) *Marxism and Morality*. Oxford: Oxford University Press.
Lyons, David, ed. (1979) *Rights*. Belmont, CA: Wadsworth.
Lyotard, Jean-François (1997) *The Postmodern Condition: A Report on Knowledge*. Trans. Geoff Bennington and Brian Massumi. Minneapolis, MN: University of Minnesota Press.
Macedo, Stephen (1990) *Liberal Virtues: Citizenship, Virtue, and Community in Liberal Constitutionalism*. Oxford: Clarendon.
Machan, Tibor (1998) *Classical Individualism: The Supreme Importance of Each Human Being*. London: Routledge.
——, and Douglas Rasmussen, eds (1995) *Liberty for the 21st Century: Contemporary Libertarian Thought*. Lanham, MD: Rowman and Littlefield.
MacIntyre, Alasdair (1981) *After Virtue*. Notre Dame, IN: University of Notre Dame Press.
—— (1987) *Whose Justice? Which Rationality*. Notre Dame, IN: University of Notre Dame Press.
Mack, Eric (1983) 'Distributive Justice and the Tensions of Lockeanism' *Social Philosophy and Policy* 1: 132–50.
Mackenzie, Catriona, and Natalie Stoljar, eds (2000) *Relational Autonomy: Feminist Perspectives on Autonomy, Agency, and the Social Self*. New York: Oxford University Press.
MacKinnon, Catherine (1987) *Feminism Unmodified: Discourses on Life and Law*. Cambridge, MA: Harvard University Press.
—— (1989) *Toward a Feminist Theory of the State*. Cambridge, MA: Harvard University Press.
—— (1993) *Only Words*. Cambridge, MA: Harvard University Press.
MacLean, Douglas, and Claudia Mills, eds (1983) *Liberalism Reconsidered*. Totowa, NJ: Rowman and Allenheld.
Macpherson, C. B. (1962) *The Political Theory of Possessive Individualism*. Oxford: Oxford University Press.
McAllister, Matthew (1996) *The Commercialization of American Culture: New Advertising, Control, and Democracy*. Thousand Oaks, NJ: Sage Publications.
McCallum, Gerald (1967) 'Negative and Positive Freedom' *Philosophical Review* 76, 3112–34.
McLellan, David (1977) *Karl Marx: Selected Writings*. Oxford: Oxford University Press.
Margalit, Avishai, and Joseph Raz (1990) 'National Self-Determination' *Journal of Philosophy* 87, 9: 439–61.
Martin, Rex (1985) *Rawls and Rights*. Lawrence, KS: University Press of Kansas.

BIBLIOGRAPHY

Marx, Karl, and Frederick Engels (1848/1998) *The Communist Manifesto*. London: Verso.
Mele, Alfred R. (1995) *Autonomous Agents: From Self-Control to Autonomy*. New York: Oxford University Press.
Mendus, Susan (1989) *Toleration and the Limits of Liberalism*. Atlantic Highlands, NJ: Humanities Press International.
Meyers, Diana T. (1987) 'The Socialized Individual and Individual Autonomy,' in Kittay and Meyers, eds (1987): 139–53.
—— (1989) *Self, Society, and Personal Choice*. New York: Columbia University Press.
—— (1994) *Subjection and Subjectivity: Psychoanalytic Feminism and Moral Philosophy*. New York: Routledge.
—— ed. (1997) *Feminist Social Thought*. London: Routledge.
Mill, John Stuart ([1859] 1975) *On Liberty*. Ed. David Spitz. New York: Norton.
Miller, David, ed. (1991) *Liberty*. New York: Oxford University Press.
—— (1989) *Market, State and Community: Theoretical Foundations of Market Socialism*. Oxford: Clarendon Press.
——, and Michael Walzer, eds (1995) *Pluralism, Justice, and Equality*. Oxford: Oxford University Press.
Miller, Richard (1991) 'Social and Political Theory: Class, State, Revolution' in Carver, ed. (1991): 55–105.
Milligan, David, and William Watts Miller, eds (1992) *Liberalism, Citizenship and Autonomy*. Brookfield, VT: Avebury.
Mills, Charles (1997) *The Racial Contract*. Ithaca, NY: Cornell University Press.
—— (1999) 'The Racial Polity,' in Babbit and Campbell, eds (1999): 13–31.
—— (2000) 'Race and the Social Contract Tradition' *Social Identities* 6, 4: 441–62.
Milton, John ([1660] 1950) *Aereopagitica*, in *The Complete Poetry and Selected Prose of John Milton*. New York: Modern Library, 677–730.
Montefiore, A. ed. (1975) *Neutrality and Impartiality*. Cambridge: Cambridge University Press.
Moon, J. Donald (1993) *Constructing Community: Moral Pluralism and Tragic Conflicts*. Princeton, NJ: Princeton University Press.
Morris, Christopher (1999) *The Social Contract Theorists: Critical Essays on Hobbes, Locke, and Rousseau*. Lanham, MD: Rowman and Littlefield.
Mouffe, Chantal, ed. (1992) *Dimensions of Radical Democracy: Pluralism, Citizenship, Community*. London: Routledge.
—— (2000) *The Democratic Paradox*. New York: Verso.
Mulhall, Stephen, and Adam Swift (1992) *Liberals and Communitarians*. Cambridge: Basil Blackwell.
Munzer, Stephen (1990) *A Theory of Property*. Cambridge: Cambridge University Press.
Nagel, Thomas (1981) 'Libertarianism Without Foundations,' in J. Paul, ed. (1981): 191–205.
—— (1991) *Equality and Partiality*. New York: Oxford University Press.
Narveson, Jan (1984) 'Equality vs. Liberty: Advantage, Liberty' *Social Philosophy and Policy*. 2, 1 (Autumn): 33–60.
—— (1988) *The Libertarian Idea*. Philadelphia, PA: Temple University Press.
—— (1995) 'Contracting for Liberty,' in Machan and Rasmussen, eds (1995): 19–40.
—— (1998) 'Libertarianism vs. Marxism: Reflections on G. A. Cohen's *Self-Ownership, Freedom and Equality*' *Journal of Ethics* 2,1: 1–26.
—— (2000) 'Libertarianism,' in LaFallotte, ed. (2000): 306–24.
Nicholson, Linda, ed. (1990) *Feminism/Postmodernism*. New York: Routledge.
—— (1995) 'Introduction,' in Benhabib, ed. (1995): 1–16.
Nielsen, Kai (1985) *Equality and Liberty: A Defense of Radical Egalitarianism*. Totowa, NJ: Rowman and Allanheld.

BIBLIOGRAPHY

Nisbet, Robert (1986) *Conservatism: Dream and Reality*. Minneapolis, MN: University of Minnesota Press.
Noddings, Nel (1984) *Caring: A Feminist Approach to Ethics and Moral Education*. Berkeley, CA: University of California Press.
Nozick, Robert (1974) *Anarchy, State, and Utopia*. New York: Basic Books.
Nussbaum, Martha (1993) 'Non-Relative Virtues: An Aristotelean Approach,' in Nussbaum and Sen, eds (1993): 242–69.
——, and Jonathan Glover, eds (1995) *Women, Culture and Development: A Study in Human Capabilities*. Oxford: Clarendon Press.
——, and Amartya Sen, eds (1993) *The Quality of Life*. Oxford: Clarendon.
Oakeshott, Michael (1991) *Rationalism in Politics*. Ed. Timothy Fuller. Indianapolis, IN: Liberty Press.
Offen, Karen (1990) 'Feminism and Sexual Difference in Historical Perspective,' in Rhode, ed. (1990): 13–20.
Okin, Susan Moller (1989) *Justice, Gender, and the Family*. New York: Basic Books.
Oliver, Kelly, ed. (2000) *The French Feminist Reader*. Lanham, MD: Rowman and Littlefield.
O'Neill, Onora (1989) *Constructions of Reason: Explorations in Kant's Practical Philosophy*. New York: Cambridge University Press.
Outlaw, Lucius (1996) '"Conserve" Races: In Defense of W. E. B. Dubois,' in Bell et al., eds (1996): 15–38.
—— (1999) 'On Race and Philosophy,' in Babbitt and Campbell, eds (1999): 50–78.
Pateman, Carole (1988) *The Sexual Contract*. Stanford, CA: Stanford University Press.
Paul, Ellen Frankel, Fred Miller and Jeffrey Paul, eds (1986) *The Communitarian Challenge to Liberalism*. Cambridge: Cambridge University Press.
—— eds (1987) *Equal Opportunity*. Oxford: Basil Blackwell.
—— eds (2000) *Democracy*. Cambridge: Cambridge University Press.
Paul, Jeffrey, ed. (1981) *Reading Nozick*. Totowa, NJ: Rowman and Littlefield.
Pearce, Diana (1992) 'The Feminization of Poverty,' in Kourany, ed. (1992): 207–19.
Pearsall, Marilyn, ed. (1986) *Women and Values: Readings in Recent Feminist Philosophy*. Belmont, CA: Wadsworth Publishing.
Pelczynski, Zbigniew, and John Gray, eds (1984) *Conceptions of Liberty in Political Philosophy*. New York: St. Martin's Press.
Pettit, Philip (1993) *The Common Mind: An Essay on Psychology, Society, and Politics*. Oxford: Oxford University Press.
—— (1997) *Republicanism: A Theory of Freedom and Government*. New York: Oxford University Press.
Phelan, Shane (1996) *Getting Specific: Postmodern Lesbian Politics*. Minneapolis, MN: University of Minnesota Press.
Pojman, Louis, ed. (1999) *The Moral Life: An Introductory Reader in Ethics and Literature*. New York: Oxford University Press.
Putnam, Robert (2000) *Bowling Alone: The Collapse and Revival of American Community*. New York: Simon and Schuster.
Rachels, James (1993) *The Elements of Moral Philosophy*. New York: McGraw-Hill.
Radin, Margaret Jane (1993) *Reinterpreting Property*. Chicago, IL: University of Chicago Press.
Rae, Douglas, and Douglas Yates (1981) *Equalities*. Cambridge, MA: Harvard University Press.
Rakowski, Eric (1991) *Equal Justice*. Oxford: Clarendon Press.
Rashdall, Hastings (1924) *The Theory of Good and Evil: A Treatise on Moral Philosophy*. London: Oxford University Press.
Rasmussen, David M. (1990) *Reading Habermas*. Cambridge, MA: Basil Blackwell.
Rawls, John (1971) *A Theory of Justice*. Revised edn. (1999) Cambridge, MA: Harvard University Press.

—— (1982) 'Social Unity and Primary Goods,' in Sen and Williams, eds (1982): 159–86.
—— (1993) *Political Liberalism*. New York: Columbia University Press.
—— (1999a) *Collected Papers*. Ed. Samuel Freeman. Cambridge, MA: Harvard University Press.
—— (1999b) *The Law of Peoples*. Cambridge, MA: Harvard University Press.
Raz, Joseph (1979) *The Authority of Law: Essays on Law and Morality*. Oxford: Clarendon Press.
—— (1986) *The Morality of Freedom*. Oxford: Clarendon.
Reath, Andrews, Barbara Herman and Christine Korsgaard, eds (1997) *Reclaiming the History of Ethics: Essays for John Rawls*. Cambridge: Cambridge University Press.
Reiman, Jeffrey (1997) *Critical Moral Liberalism*. Lanham, MD: Rowman and Littlefield.
Rhode, Deborah, ed. (1990) *Theoretical Perspectives on Sexual Difference*. New Haven, CT: Yale University Press.
Riley, Patrick (1983) *Kant's Political Philosophy*. Landham, MD: Rowman and Littlefield.
Ripstein, Arthur (1987) 'Foundationalism in Political Theory' *Philosophy and Public Affairs* 16, 2: 115–37.
—— (1999) *Equality, Responsibility, and the Law*. New York: Cambridge University Press.
Roemer, John E. (1982) *A General Theory of Exploitation and Class*. Cambridge, MA: Harvard University Press.
—— (1985) 'Should Marxists be Interested in Exploitation?' *Philosophy and Public Affairs* 14, 1: 30–65.
—— ed. (1986) *Analytic Marxism*. Cambridge: Cambridge University Press.
—— (1988) *Free to Lose: An Introduction to Marxist Economic Philosophy*. Cambridge, MA: Harvard University Press.
—— (1996) *Theories of Distributive Justice*. Cambridge, MA: Harvard University Press.
—— (1998) *Equality of Opportunity*. Cambridge, MA: Harvard University Press.
Rorty, Richard, ed. (1967) *The Linguistic Turn*. Chicago: University of Chicago Press.
—— (1989) *Contingency, Irony and Solidarity*. Cambridge: Cambridge University Press.
—— (1991) *Objectivity, Relativism, and Truth*. Cambridge: Cambridge University Press.
Rosenblum, Nancy L. (1989) *Liberalism and the Moral Life*. Cambridge, MA: Harvard University Press.
Rothbard, Murray (1978) *For A New Liberty: The Libertarian Manifesto*. Lanham, MD: University Press of America.
Rousseau, Jean-Jacques ([1755] 1987) *Discourse on the Origins of Inequality*, in *Rousseau: Basic Political Writings*. Trans. Donald Cress. Indianapolis, IN: Hackett Publishing Co.
—— ([1760] 1987) *On the Social Contract*, in *Rousseau: Basic Political Writings*. Trans. Donald Cress. Indianapolis, IN: Hackett Publishing Co.
Ruddick, Sarah (1990) *Maternal Thinking: Toward a Politics of Peace*. New York: Ballantine Books.
Sandel, Michael J. (1982) *Liberalism and the Limits of Justice*. Cambridge: Cambridge University Press, 2nd edn 1999.
—— (1996) *Democracy's Discontent: America in Search of a Public Philosophy*. Cambridge, MA: Belknap Press.
Satz, Deborah (1992) 'Markets in Women's Reproductive Labor' *Philosophy and Public Affairs* 21, 2 (Spring): 107–31.
Scanlon, Thomas (1982) 'Utilitarianism and Contractarianism,' in Sen and Williams, eds (1982): 103–28.
—— (1998) *What We Owe to Each Other*. Cambridge, MA: Harvard University Press.
Scheman, Naomi (1993) *Engenderings: Constructions of Knowledge, Authority, and Privilege*. New York: Routledge.

BIBLIOGRAPHY

Schneewind, J. B. (1998) *The Invention of Autonomy.* Cambridge: Cambridge University Press.
Sen, Amartya (1992) *Inequality Reexamined.* Cambridge, MA: Harvard University Press.
—— (1997) *On Economic Inequality.* Oxford: Clarendon.
——, and Bernard Williams, eds (1982) *Utilitarianism and Beyond.* Cambridge: Cambridge University Press.
Sher, George (1987) 'Other Voices Other Rooms: Women's Psychology and Moral Theory,' in Kittay, ed. (1987): 178–89.
—— (1997) *Beyond Neutrality: Perfectionism and Politics.* Cambridge: Cambridge University Press.
Simmons, A. John (1979) *Moral Principles and Political Obligations.* Princeton, NJ: Princeton University Press.
—— (1992) *The Lockean Theory of Rights.* Princeton, NJ: Princeton University Press.
—— (1993) *On the Edge of Anarchy: Locke, Consent, and the Limits of Society.* Princeton, NJ: Princeton University Press.
—— (1999) 'Justification and Legitimacy' *Ethics* 109, 4: 739–71.
Singer, Peter (1993) *Practical Ethics.* New York: Cambridge University Press.
—— ed. (1991) *A Companion to Ethics.* Cambridge, MA: Basil Blackwell.
Skinner, Quentin (1978) *The Foundations of Modern Political Thought.* Cambridge: Cambridge University Press.
Slote, Michael (1992) *From Morality to Virtue.* New York: Oxford University Press.
Sommers, Christina Hoff (1987) 'Filial Morality,' in Kittay, ed. (1990): 69–86.
—— (1995) *Who Stole Feminism? How Women Have Betrayed Women.* New York: Simon and Schuster.
Spelman, Elizabeth (1997) 'Woman: The One and the Many,' in Meyers, ed. (1997): 160–79.
Spencer, Herbert (1972) *On Social Evolution: Selected Writings*, Ed. J. D. Y. Peel. Chicago, IL: University of Chicago Press.
Sreenivasan, Gopal (1995) *The Limits of Lockean Rights in Property.* New York: Oxford University Press.
Sterba, James (1986) 'Recent Work on Alternative Conceptions of Justice' *American Philosophical Quarterly* 23, 1: 1–22.
—— (2001) *Three Challenges to Ethics: Environmentalism, Feminism, and Multiculturalism.* New York: Oxford University Press.
Stocker, Michael (1987) 'Duty and Friendship: Towards a Synthesis of Gilligan's Contrastive Moral Concepts,' in Kittay, ed. (1987): 56–68.
Sumner, L. W. (1996) *Welfare, Happiness, and Ethics.* Oxford: Clarendon.
Tamir, Yael (1993) *Liberal Nationalism.* Princeton, NJ: Princeton University Press.
Taylor, Charles (1979) *Hegel and Modern Society.* Cambridge: Cambridge University Press.
—— (1985) *Philosophy and the Human Sciences: Philosophical Papers, II.* Cambridge: Cambridge University Press.
—— (1989a) 'Cross-Purposes: The Liberal-Communitarian Debate,' in Rosenblum, ed. (1989): 159–82.
—— (1989b) *Sources of the Self: The Making of Modern Identity.* Cambridge, MA: Harvard University Press.
—— (1991) *The Ethics of Authenticity.* Cambridge, MA: Harvard University Press.
—— (1992) *Multiculturalism and the 'Politics of Recognition.'* Princeton, NJ: Princeton University Press.
—— (1995) *Philosophical Arguments.* Cambridge, MA: Harvard University Press.
Temkin, Larry (1993) *Inequality.* New York: Oxford University Press.
Thomas, Laurence (1999) 'Split-Level Equality: Mixing Love and Equality,' in Babbitt and Campbell, eds (1999): 189–201.
Thomas, William (1985) *Mill.* New York: Oxford University Press.

BIBLIOGRAPHY

Tong, Rosemary (1989) *Feminist Thought: A Comprehensive Introduction.* Boulder, CO: Westview Press.
Tuck, Richard (1979) *Natural Rights Theories.* Cambridge: Cambridge University Press.
—— (1989) *Hobbes.* Oxford: Oxford University Press.
Tucker, Robert C., ed. (1978) *The Marx Engels Reader.* New York: Norton.
Tully, James (1980) *A Discourse on Property: John Locke and His Adversaries.* New York: Cambridge University Press.
Vallentyne, Peter, and Hillel Steiner, eds (2000a) *Left-Libertarianism and Its Critics: The Contemporary Debate.* New York: St. Martin's Press.
—— (2000b) *The Origins of Left-Libertarianism: An Anthology of Historical Writings.* London: Palgrave.
Vlastos, Gregory (1962) 'Justice and Equality,' in *Social Justice.* Ed. Richard Brandt. Englewood Cliffs, NJ: Prentice-Hall, 31–72.
Waldron, Jeremy (1988) *The Right to Private Property.* Oxford: Oxford University Press.
—— (1992) 'Minority Cultures and the Cosmopolitan Alternative' *University of Michigan Journal of Law and Reform* 25, 3: 751–93.
—— (1993) *Liberal Rights: Collected Papers 1981–1991.* New York: Cambridge University Press.
—— (1999) *The Dignity of Legislation.* New York: Cambridge University Press.
Wall, Steven (1998) *Liberalism, Perfectionism and Restraint.* New York: Cambridge University Press.
Walzer, Michael (1983) *Spheres of Justice.* Oxford: Blackwell.
—— (1987) *Interpretation and Social Criticism.* Cambridge, MA: Harvard University Press.
—— (1990) 'The Communitarian Critique of Liberalism' *Political Theory* 18, 1: 6–23.
Ware, Alan, and Robert Goodin, eds (1990) *Needs and Welfare.* London: Sage.
Warnke, Georgia (1989–90) 'Rawls, Habermas, and Real Talk: A Reply to Walzer' *The Philosophical Forum* 21, 1–3: 197–203.
Weinreb, Lloyd (1987) *Natural Law and Justice.* Cambridge, MA: Harvard University Press.
Weitzman, Leonore (1985) *The Divorce Revolution: The Unexpected Social and Economic Consequences for Women and Children in America.* New York: Free Press.
West, Cornell (1994) *Race Matters.* New York: Vintage.
Westen, Peter (1990) *Speaking of Equality.* Princeton, NJ: Princeton University Press.
Wheeler, Sam (1980) Natural Property Rights as Body Rights' *Nous* 14, 2: 171–93.
White, Stephen (1988) *The Recent Work of Jürgen Habermas.* New York: Cambridge University Press.
—— (1991) *Political Theory and Post Modernism.* Cambridge: Cambridge University Press
Williams, Bernard (1962) 'Justice and Equality,' in *Philosophy, Politics and Society.* Ed. Peter Laslett and W. G. Runciman. Oxford: Blackwell, 110–31.
Williams, Patricia J. (1991) *The Alchemy of Race and Rights.* Cambridge, MA: Harvard University Press.
Wright, Eric Olin, Andrew Levine and Eliot Sober (1992) *Reconstructing Marxism.* London: Verso.
Wolff, Robert Paul (1970) *In Defense of Anarchism.* New York: Harper & Row.
—— (1984) *Understanding Marx: A Reconstruction and Critique of 'Capital'.* Princeton, NJ: Princeton University Press.
Wood, Allen (1972) 'The Marxian Critique of Justice' *Philosophy and Public Affairs* 1: 244–82.
—— (1981) *Karl Marx.* London: Verso.
Young, Iris Marion (1990a) *Justice and the Politics of Difference.* Princeton, NJ: Princeton University Press.

BIBLIOGRAPHY

——(1990b) 'The Ideal of Community and the Politics of Difference,' in Nicholson, ed. (1990): 300–23.
——(1997a) *Intersecting Voices: Dilemmas of Gender, Political Philosophy and Policy*. Princeton, NJ: Princeton University Press.
——(1997b) 'Is Male Gender Identity the Cause of Male Domination?' in Meyers, ed. (1997): 21–37.
——(2000) *Inclusion and Democracy*. Oxford: Oxford University Press.
Zack, Naomi, ed. (1997) *Race/Sex: Their Sameness, Difference, and Interplay*. London: Routledge.
——(1999) 'Philosophy and Racial Paradigms' *Journal of Value Inquiry* 33: 299–317.

Index

abortion 115–16
Adorno, T. 191
affirmative action 5, 156 n. 3, 161, 163
alienation 193–4
analytic philosophy 4
anti-paternalism *see* paternalism
anti-perfectionism *see* perfectionism
Aristotle 16, 60, 61, 103, 104, 131 n. 6
Arneson, R. 84 n. 16
authority: political 7, 8, 25–59, 96, 103, 108, 116, 127, 128; and conservatism 127–9, 153; *de facto* and *de jure* 25
autonomy 7, 15, 17, 27, 66, 94, 95–7, 101, 102–3, 104–5, 113, 119, 125, 127–8, 131, 134–5, 139, 140, 144, 149, 178–9, 182, 193 n. 7, 206, 209–10; and care ethics 170, 174; and communities 139; and culture 146–7; and feminism 166–7, 168–9; and ideology 193; and marriage 168; and race 159–60

Bell, D. 131 n. 6, 142 n. 10
Benjamin, W. 191
Boxill, B. 156 n. 3
burdens of judgement 112; *see also* Rawls, J.
Burke, E. 126
Butler, J. 206, 207 n. 17

capitalism 1, 20, 47, 62, 66, 67, 141, 149, 175; and Marxism 186, 188–99
care ethics 16–17, 170–3
categorical imperative 15, 50; *see also* Kant, I.
Christiano, T. 41 n. 8

civic education 142
civic republicanism 142
class 188–9, 196
collective choice 142–3; *see also* democracy
commodity fetishism 190
communitarianism 16, 130–45, 209; as a positive political view 141–5
communities: definition of 145; effect of liberalism upon 139–41
conceptual analysis *see* philosophic method
consent 39, 44–6, 48, 51, 52–6; tacit 44
conservatism 6, 126–30, 142; and perfectionism 127
constructivism 95, 110, 136, 209
contracts 26, 54, 65, 168; and libertarianism 71–4; *see also* social contract
coordination game 38–9
critical race theory 157–63
critical theory xii, 191

democracy 34, 56, 86, 87, 117–19, 120, 178, 179–80, 186, 211, 212–13; and communitarianism 142–3; constitutional 112–13; in Hobbes 34; and legitimacy of political power 119; liberal 6–9, 95; in Rousseau 49
deontology 15–16, 50; *see also* Kant, I.
Descartes, R. 201
desert of economic advantages 64
difference principle 53, 76–8, 79–80, 91, 111; *see also* Rawls J.
discrimination 75, 86, 155–7, 160–3, 164, 165, 181

INDEX

distributive justice 60–90; egalitarian theory of 80–7; and equality of opportunity 62–4; libertarian theory of 65–74; Rawlsian view of 74–80
diversity 7, 99, 108, 120, 146–7, 163; *see also* pluralism
Dworkin, R. 80, 81, 82–5, 84 n. 15, 88

egalitarianism 64, 80–7, 90, 156, 166; critique of 88–9; and Marxism 195–7
egoism 37; *see also* psychological egoism
Elster J. 192 n. 6
entitlement, historical theory of 67–9; *see also* libertarianism
equal opportunity 18, 62–4, 80, 137, 161, 165–8; in Rawls 53, 75; for welfare 84–5
equality 56–7, 62, 88–9, 90, 94, 95, 101, 102, 112–13; of resources 82–5; of welfare 81–2
expensive tastes 81, 83–4
exploitation 194–7

fact-value distinction 11–12, 153
feminism 163–79; characterizations of 163; and equality of opportunity 164–7; and families 167–9; liberal 164; and objectivity 176
Foucault, M. 4, 204, 206
Frankfurt School xii, 191
freedom 10, 20, 26, 66, 72, 85, 112–13, 136, 142, 155, 166, 189; and culture 145–8; in Kant 50–1; in Locke 43; in Rawls 54, 56, 57, 75, 77, 79; in Rousseau 48–9; *see also* liberty

Gauthier, D. 33 n. 4
Gilligan, C. 170–3, 182

Habermas, J. xii, 117–18, 120
Hampton, J. 29 n. 2, 33 n. 4, 37 n. 5, 39
Haraway, D. 205 n. 15
Hegel, G.W.F. 4, 131 n. 6, 189

heterosexism 164
historical materialism 186–9
Hobbes, T. 28–37, 41, 43, 45, 46, 49, 51, 72, 153; view of state of nature 29–34
Horkheimer, M. 191
human nature 104, 107
human rights *see* natural rights
Hume, D. 11, 35, 107–8, 126

identity 6, 19, 20, 77, 131, 133, 135; and culture 145–7; and democracy 179–80; and gender 173–6; and political theories 154–5; post-modern view of 205–7; and race 159–60
identity politics 204–5
ideology 189–93; and justice 197–9
individualism 86, 96, 137–8, 167
injustice 179–80, 210; and political theory 153–7

justice 7, 60, 65–6, 88–9, 96–7, 102, 104; and care ethics 170–3; and citizen motivation 137; communitarian view of 132–3; and conservatism 126–30; and democracy 211; Habermas's approach to 117–19; in Hobbes 32; and injustice 153–7; and Marxism 197–9; and race 159–63; Rawls's theory of 52–6, 74–80, 111–17; and utilitarianism 110
justice as fairness 111, 112; *see also* Rawls, J.

Kant, I. 15, 48, 50–1, 56, 111, 113, 153, 210
Kekes, J. 126, 127 n. 3
Kim, D.H. 158 n. 5
Kristeva, J. 203
Kymlicka, W. 97, 98, 134

labor theory of value 194
language 131–2; post-modern view of 202–6
laws of nature 32–3
legitimacy: liberal principle of 102–3,

INDEX

106, 116–17, 208; of political power 26, 37, 39–41, 45–8, 51, 52–6, 89, 96; *see also* democracy
liberalism 5, 6–9, 41, 52, 94–119, 207–12; and breakdown of communities 139–41; canonical account of 74–6; communitarian critique of 130–9; and conservatism 126–9; and culture 145–8; feminist 164–7; and identity formation 175–6; and Marxism 198–9; and post-modernism 204; and racism 159–63
libertarianism 18, 46–8, 62, 65–74, 192
liberty 7, 26 n. 1, 65, 68, 69–71; and libertarianism 65, 69–71, 73; Locke's conception of 43 n. 9; Mill's principle of 108; priority of 115; in Rawls 78, 111; *see also* freedom
Locke, J. 4, 34, 39, 41–6, 49, 51, 56, 65, 66, 67–8, 106, 153, 210; view of state of nature 43–4
Lyotard, J.-F. 200

MacIntyre, A. 130
Marx, K. 4, 186–99; *see also* Marxism
Marxism 130–1, 186–99, 208–9; critique of capitalism 193–7; and justice 197–9; and racism 192
Mill, J.S. 4, 14, 108, 204, 207; doctrine of liberty 108; *see also* utilitarianism
Mills, C. 153 n. 1
moral powers 113–14
moral theory 14–17

Narveson, J. 65 n. 4, 69–70, 73, 81
natural rights 27–8, 46
neutrality 7, 98–103, 137, 207; of political theory 154–7
Nisbet, R. 126
Nozick, R. 47, 65–6, 67–9
Nussbaum, M. 85 n. 17

Oakeshott, M. 126
objectivity 2–3, 4, 8, 12, 21; feminist critique of 176–9; post-modern critique of 199–201, 202–6

original position 75, 78, 118, 132–3; *see also* Rawls, J.
overlapping consensus 112, 114; *see also* Rawls, J.

paternalism 15–16, 97, 109
patriarchy 164
perfectionism 97, 103–8, 116, 118, 144, 149, 209; and utilitarianism 108–11
person, conception of 7, 119, 130–5, 201, 204–5, 209–10; in Hobbes 41
philosophic method 9–13
pluralism 95, 101–2, 109, 111–12, 116, 147, 149, 173, 209–10; *see also* diversity
political liberalism 111–17, 162, 211
political philosophy characterized 3
post-modernism 2, 199–207, 208; and liberalism 204
post-structuralism *see* post-modernism
power: and formation of self 203–4, 206; political 3, 26; political, conservative view of 127; political, Hobbesean justification of 30, 33, 39–40; political, Kantian justification of 51; political, liberal justification of 102–3, 106, 131; political, Lockean justification of 41–6; political, Rousseau's justification of 48–9; *see also* authority
primary goods 78, 82; *see also* Rawls, J.
priority of justice 101, 125, 139; *see also* priority of right
priority of right 96–7, 101–2, 162, 170, 176, 208; *see also* priority of justice
Prisoner's Dilemma 30–2, 38, 72
privacy 98, 138, 167–9; *see also* public–private distinction
property rights 35, 47, 65, 71, 72–3; and exploitation 193–6; and self-ownership 66–9
Protestant Reformation 27, 112
psychoanalysis 176, 182, 200, 201, 206

247

INDEX

psychological egoism 29, 37
public–private distinction 167–9; *see also* privacy
public reason 114; *see also* Rawls, J.

race 145; definitions of 157–9; *see also* racism
racism 157–63; definition of 158; and Marxism 192
Rashdall, H. 126
rationality 72 n. 10, 73–4
Rawls, J. 4, 5–6, 12–13, 52–5, 74–80, 82, 88, 111–18, 130, 132, 155–6, 162, 165; and equality 74, 75, 77 79–80, 80–7; and freedom 74, 77, 79, 210–11
reflective equilibrium 12–13, 54, 77; *see also* Rawls, J.
responsibility 84–5
revolution 187, 188
rights: group-based 146–7; liberal emphasis on 140–1, 170–1, 174, 179, 188, 205–6; libertarian view of 65–6; natural 27–8, 46–8; negative 47, 65; in Rawls 53, 75, 78; *see also* property rights
Rousseau, J.-J. 26, 48–59, 51, 55, 56, 143; theory of general will 48–9

Sandel, M. 130, 142, 144–5
self-ownership 66–9
Sen, A. 15, 62, 85–6, 89
Simmons, J. 45 n. 10
skepticism 95, 100–1; and relativism 95

social contract 8, 26–8, 25–57; *see also* contracts
socialism 186, 188, 196–7; efficiency of 196
sovereignty 48; by acquisition 34, 36; by institution 34, 36; popular 6, 51, 56, 95, 126
standpoint theory 177–8
state of nature *see* Hobbes, T.; Locke, J.

taxation 47, 65, 66, 69, 70–1, 76, 83; and public support of institutions 137; *see also* property rights
Taylor, C. 130
toleration 7, 27, 95, 98–9; Locke on 42

utilitarianism 14–15, 79, 81, 82; and perfectionism 108–11
utility, definitions of 109–10; *see also* utilitarianism

value, conceptions of 105–6
veil of ignorance 118, 143; *see also* Rawls, J.
virtue theory 16

Walzer, M. 142 n. 10
Wars of Religion 27, 112
welfare 80 n. 14, 82, 89, 109–10; equality of 81–2; *see also* utility
welfare state 87–90

Young, I. 161, 171 n. 14, 205–6, 207 n. 17